The BMW
5 Series and X5

Also by Marc Cranswick

Porsche 928, 924, 944 and 968: The Front-Engined Sports Cars (McFarland, 2008)

The BMW 5 Series and X5

A History of Production Cars and Tuner Specials, 1972–2008

Marc Cranswick

McFarland & Company, Inc., Publishers
Jefferson, North Carolina, and London

Library of Congress Cataloguing-in-Publication Data

Cranswick, Marc.
The BMW 5 series and X5 : a history of production cars and tuner specials, 1972–2008 / Marc Cranswick.
p. cm.
Includes bibliographical references and index.

ISBN 978-0-7864-4351-2
softcover : 50# alkaline paper ∞

1. BMW 5 series automobiles — History. I. Title.
TL215.B25C73 2010 629.222'2 — dc22 2010017738

British Library cataloguing data are available

On the cover: The 2009 BMW E60 M5 sedan (Bayerische Motoren Werke AG)

Manufactured in the United States of America

McFarland & Company, Inc., Publishers
Box 611, Jefferson, North Carolina 28640
www.mcfarlandpub.com

Table of Contents

Introduction

In the late 1960s racer and businessman Gordon Spice familiarized himself with the Nürburgring using a rented BMW 2002. He went through a couple of sets of tires and three sets of brake pads during the exercise and covered the cost of such consumables by charging folks to ride with him! The rental company was somewhat puzzled by the fact their car was returned with a different tire brand fitted, but the use of a BMW was no surprise, since BMW built good sports sedans.

Formula 1 and CART champ Nigel Mansell once owned an e12 M535i too, but BMW's road to success quickly took it beyond sports sedans that appealed to professional racing drivers. As a niche player grows, it edges closer to the business of rivals on either side of the divide. This tenet has proven true as BMW turned its attention outside the realm of the diehard enthusiast. However, in every new activity the Bavarian firm has maintained its dignified sporty character. The 5 series is no exception.

The oldest of BMW's "series" models, the 5 series dates back to September 1972. As BMW's middle child the 5 series has featured the company's power teams and technical devices from its smallest and largest models, with the e12 M535i being the first car after the e26 M1 to wear the "M" badge. There has been more to the 5 series than just BMW Motorsport versions, with the 6 series coupe and X5 SUV (SAV or Sports Activity Vehicle, in BMW parlance) as notable related technical spinoffs.

BMW is a company associated with motoring firsts. The idea of a sports sedan was a novelty at one time; so was the top safety rating bestowed by the Swedish insurance company Folksam upon the e12 5 series. Rewards are rarely given immediately to trendsetters, but eventually people come around. This has been the case with BMW's various gadgets, usually cryptically denoted using acronyms. The Bavarian concern has introduced a fair number of these technical newbies over the decades, and these items are examined herein.

It should be noted that this book doesn't cover just one car maker ... it covers ten. Tuners or speed shops, as they pertain to BMW and other prestige marques, are best described as low-volume specialist manufacturers and are regarded as such by the central German TÜV authority. Compared to the operations that catered to U.S. makes up to the early '70s, the mostly German BMW tuners adopt a more holistic approach to the art of performance improvement.

The extent of alterations carried out by companies like Alpina, Hartge and others results in vehicles discernibly different in nature from the BMW started with. They cater to a niche within a niche where serious modifications and sizable price increases prove small hurdles to enthusiasts determined to get a car just right for their personal requirements. The relationship between BMW and the tuners has been a harmonious one. The giant looks at the specialist's efforts and sometimes sees something that would work well on normal BMWs. For convenience and cost, tuners have been known to raid the BMW parts store and fit items in new combinations never thought of before.

BMW and its products are often the subject of the popular press, as the references in this account bear out. For raw data and archive materials a number of parties have provided key assistance, and thanks is offered to the following: Susanne Müllejans of AC Schnitzer & Kohl automobile GmbH; Kris Odwarka of Alpina Burkard Bovensiepen GmbH + Co. KG; Diane Clancy of BMW North America LLC; Birgit Pausch of BMW AG GmbH; Bob Harper of *BMW Car* magazine; Dinan Engineering Inc.; Uli Schwarz of Hamann GmbH; Allen Hardy of H&B Inc.; Anne-Christine Blasen of Herbert Hartge GmbH & Co. KG; Walter Koenig of Koenig Specials; Mary Rowe of Metric Mechanic Inc.; and Oktavia Krankenberg of MK-Motorsport Krankenberg GmbH. I would also like to say a special thanks to the Ulrich Thieme Collection, to Christian Hartmann, and for the professional photographic skills of Paul Baylis, Max Earey and Julie Knapman.

1

Triplanes, Trucks and Eggmobiles

BMW's Rocky Road to the Top

Today BMW has a clear public image recognized all over the world. Even though the company's vehicle portfolio is now more diverse than ever, covering small 4-cylinder cars (1 series) to large V-12 sedans (7 series), the identity is clear. The BMW message is obviously exclusive sports luxury. It is of no consequence that BMW is no longer a small manufacturer, or that the Bavarian company offers diesels and off-road vehicles; everyone knows that a BMW is an ultimate driving machine. Diesel-powered, U.S.–built X5s may be a common sight on the street, but the core message still rings true. However, there were times when BMW's nature was less clear, and in the beginning cars weren't even in the picture.

Before it was the Bayerische Motorenwerken (Bavarian Motor Works), BMW was the Bayerische Flugzeugwerke (Bavarian Aircraft Works). BMW was an aero engine manufacturer formed by the merger of two companies in 1916. One of the companies was started by Gustav Otto, the son of Nikolaus August Otto, who invented the 4-stroke engine. Indeed, a BMW engine powered the infamous Red Baron's aircraft. Naturally the Treaty of Versailles knocked the aero engine business on the head, so after World War I, BMW explored other areas: engines for boats and trucks, as well as another mode of transport the company specializes in to this day, motorcycles.

The year was 1923 and Max Friz's R32 had two features BMW bikes would utilize for the following 60 years, namely a flat air-cooled twin and rear shaft drive ... no chain, no worries![1] The next step was automobiles, specifically a series of BMWized license-built versions of the English Austin 7 that commenced with the 1928 BMW 3/15. The first original BMW design occurred in 1933 with the worthy 303 motivated by an 1,173 cc inline six of 30 bhp. Indeed, the 1930s would see BMW evolve through a fine line of I6 powered sedans, coupes and convertibles that culminated in the iconic 1940 Mille Miglia–winning 328.

BMW got back into aero engines and even came up with a jet engine, but the Second World War messed everything up. Factories were bombed out, the car plant was located in East Germany and BMW's great people were involved in war reparations. However, the company rebounded; BMW motorcycles in the form of the 1949 MY R24 roared back, but BMW was keen to return to cars. In this vein the company had something ambitious, and all new, something that recalled their classy prestige models of the 1930s. The new car was

Representative of the sort of bike BMW made between 1923 and 1983, we have a 1972 BMW R75/5 "U.S. Toaster," accompanied by a Velorex sidecar (courtesy Hans Vaalund).

the 6-cylinder 501, which made its debut at the 1951 International Automobile-Ausstellung.

The ambitious nature of the 501 came from the fact that there was barely any luxury car market in war-ravaged Germany, and there was the somewhat minor issue that BMW didn't have the productive means to build the car. In spite of these obstacles the 500 series moved along; Baur did the bodies for BMW, and in 1954 Germany witnessed its first postwar V-8 with the 2.6 liter all-alloy V-8-powered 502. Very extravagant, in fact the 501/2 was nicknamed the Baroque Angel because of its voluptuous lines. The transatlantic character of the model was heightened in 1955.

In 1955 General Motors introduced a new, modern OHV small-block V-8 into the tri-year Chevrolet sedan; it was known as "The Hot One." The same year BMW brought out a bigger, more powerful version of their new OHV V-8, creating the 502 3.2 liter. By 1960 the 502 S (Super) 3.2 was rated at 160 bhp and capable of 118 mph, making it the fastest production sedan available in West Germany, faster than a Mercedes-Benz. BMW were always confident rivals of the stodgy Swabians. The BMW 501, with pre-war I6, cost $1,000 more than a Mercedes 220S. That's confidence!

Isetta 250/300—BMW Is the Egg Man

Even in its weak economic state BMW offered more glamour than its Stuttgart nemesis. In 1955 BMW revealed the 507 sports car and 503 grand tourer, both V-8 powered and

The Isetta family helped BMW weather the '50s, but it was the New Class 1500 that opened the door to worldwide success. The e12 5 series replaced the New Class sedan in 1972; a 1980 U.S. model is shown (courtesy Greg and Colleen Johnson).

based on the 501/2 family. Elvis had a 507, and there is no doubt that Bavarians all loved the V-8 models, a great morale booster in the fifties. The sad thing was that in spite of high prices, BMW was losing money on the V-8 luxo/sports line. BMW's portfolio was rather limited, catering to two-wheel devotees and those who could afford the very best. However, getting into the 1950s, German buyers wanted more practicality than a motorcycle/sidecar affair could provide; they wanted a microcar.[2]

Low cost, simple motoring with weather protection superior to a motorcycle was offered by the fifties microcar. Often including a motorcycle-derived engine, and being of a nature to attract road tax commensurate with said motorcycle, the microcar universe was comprised of names like Heinkel, Goggomobil, Messerschmitt, Bond and Iso. The last name was key to BMW. The Iso Isetta was a successful Italian microcar, resembling a bubble or egg, and as with the earlier Austin Seven, BMW decided to enter the microcar business by building the Isetta under license.

So it was that the 1955 BMW Isetta 250 was born, incorporating the BMW roundel and BMW R25 motorcycle power plant, but otherwise close to its Italian cousin. The Isetta did well in sales, and BMW supplemented the Isetta 250 with the up-gunned 300! As successful as the eggmobile was, the public in West Germany and elsewhere were soon looking for a more refined vehicle to spend their postwar prosperity on, like the Fiat 500, the VW

Beetle and the new BMC Mini. Not being one to stand still, BMW penned an expanded and re-engineered version of the Isetta using the services of Willy Black. The 1957 600 had a side door to admit passengers to rear seating, wider spaced rear wheels and independent rear suspension.

While the BMW 600 was a tough not-so-little device, BMW produced a real small car with the all-new 1959 700. The 700 sedan and coupe were more engineering must-haves, styled by Michelotti, powered once again by BMW flat twin knowhow, and guided to fruition by Alex von Falkenhausen. The 700 was an instant classic and a commercial success. Unfortunately, BMW was at a crossroads by 1959. The Isetta family had done its best to fill BMW's money box, but the microcar sector was over. The V-8 cohort was advancing in years, and BMW was in financial trouble. Takeover fever was in the air, and the wolves were at the gates.

Takeover Trouble — Barbarians at the Bavarians' Gates

Interested parties included Britain's Rootes Group and American Motors, in rude financial health through making solid, frugal Ramblers. But the front-runner for buying BMW was Daimler-Benz. Daimler-Benz was on a little shopping spree, having bought DKW (Auto Union) in 1958, and at an historically important shareholder meeting in December 1959 it seemed like BMW would be their next acquisition. Fortunately discontent with the sellout was strongly expressed by a certain shareholder called Dr. Mathern. The doctor's verbal counterpoint bought time, and Harald Quandt bought shares — BMW shares. What was thought to have been a slam-dunk MB takeover was stopped cold; the danger had passed, and BMW was safe.

BMW was now independent and free to complete the car that would place the Bavarians back on the right road, a car that would be the blueprint for all BMW's new models up to and including the 1988 e34 BMW 5 series. It was the BMW 1500. Entering the 1960s there was room in the West German market for a sharp middle-class sedan. The public had sober VW and German Ford sedans, but between these cars and expensive Mercedes there was a niche. The 1500 would meet this need for a moderately sized prestige sedan designed and marketed for those who loved driving.

BMW's Wilhelm Hofmeister was doing the styling, Alex von Falkenhausen the engineering, but the marketing was accomplished by Paul Hahnemann, also known as "Niche Paul." This exuberant super-salesman drove home the message that BMWs offered a unique driving experience in the European market, as unique as the Hofmeister kinked-C pillar. The European public received and agreed with the message. The 1961 1500 sedan was BMW's new beacon.

BMW's new model family was called the "New Class," naturally, and with it there was little need or room for the old class. The Isetta ground to a halt in 1962, the 501/2 chugged on to 1964, and the 700 crossed the finish line in 1965. However, with the success of the New Class, BMW had little time to mourn their respective departures. Front and center in their arsenal was the 1963 1800; a larger-engined version of the 1500 with the gremlins ironed out, it was a true volume seller. From now on BMW would play with variations on the winning 1500/1800 range, even adding glamour with the new four-place 2000CS in 1965.

If the coupe could have a 2-liter version of BMW's new 4-cylinder motor, so too could the sedan giving rise to the 1966 100 bhp 2000. However, bigger is not always better, and what really got the BMW volcano to blow its top was a smaller 2-door car. A further derivative of the 4-door sedan, the 1966 1600-2 was a shortened version using the 1600cc engine from the 1500–2000 sedans. It was lighter and faster than a 4-door 1600. Suddenly it was possible to get the BMW qualities of driver involvement and quality construction for a lot less money.

U.S. buyers became well aware of the 2-door 1600's value for money during the 1967 model year. Offering a base price of just $2,477, importer extraordinaire Max Hoffman had the right car to explode North American interest in BMWs. The situation only improved into 1968, when tightening emissions control precipitated one of the best-known Bimmers of all time, the 2002. Dropping the unstressed 2-liter mill into the diminutive 2-door gave rise to an enthusiast's dream that was a sales triumph the world over.

With this welcome change of fortune BMW's latest problem was where to build all these popular new models. The company was hungry for production capacity and did a little takeover activity of its own. BMW bought out Hans Glas GmbH. Glas was a 1950s pioneer of the rubber-toothed cambelt, he was behind the Goggomobil, and he also had an excellent modern factory in Dingolfing. Glas's range of quality sedans and coupes would soon be BMWized, and the Dingolfing factory would be utilized to make the upcoming 1972 BMW 5 series, but before that BMW had some grand designs.

Benz Bashing

The 1500–2000's success was in leaving Daimler-Benz alone, but that temptation could only be resisted for just so long. In 1968 BMW introduced a brand-new large sedan, powered by a 6-cylinder derivative of the current BMW I4. This new car was coded e3, with the opening models called 2500 and 2800. The model names denoted metric engine size. At 185 inches in length, this was a big car by European standards, and BMW obviously had an eye out for export markets, given the car's luxury equipment and power.

The 2500/2800 offered power steering, power windows, and automatic transmission, and it was the first BMW available with factory air conditioning. The size, the features, and the 6-cylinder motors hinted at obvious competition, the W108 Mercedes 250/280S of 1965. The Mercedes S class also had a choice of 2.5 and 2.8 liter I6 engines. To underline their impudence BMW simultaneously readied a sporting companion coupe, to fire shots at the MB 280SL. Using the 2000CS as a base, BMW inserted their new 2.8-liter six into a body with a lengthened nose and revised visage to create the e9 2800CS.

The 2800CS had the same 170 bhp rating as the MB 280SL, and the BMW 2500/2800 had more power than their Daimler-Benz S class counterparts. In the face of such similarities, there were important differences that made BMW special. The BMW sedans offered much more driver appeal; the MB S class offered a bench front seat. The 280SL was a 2-seater with removable top; the 2800CS was only ever a 2+2 coupe. In all versions the BMWs were happier with manual transmission. BMW was always closer to the stick shift than Daimler-Benz, and this characteristic continues to the present; plus, BMW didn't do diesels back then.

The manual-transmission-only Euro spec 3.0Si was a 140 mph sedan MB had no answer for. A 1973 UK 3.0Si is shown wearing Alpina B9 rims (courtesy Jamie Myles).

How Mercedes management must have rued the day in December 1959 when BMW escaped, permitting the mini upstart to poach sales away from the establishment. Such audacious behavior could only arise through careful planning and a degree of uniformity. Compared to the pre-war and early postwar periods, new BMWs from 1961 to the mid 1990s have displayed a strong family likeness in styling and engineering. This is not platform sharing in the modern sense, but shared engines, components, and suspension layout, as well as appearance. Thus, the small BMW 3 series under a magnifying glass looked like the company's large 7 series.

This uniformity has been criticized for its blandness, the claim being that luxury and class can't be attained by simply scaling up, but the formula worked. On occasions when BMW strayed too far outside the box, as with the e31 8 series, the commercial results were less than stellar. This systematic approach was also reflected in management. It was only natural that the Quandt group wished to look after its investment in BMW. Arriving from

Opposite, top: **BMW has had a long presence in racing. In 1985 the Bavarians put forward a sports car for the IMSA GTP (Grand Touring Prototype) class. The BMW GTP used a version of the turbo I4 seen in the World Championship–winning Brabham F1 car (courtesy Mel Abrahams).** ***Opposite, bottom:*** **Bavaria's challenge to the MB 450SE, the e23 733i. The 7 series replaced the e3 sedan in 1977, offering luxo living with driver involvement not found in MB's S class (courtesy Bruce and Donna McDonald).**

BMW M Team

Quandt, Eberhard von Kuenheim became BMW's new chairman in 1970, and held the post going into 1993, when he was succeeded by Bernd Pischetsrieder.

The reborn BMW knew itself in all aspects of operation. To formalize the vision, six-year corporate plans were initiated in 1974. There was also the business of selling cars overseas. Sales, service and distribution were entrusted to a foreign agent, as was normal practice, but a superior situation would result if the car maker itself controlled operations in the overseas market. So it was that BMW North America started in 1975, to sell and service BMWs, taking over the activity from Hoffman Motors Corporation. Similarly in the UK, BMW GB covered such matters from 1980; formerly sales and service had been carried out by importer BMW Concessionaires GB.

Did order triumph over chaos? Did BMW's reordering work? The Munich-based concern certainly expanded their sales base. In 1966 BMW celebrated its 50th birthday at the Bavarian State Opera House, with annual production breaking the 60,000-unit barrier. The Bavarian's production total for 1986 was 432,285, a substantial technical jump from small car maker to being a medium-sized one. This was a great achievement in selling cars designed for no speed limits, in countries where national speed limits do exist. In that sense BMW has been the most successful German manufacturer in selling the idea of high-speed driving to overseas buyers. VW introduced the world to the economy car, Daimler-Benz brought luxury, Porsche made sports cars, but BMW has made popular the idea that a sedan can be more than mere family transport.

2

The Original BMW 5 Series (e12)

A Sedan in the Fastback Era

The 1960s had been a great time for BMW, but would it be able to remain independent by the close of the next decade? The oldest member of the new BMW range, the 1500–2000, was now a decade old and in need of replacement. Its successor would have to be good, for BMW's survival still hung in the balance, according to *Management Today* in 1971. The quality of the new mid-size BMW, and its companions, would decide whether West Germany's littlest automaker finished the 1970s as an independent.[1]

Clues as to the new car's nature came from inside and outside BMW. Inside the e3 2500–3.3Li range pointed to the newcomer being 6-cylinder powered, and larger to accept the longer I6. Outside, Daimler-Benz provided a target with the W114 sedan. This wildly popular small Mercedes had arrived in 1968, offering a bewildering array of engines, including the ubiquitous diesel taxi. It also proved instructive that BMW's new in-house stylist, Paul Bracq, had just moved in from Daimler-Benz, where he had completed the styling of their contemporary models.

Naturally, the new BMW would incorporate the Hofmeister C pillar, and the traditional BMW kidney grille couldn't be omitted, but other influences also abounded. At this time the long hood, short rear deck, fastback-coupe look was in vogue, and designers felt duty-bound to incorporate it on anything and everything from vacuum cleaners to sedans. Specifically, the 1500–2000's replacement was influenced by Garmisch, a Bertone coupe-styling exercise based on the BMW 2000TI and displayed at the 1970 Geneva car show.

BMW's sixties new wave cars had a style reminiscent of the Chevrolet Corvair. The new middle model deviated from this with a trimmer line. There was less bulk about the sides, and a neat slight wedge shape that fell with subtlety towards the front. The only bit of ornamentation was a black horizontal vent on the C pillar that allowed the extraction of stale air. The slimline double rubber bumper look was similar to that seen on the new 1972 MB S class, a sign of Paul Bracq's influence, but it looked neater on the BMW. To curb fussiness the new sedan also adopted the early 1970s BMW practice of having purely black grilles around the kidney.

Reflecting the new car's neat nature was a new 3-digit BMW naming system. BMW's New Class cars were named in accordance with their metric engine capacities. This was somewhat confusing given the rising number of BMW variants. The company even resorted to calling the e3 2500–3.3Li the Bavaria in the U.S. market, with some success. There was

The 1972–75 Kugelfischer injected 520i had a top speed of 114 mph, and could do 0–60 mph in 10.5 seconds (courtesy Ulrich Thieme, http://www.e12.de).

logic in calling BMW's new medium-size car the 520: five because it was the fifth New Class range after the 1500–2000/02/e3/e9; the "20" referred to engine size, in this case a starter 2-liter 4-cylinder.

It was easy to refer to the new car as the 5 series, or was it? Some difficulty arose concerning the German language and the fact BMW HQ wanted the car to be known as "five-twenty." This was a natural assumption for English speakers, but in German it was normal to say "five hundred and twenty." To obviate the problem BMW made early 520/520is have badging with a large "5" digit. However, the growing popularity of BMW cars and the increasingly global nature of life soon made the correct version obvious and BMW made the badge digits of the next new 5 series version, the 525, all the same size.

When the e12 5 series started life as the 520, the model name made little sense because the 02, e3 and e9 were still living. However, once BMW's other new '70s ranges arrived (1975 e21 3 series, 1976 e24 6 series, 1977 e23 7 series), the public were in no doubt. Quickly these new ranges became icons in their respective model segments. Synonymous with the successful sports sedan concept, if one wanted this type of car then BMW was the automatic choice.

From the onset it must be made clear that the 520 was not revolutionary in the manner of Citroen's contemporary CX. As with other BMWs the 181.9-inch-long 520 was a con-

The 130 bhp injected I4 M10 shared by the BMW 2002tii and 520i. The cylindrical metal container in the middle of the intake manifold is the throttle butterfly housing (courtesy Ulrich Thieme, http://www.e12.de).

ventional front-engine, rear-drive 4-door sedan using a steel unibody. The features that made the 520 stand out were good build quality, fun driving character and well-executed engineering with some thoughtful design touches. The 520 brought items to make European motoring easier.

The 5 series dashboard was an avant-garde one-piece molding, unobtrusive and designed to answer a chief problem with dash fresh-air supply, namely drafts. Since the late '60s new cars were being introduced without vent wings, relying instead on interior adjustable dash vents to admit fresh air, but this tended to bring drafts. The BMW solution was to have large dash vents that allowed a large volume of fresh air to be moved at slow speed, on the 3-speed fan's first speed. The vents were fixed, so the air filled the cabin in a diffuse manner without air directly blowing upon occupants and causing drafts.

The cutting-edge nature of dash arrangements was continued with the provision of three rotary heat/vent controls. The middle knurled ring controlled fan speed, the left dial did temperature and the right one did distribution. Stratified heating with warm feet and a cool head was a snap ... once one had studied the owner's handbook. European HVAC controls in the pre-climate-control era were never exactly intuitive. Two sliders even allowed the amount of fresh air to each half of the interior to be regulated, and there was more. For the first time a medium-size BMW was available with factory-installed air conditioning.

The traditional BMW pairing of a large circular speedo and tach, with reliance on warning lamps rather than gauges, and reddish-orange illumination at night (courtesy Ulrich Thieme, http://www.e12.de).

The e12's a/c came courtesy of German manufacturer Behr, and was available on 5 series cars from the start of the 1974 MY. The downside with this option was that it filled the storage cubbyhole in the center console, and forced the radio onto the base of the transmission tunnel behind the shifter. There was still a useful storage tray with dividers on the dash's passenger side, and BMWs of this era had a huge glove box. Air-conditioned e12s had two additional dials at the console base to regulate the a/c's blower speed and temp.

Due to the add-on nature of a/c on European cars of this period, the e12 had two fan motors, one in the bulkhead for the fresh air/heater mode and a second squirrel-cage blower under the dash for the a/c. It was neat-looking, if not truly integrated, with BMW blending the evaporator/blower box housing into the dash/shifter surround. There was a neat plastic pod with swivel vents available for a/c e12s. This fixture sat in the center of the dash, attached with the four screws of the removed standard central dash grille. The pod has always been

Opposite, top: **The BMW 4-cylinder tower HQ and e12 5 series were both 1972 newcomers (courtesy Ulrich Thieme, http://www.e12.de).** ***Opposite, bottom:*** **A yellow e12 unibody in the BMW Mobile Tradition workshop. Mobile Tradition looks after BMW's museum fleet of classics, displays them on show tours and handles the historic BMW angle (courtesy Ray Coldwell).**

BMW Group
528i
M-WS 3897

listed in the BMW parts catalogue, but only seems to have been fitted to pre–1982 U.S.–spec 5 series cars.

Sitting in this climate-controlled box, the driver was master of all he surveyed, and a great deal was surveyed thanks to BMW's traditional tall greenhouse. A clear view of the 520's instruments was also provided thanks to a tidy raised pod. BMW believed in minimal instrumentation; after all, how many gauges can one take in at a glance? Contrary to then current sports/GT flight-deck car practice, BMW provided two large circular gauges (speedometer and tachometer) flanked by two smaller ones (gas and water temp); the latter two were angled for a better view. The rest of the information came from warning lights. There were two warning lamps high in the display for low gas and oil. The remainder were at the base and took care of items like directional flashers, low battery charge, headlamp high beam and shift quadrant position for automatic e12s.

Pod instruments were shielded by a single pane of antireflective glass. Night illumination was of a gentle aviation-inspired orange, contrasting with the green lighting that Daimler-Benz was using at the time. However, BMW did copy the 1971 MB 350SL by fitting a mini rechargeable flashlight to the e12's glove box. BMW continued a recent tradition, first seen on the e3 and e9, of fitting a tool kit to the inside of the trunk lid. Previously cars like the 2000 and 02 had a simple trunk tool pouch. In short order the drop-down tool kit became a Bimmer icon, and a favorite with BMW salesmen when wowing customers.

In a break with tradition the e12 520 became the first BMW to have its turn signal column stalk mounted on the left, thus leaving the right hand free to operate the shifter. Unfortunately BMW didn't swap the stalks over for right-hand drive e12s, so in certain export markets the driver had to coordinate shifting and signaling with the same hand. A few more buttons and pullout knobs for hazard warning lights, headlamps and fog lights lay beneath the instrument binnacle, an obscure location.

For this generation of 5 series there was no power seat option, but it was possible to manually adjust the front seats over a great range. Naturally fore/aft adjustment and reclining seats were standard, and for a little extra the driver's seat could be height-adjustable, and the steering wheel would telescope over a 1.6-inch range. Indeed, if the front seats were put all the way forward, fully reclined with head restraints removed, the e12 could provide comfy sleeping accommodation. Little wonder such a feature was omitted from U.S. sport compacts! In truth, occupants may have been more comfortable reclining than sitting in or driving an e12. The 520 was a Teutonic device, after all.

BMW could rightly claim the seats were biomechanically sound, but as per German car practice the front seats were very firm with a flat seat squab. This was especially noticeable with the perforated Skai leatherette, BMW's equivalent of Mercedes' MB Tex vinyl, and even with the optional real leather interior available from the start of the 1974 MY. It seemed like the seat bases were designed for affluent German businessmen that looked forward to Oktoberfest. Chancellor Helmut Kohl would have been comfy in an e12 520, but what of thinner types? German cars have long been known for their lengthy options lists, but did the drivers really have to bring their own padding?

Overseas newcomers to the marque would have to adjust to the Spartan nature of the e12's luxury. Regardless of the number of option boxes ticked, the interior wasn't plush; even the wood on the dash had the dull silk finish so typical of German cars. This was the only bit of forest found on e12s, unless one had purchased the top model variant (528/528i/

In BMW's own words, "Many features need no maintenance ... on your BMW. Including the advanced design safety chassis, with its ability to cope with far more power than even this lively four can develop" (courtesy Peter Kilner and Peter Hackney, http://team-orange.blogspot.com/).

530i), which added wood door cappings ... but it still wasn't a Jaguar, and didn't wish to be.

Lovers of auto sound were shocked to find a radio was extra. There was a single solitary dash speaker grille on the passenger side, and even the speaker that lay behind it was an option. BMW offered a fine line of Blaupunkt and Becker radio or radio/tape decks, at additional cost. For those wishing to escape mono mediocrity, two rear parcel shelf and two front footwell speakers could be fitted, but once again they resided on the options list. The e12 was designed to accommodate DIN standard audio fittings, something to consider before trying to install bulkier appliances.

At least large objects could be carried in the trunk. A capacity of 16 cu. ft. and a flat loading space meant that this was one fast compact capable of carrying more than a toothbrush. The only problem was that the space sat over a wheel well. If there was a puncture, trunk contents would have to be moved before getting to the spare tire. At least it was a real spare and not a space saver, although the owner's back would be wishing it were as he lifted the spare over the e12's high loading sill! One needed a high sill to maintain body torsional rigidity, but while the driver may have put his back out lifting a load, the e12 wouldn't, thanks to Nivomat. Taking a leaf from the e3's option book, the e12 offered hydraulic Nivomat self-leveling rear suspension.

Regardless of the load being carried, the correct ride height would be maintained. There was a safety cut-out switch that turned off the system if its capacity was exceeded.

Many thought BMW had achieved the perfect compromise in the melding of the 520 body with the 2.5-liter M30. A 1974 525 is depicted (courtesy Christian Hartmann).

Boge Nivomat was a rarely specified option, but recommended if the owner towed frequently. Nivomat was a new option for a middle-order Bimmer, made possible because the rear springs/shocks were now mounted together on a strut. On the BMW 2000 they were separate. Once again the BMW 520 used front MacPherson struts and rear semi-trailing arms, but with evolutionary development.

The front suspension's struts were tilted 12 degrees rearwards, like on the e3. Suspension travel was also increased compared to the BMW 2000; the range now went from 4.13 inches up to 4.53 inches down. The changes were meant to cut road shock, improve ride comfort and reduce steering effort. However, e12s with manual ZF Gemmer worm and roller steering were still heavy to park, as with all non-power-steering Bimmers. Even on 175 section tires and a 5½ inch rim (standard 520 issue), the e12 was a handful at low speed.

Power steering was a welcome new feature on the e12. Never available on the I4-powered 1500–2000, it was much needed on six-pot versions of the e12, given the extra weight carried in the nose. Unfortunately the ZF recirculating ball power assistance was only stock equipment on the top e12 in any given market (528/528i/530i), that being the only version that came with 6-inch-wide rims and 195 section tires as standard equipment. The steel rims used on the e12 5 series were of a new design with larger brake cooling slots than those found on the 2000 sedan, but a more noticeable change was the e12's four-headlamp grille.

Four equal size quartz iodine lamps graced the 520's visage, just like those seen on the

BMW became well known for sound ergonomics. The only fly in the ointment was the organ-style gas pedal, that made one's ankle bend back uncomfortably with small throttle openings. The solution was to drive faster (courtesy Christian Hartmann).

e3 sedan and e9 coupe. It looked good, but it also made the new 5 series easier to sell overseas. Only equal-sized round or square lamps were legal in the U.S.; rectangular reflectors weren't allowed. The 2000 and 2000CS had interesting trapezoidal headlamps, but for the U.S. they were forced to keep the frame and substitute four round lamps. The new 520 was none the worse for adopting the e3/9's look, and had the useful feature whereby removing the key from the ignition would extinguish the headlights and turn on the parking lights. This prevented a dead battery due to leaving the headlamps on overnight. Plus, by using the turn signal, it was possible to leave the parking lights operational on one side of the car, preventing the 5 series from getting bashed when parked on a street corner at night.

An executive car should always have gadgets for the busy entrepreneur to amuse himself with. The e12 offered a choice of manual steel or power sunroof from the 1974 MY, as well as power windows from the same time. The latter was a new feature for BMW's middle car. A control panel with 4 identical black rocker panel switches, and a child disabler button in between to knock out the rear windows, was placed on the driver's door trim, with one button on each remaining door. This control panel was taken from the e3 sedans. Which window did each panel rocker switch operate? The uninitiated driver had to consult the owner's handbook, or just experiment. It was normal in the 1960s and '70s for such buttons to be placed in a row and unlabeled.

BMW's engineers were anxious to make life easier for the driver with warning lights, rather than rows and rows of gauges. Indeed, they thought aircraft-style audible voice warnings, like the Boeing 707's low altitude message, were the way forward. The engineers were also making life easier for themselves by including a service diagnosis socket on all e12s. Plug the BMW dealership's SUN diagnostic engine analyzer into the socket of the e12's fusebox and all would be revealed. The service technician could glean a speedy readout of carb, distributor setting, even flywheel alignment in under 10 minutes.

The electronic diagnosis plug was first seen on 1971 MY BMW e3 sedans. The new BMW sedans were paving the way to the present, when cars work out what attention they need. Of course a car should look after not only itself, but also its occupants, and not just in terms of trinket accessories that make driving easier, but true safety. BMW had an idea on car safety that was represented by the BMW Turbo show car of 1972. The first styling exercise of BMW's new in-house designer Paul Bracq, and arguably more original of line than Giugiaro's later M1, the BMW Turbo's message was that a safe car needn't look, or drive, like a tank.

In cars, cuisine and culture, Bavaria has a unique nature in Germany. People in Italy and Spain even call Munich Monaco di Bavaria. Observe also Aloisius, the cantankerous but lovable character from Ludwig Thoma's 1911 work *A Municher in Heaven.* Aloisius was a typical Bavarian railway worker who died at Munich central station. Angels whisked Aloisius off to Heaven, where singing and behaving angel-like weren't to his taste. Aloisius much preferred a beer and some smokeless tobacco, so God sent him on a mission to earth once a week to give divine advice to the Bavarian government. Unfortunately Aloisius, now in human form, was too busy enjoying a few beers to offer any advice. Here Munich BMW dealership Schorsch Meier's 1970s advertising decal announced that real Bavarians drive BMWs, and the place to buy BMWs was Schorsch Meier (courtesy Christian Hartmann).

Safe at Any Speed—1970s Experimental Safety Vehicles

Established thinking said that one needed something like a Hummer to be safe. Safety car design proposals put forward at the time were large, heavy, cumbersome devices that

Opposite, top: Because of the trade embargo, this 518, originally destined for Iran, was exported to Belgium. Such left-hand-drive export 518s were called "Deluxe" (518 with 525 interior), and were assembled by BMW South Africa. Opposite, bottom: With its smaller bores the 518's 1.8-liter suffered fewer blown head gaskets than the 2-liter 520/4 (courtesy Christian Hartmann).

BB L1975H

The injected 2-liter M10 with Bosch L-jet AFM, plus many electric ancillaries, help the I4 function on hydrogen (courtesy Ulrich Thieme, http://www.e12.de).

were fuel inefficient, unless compared to a tank. ESV (Experimental Safety Vehicle), rather than SUV, fever was on as companies tried to design the cars of the future that would meet stricter national crash-testing laws. The proposals advanced by GM, AMF and Fairchild Corporation would have made any owner of a chrome-bumpered MGB nervous![2] Realizing that if everyone drove a 6,000-lb. behemoth we would all be doomed to ecological hell, Mercedes' and Volvo's studies were based on actual cars, not tanks.

Mercedes' 1972 ESF 13 was a modified W123 sedan with a 350SL nose and padding. Volvo's 1972 car had an exterior and dashboard similar to those of the future 740/760 models. These examples wouldn't win any beauty contests, but they did weigh closer to 3,000 than to 4,000 lbs., and had as good a chance as any in meeting ESV guidelines. BMW wasn't in the process: its 1972 car didn't even pretend to try to meet the National Highway Traffic and Safety Administration's goals. Its engine, an uprated 200 bhp version of the BMW 2002 Turbo motor, was certainly never going to be 1974 emissions legal. This was especially so since the 2002 Turbo was never emissions legal in any other year.

Opposite, top: **The future has arrived when one is at the wheel of a Hydrogen 5, with an electronic dash box doing a passable impression of an Altair 8800.** ***Opposite, bottom:*** **That blue box helps the Hydrogen 5 keep the world green. To battle big oil one needs a little e12 (courtesy Ulrich Thieme, http://www.e12.de).**

Top: **The trunk-mounted hydrogen tank doesn't leave room for a toothbrush, let alone the e12's usual spare wheel well.** ***Bottom:*** **Notice the absence of the rear gas filler flap from this series 1 e12's rear deck. That's because the Hydrogen 5 runs on hydrogen alone, so there is no gasoline tank (courtesy Ulrich Thieme, http://www.e12.de).**

BMW's 1972 Turbo did try to see what level of safety could be built into a road car, so it had that much in common with the ESV. BMW was on its own safety mission. It was as though BMW and the other manufacturers went to the same book club, but BMW decided to read a different book! The Bavarians came up with a 2-seater gullwing mid-engined sports car. Powered by the aforementioned 2-liter turbo it was capable of 0–62 mph in 6.6 seconds with a top end of 155 mph. These figures wouldn't have been possible unless the Turbo was light, which it was at 2,160 lbs. Somewhere in this package the designers managed to include 8.8 cu. ft. of trunk space, more than many sport compacts of the day.

The hardest thing to believe was the gullwing's incorporation of active and passive safety elements that were visible in BMW cars present and future. Front and rear nose sections were composed of foam with plastic cappings and retractable steel beams. Such construction created minimal or zero damage in low-speed collisions, plus absorbed impact force in serious crashes. The gullwing door posts acted like a roll bar, and the interior was a human-friendly zone of compliant materials. Grouping of related instruments and controls into logical areas promoted driving efficiency.

The driver wasn't going anywhere unless he buckled up for safety. Preceding 1974's Interlock system, the BMW Turbo's engine wouldn't fire unless the driver was wearing a seat belt. This was a feature that would save many lives if car makers were brave enough to productionize it. No doubt road users would have been moving more efficiently and safely if they had access to a BMW Turbo. Sadly the Munich concern didn't put the car into series production, although it can be viewed in BMW's museum.

For a company that was rising on the strength of its sedans, why make a safety car that looked like a DeLorean? The BMW Turbo and e12 520 may have looked dissimilar, but the production sedan put BMW's safety lessons into practice. Proof of this can be seen from the fact that BMW ran a crash test program whereby 520s were introduced head-on into a barrier at 50 kph. In the early 1990s, U.S. FSS (Federal Safety Standard) 208 still only mandated that this test be conducted at 48 kph. The alarming thing was that many new cars on the market at the time still couldn't pass FSS 208! This makes the crashworthiness of the e12 all the more remarkable.

BMW wasn't just throwing 520s into walls, they were flinging them through the air as well! It was also part of BMW's study to hurl e12s off test rigs sideways at 50 kph onto their roofs as part of rollover testing. Naturally the 520 was up to coping with such abuse, thanks to an integral central roof roll bar, plus reinforced front and rear roof pillars. BMW and others were highly concerned over the roof strength of their cars, in view of possible mandatory U.S. rollover tests. They were conducting in-house roof strength tests on the e3, and removed the pillarless e9 coupe from U.S. sale altogether.

The possible ban on ragtops didn't matter if one was a sedan man. The e12's unibody with collapsible crumple zones and rigid passenger center section had things covered. The logic of the energy-absorbing, low-set e12 dashboard was now clear. Apart from the raised instrument binnacle, the rest of the dash was low enough to remove the chance that the front passenger's head would make contact. The driver faced a new smaller four-spoke safety steering wheel. This was a new BMW design for the 1973 MY and featured a flexible rim and deeply dished padded hub.

From a servicing/repair angle the new tiller was helpful in having a flip-off hub that unclipped. Unlike later Bimmer steering wheels, it wasn't necessary to prize out the wheel's

For 1977 BMW decided to mount its trunk-lid model i.d. badge on a black plaque, for U.S. and Euro e12s. Even so, the 530i continued with 176 bhp (courtesy David Scott).

roundel badge with a flathead screwdriver to adjust the locking nut if the wheel was off center. It was also good to know that, like the BMW Turbo, the e12 had a collapsible steering column, and that this was improved over the one on the BMW 2000. However, there were some odd omissions from early e12s. Three-point inertia reel front seat belts and front seat head restraints weren't standard equipment until the 1974 MY.

Standard seat belts on the very early 520s were awkward to use, as per many cars of the time, and those wishing to avoid whiplash were wise to specify the front headrests. The inertia reel belts and front headrests shouldn't have been optional on such an expensive car. However, right from the get-go all e12s had a rear fog lamp built into the taillight cluster on the driver's side. From the 1974 MY onwards dual front halogen fog lamps were available, and the e12's front headlamps were upgraded from quartz-iodine to halogen spec at the same time.

Clear lights are just as important as powerful lights. From the start of the 1974 MY e12s could be fitted with a front headlamp wash/wipe system. This device worked when the normal windshield washer function was activated, and brought with it an auxiliary fluid container with a capacity of 2.5 liters. The e12s generally had a larger washer fluid container for the windshield, as well as a more powerful wiper motor and longer windshield wiper blades compared to the outgoing 2000.

Moving on from past practice, the e12 had its gas tank located under the trunk floor. Older sedans often had the top of the tank act as part of the trunk floor, with filler neck plumbing running inside the trunk to the top of the tank. On the 520 all the plumbing

The 1978 BMW 520/6, with M60 baby six, replaced the 1972–77 dual carb M10-powered 520/4. The new motor was also shared with the e21 3 series (courtesy Zoltan Udvari).

was kept out of the trunk. In a rear end collision there would be no gasoline spillage in the trunk in spite of the pre–1977 e12's rear-deck-mounted gas filler. The e21 3 series improved on this by using a saddlebag gas tank ahead of the rear wheels and under the rear bench seat.

On BMWs of this era the manufacturer claimed that having the spare in a trunk wheel well was a bonus in rear-end collisions because the tire acted as a shock absorber. BMW was also referring to the front MacPherson strut/rear semi-trailing arm chassis, which they had been chipping away at since the 1500, as their famous advanced design safety chassis. BMW avoided a chassis that would understeer the driver into oblivion. Final oversteer wasn't such a bad thing, so the engineers persisted with a setup that allowed a BMW to become the first sedan in the world to lap the Nürburgring in under 10 minutes.

The 5 series may have run off the road, but never out of brakes. Using ATE components, the e12s with small engines had front disks and rear drums, e12s with the "Big Six" came with 4-wheel disks. All e12s had 4-pot front brake calipers and dual brake circuits, split front and back. The driver could always rely on the full braking power of the front brakes, even when one circuit failed. Big-six e12 had an auxiliary set of drums to take care of hand-brake duty, but this arrangement, as expected, wasn't as effective as on the e12s with rear drums.

BMW had a few options to improve active safety, and the joy of motoring. As per the 02 and CS ranges one could order an e12 with a limited slip differential. The ZF disk-style Lok-O-Matic LSD transferred the traction from the wheel that slipped to the one that

The 2-liter 520/6 was the most popular Euro e12 of its time, chalking up 140,031 sales during 1977–81 (courtesy Dennis Van Kessel).

gripped, ensuring no lost time on the way to work should one have accidentally lifted an inside rear wheel when pressing on! There was also heavy duty suspension (HD) available on e12s from the 1974 MY. The HD option involved one set for the small-engined cars, and one for the big-six editions. A 5-speed manual gearbox was also offered on e12s, but in the early years it was only a close ratio box.

The CR dogleg 5-speeder had a direct fifth, which didn't bring better economy or quieter cruising, just more closely spaced intermediate ratios and snappier in-gear acceleration. The dogleg shift pattern involved placing 1st under reverse, with 2nd through to 5th in the "H" pattern. When racing, one mostly lives within the H, 1st being used to get rolling out of the pits. BMW has actively tested all 5 series cars on the dangerously exciting Nürburgring. The CR 5-speed would have been useful keeping the engine on the boil when negotiating the twists of the Old Ring.

The Grand Unveiling: Munchen 1972—520 Meets World

BMW unveiled the new 520 soon after the close of the 1972 Munich Olympic games, and there was some connection between the e12's I4 motor and the Olympics, and recent Bimmer history. The initial BMW 520/520i cars were powered by 2-liter versions of the BMW M10 I4, the same engine that powered the 1961 1500 and its successors, plus formed the basis of BMW's new I6 (M30). It was a big relief after BMW's V-8 era, and there was

A 1978 UK spec 518 4-speed manual, with BMW's optional 14-inch turbine alloys. The UK market's BMWs have long been better equipped than their Continental counterparts (courtesy Ray Coldwell).

a good way to celebrate the M10 and look to the future with a new building to serve as BMW's HQ. The rush was on: in 1966 Munich was chosen to host the 1972 Olympics, and the eyes of the world would soon be on the city.

The Olympic complex featured a clear canopy, and this raised the bar somewhat when it came to BMW's planning its HQ reply. The answer came from Austrian architect Karl Schwanzer, whose solution was the "4-cylinder tower." BMW became unbeatable in modern times not from V-12s or jet engines, but from a humble I4, so why not reflect that fact with the new HQ? Legend has it that the genesis of the tower came from Schwanzer's clinking 4 beer mugs together. Working lunches even take place during Oktoberfest, apparently.[3]

In technical terms the cylinder was the correct choice in terms of office efficiency. When the office floor is a circle there is less walking distance to reach things, and the building as a whole lets in more light. TV coverage of the 1972 Olympics showed Frei Otto's canopy complex and, ready in time for the Games, the equally modern Schwanzer 4-cylinder tower nearby. Along with the new tower, BMW also had an adorable little "egg cup" museum next door. With both structures the BMW logo was very prominent.

The roof of the egg cup was a split-level blue and white roundel, and perched at the tower's top, BMW's badge was like the star on a Christmas tree. However, the logo and tower looked much more sinister glowing red against the darkness in the 1975 sci-fi film *Rollerball*, where the tower was a symbol of a future world where corporations governed every aspect of human destiny. The tower was also a beacon showing the new BMW. A coldly efficient structure, it displays corporate identity running on the four cylinders of an engine. It's no coincidence that BMW's middle name is motor.

It took BMW 55 years to make its one millionth car; today it makes 1,500,678 cars per annum (2007 BMW Group production total). The M10 I4 was the company's first engine in the drive for volume expansion. It was originally created by a 6-man team headed by Alex von Falkenhausen. Time was tight, but no stone was left unturned in the quest for a powerful and durable engine, because the BMW 1500 had to be a winner. The engine featured a single overhead camshaft with chain drive off a 5-bearing forged steel crank, aluminum crossflow head and cast iron block. It was a sound engine that soon grew into a 90 bhp 1800, but BMW didn't have all the answers. The 2-liter used in the 520 got a start thanks to Britain.

In the early to mid 1960s there was a dearth of good tuning work being done on the BMW I4 at home. Attempts to stoke the fires of the BMW 1800 came courtesy of British tuners like Bill Blydenstein: gas flowing heads, reprofiling cams, playing around with distributors and even a 2-liter engine. BMW didn't think it could be done, that there wasn't enough room left in the block to reach 2,000 ccs, until the British presented them with just such a bored-out block. BMW was stunned and inspired to introduce a modified block for a factory 2-liter version which would debut in the 1965 2000CS coupe, and the 1966 2000 sedan. The sedan application featured an even 100 bhp output.[4]

BMW had some new 2-liter developments for the 520. In place of the 2000's single Solex 40 PDSI, BMW introduced a dual carb setup for the 520 and 520 automatic. The 520's two Stromberg 175 CDET carbs were new hardware to BMW, and were only used on the 520; they weren't used on the 2002, 320/4 or any other Bimmer. The Strombergs had automatic choke action and were designed to give hassle-free running, even in cold weather. The new 2-liter was rated at 115 bhp at 5,800 rpm with 119 lbs/ft at a lowish 3,700 rpm. This was the even-tempered, trouble-free dual carb 2-liter, not the high-performance 2000TI with 2 Solex 40 PHH carbs of the '60s.

Those looking for an audacious 520 had to try the injected 520i. This e12 had the 130 bhp version of the 2-liter M10 well known from the 2000tii and 2002tii road burners, where fuel injection stood for performance. This engine didn't have some black box monitoring nanny system; this was racing fuel injection for the road! The 2000tii was the first BMW to be sold with fuel injection in 1969, followed by the 2002tii in 1971. The Kugelfischer PL04 had an electric pump to move the fuel along, with a mechanical injector pump boosting the pressure to a huge 500 psi at the point of injection.

By the early '70s fuel injection was expected on a fast European sports sedan. Every BMW rival offered a fuel injection variant. The Volvo 144E, Peugeot 504TI, Citroen DS 23, Triumph 2.5 PI and the MB 280E, which was in the same size class, but in a different engine size/price sector. The cars had mechanical or electronic systems by Bosch, Kugelfischer and Lucas, but they all had one thing in common: mechanics didn't like them! Fuel injection was considered the work of the devil, mainly because the trade was unfamiliar with the hardware in those early times. Whether it was the vacuum leaks of electronic systems, or improperly set-up mechanical injection, the car usually got blamed.

The Lucas injection on the Triumph TR6 and 2.5 PI was seen as some form of witchcraft, and the Kugelfischer system of the BMW 2002tii/520i needed fine adjustment to perform properly. The choke was automatic, initial idling enrichment being taken care of by the injection; just turn the key and go, don't touch the throttle before ignition! So life was supposed to be easier, but that didn't stop complaints of rough running and difficult starting. Much of this was due to incorrect idle speed and mixture settings. The latter on the U.S. 2002tii was set lean to pass emissions testing.

The 520i was never sold in the U.S., but it did welcome the attention of an expert. A dealership was the best place to start, and one has to question the ability of some overseas BMW service centers concerning looking after the BMW 2002tii/520i. This was one of the most advanced and best performing 2-liter engines in the world, especially after BMW's M10 head modification for the 1973 MY. All e12s featured M10s with the tri-hemi combustion chambers introduced with the 1968 M30 I6. BMW was using its head to make a cleaner-burning M10.

The tri-hemisphere arrangement was now used on the 4-cylinder to maintain power in the face of lower octane gas. Even in Europe lead was being phased out and BMW wanted to keep the M10's compression ratio, or efficiency, up, even though the octane boosting ingredient lead was being eliminated. The change was of great benefit to U.S. spec 1973 2002s, which were able to dump their air pumps while having a cleaner exhaust and restored pre-emissions acceleration. There were benefits too for the e12 520/520i.

In Europe less lead meant the 520i's engine was down to a 9.5 CR, from earlier 2002tiis' 10 to one, but the 520 was up to a 9 CR compared to the 2000's 8.5 to one. The later tri-hemi M10 can be identified by an "E12" casting mark on the intake side of the cylinder head; look to the right-hand side. This new version of the M10 was used on the 2002, the subsequent e21 3 series and the e12 5 series. One thing to consider about the 2-liter M10 is the heat generated by its larger bores.

The 2-liter's 89 × 80 mm dimensions, versus the 84 × 80 mm of the 1800, seems associated with more cases of blown head gaskets and cracked heads than the 1.8 liter M10. The reduced gasket area of the 2-liter makes cooling system inspection crucial. However, there was no need to stop at 2 liters with an e12. The 2-liter M10 tested the waters, just like Jaguar tried out the old XK I6 in the XJ sedan before introducing the V-12. The e12 had always been intended to take BMW's big six, and so it was that the 520 was joined by the 525 in late 1973. The later variant made its debut at the 1973 Frankfurt auto show as a 1974 MY entrant.

For the 1975 MY the 525 was accompanied by the up-engined and more lavishly trimmed 528. These latest e12s underlined the 5 series' business: it was BMW's middle model that borrowed from the small and large car ranges. The 520 sourced its engine and gearbox from the 2002; the 525/528 took their drive train from the big e3 sedan. The 2,494 cc and 2,788 cc motors from the 2500 and 2800 were selected, and that included use of 2bbl Zenith 32/40 and 35/40 INAT carbs. However, on the 525 and 528 these engines were detuned, giving 145 and 165 bhp at 6,000 and 5,800 rpm, rather than the 150 and 170 bhp at 6,000 rpm provided in the 2500/2800.

The car insurance and road tax laws in Germany, and continental Europe as a whole, involve different rates depending on engine horsepower and size. This leads to slight differences in displacement and advertised horsepower that really do affect the cost of car ownership. In Europe 2.8 liters is a limit above which the cost of motoring steps up appreciably, while in Italy the limit is 2 liters, which explains the great number of Ferrari 208 GT4/GTB/GTS in the home market. Ordinarily such small differences shouldn't have made much difference to the e12, but they did.

Something wasn't quite right with the 525 and 528. Mechanically they were very close to the 520/520i. The main differences were 4 wheel disks, different spring rates to cope with the weight distribution of a six, plus a larger radiator. The bigger radiator sat flush with the sheet metal, and the steel surround the small radiator was mounted on with I4 e12s was eliminated to give the longer I6 fan clearance. The I6 e12s weighed 100 lbs. less than an equivalent engined e3, so why were the 525 and 528 slower?

Using data from the same magazine the manual 525 did 0–60 mph in 10.6 seconds with a top end of 117 mph. This sounds quite respectable until one realizes that UK's *Autocar* also got 9.3 seconds and 121 mph out of a BMW 2500 tested earlier! However, the 525 proved more economical, achieving 23.7 mpg compared to the 2500's 21.8 mpg.[5] So what was going on here? It's true that the 525/528's M30s were artificially restricted to attain their bhp ratings, but the lighter e12s should have at least matched the e3's zip. Even in Europe low lead and "green" engine tuning were taking their toll.

Right to the end of production in 1977 the BMW 2500 was rated at 150 bhp, but if a later version was retested it would have been unlikely to have matched an older toxic edition. It would have been more economical, though, since from 1973–74 onwards, emissions and economy weighed heavily in BMW's thinking. This change in priorities didn't harm the e12, since BMW was on its way to star status.

By the mid '70s in Europe it didn't matter if the M30 wasn't the fireball it was in 1968–72; BMW's rivals were slower too, and they didn't have the prestige of a 525 or 528, unless they were wearing the three-pointed star. Still, turning up to a business meeting in a 525 made a much greater impact than arriving in a Ford Granada or Opel Senator. Both were worthy cars, and both German designed and built, but the BMW roundel had more authority.

There was an unobtrusive quality about the e12 5 series, and it was a known quantity. The understated, quiet assurance of the range was just right for this stage in BMW's history. *Thoroughbred & Classic Cars* summed it up well when reminiscing about a 525 they tried in 1974: "The following month it was the BMW 525's turn: a neat, efficient car and good value for money as a new machine, there was little to criticise."[6]

The 525 and 528 took the game right to the MB 250 and 280E compacts, which was the plan from the start. Jaguar XJ6 territory was also in sight. In this move upmarket it was understandable that BMW's new e12 5 series and e21 3 series ranges started off with soft suspension settings, discernibly cushier than those found on the 02 and e3. Those used to the older Bimmers were miffed at this development, but the e12 525/528 did set a new standard for handling/road shock absorption compromise. The e12 was more comfortable than MB's offerings, and more confidence-inspiring than those from Browns Lane Coventry.

The 528's standard power steering had a lot more feel than Jaguar's two-finger tillers. This level of driver involvement was a new development in this 6-cylinder size and price class. The closest precedent was the Triumph 2.5 PI, but that model didn't have the global market of the e12. Don't expect to be bowled over by luxury, though; BMW's trim was of the simple and durable kind.

The top e12 versions (528/528i/530i) provided the purchaser with a wooden console insert in front of the shifter, if the car didn't have a/c. This matched the trim piece seen on the e3 sedan and e9 coupe. From the 520i and up, one received a standard rev counter, plus a natty analogue-faced quartz timepiece built into the center dial of the HVAC controls. 520s made do with a large clock next to the speedo. Apart from these inventory changes, wooden door cappings and deluxe tool kit for the top model, trim spotters were disappointed.

One e12 looked much like another; even the leather was hard to tell from the leatherette. The gulf between Ford "L" and "Ghia" or Volvo Deluxe and Grand Luxe trim packs was somewhat greater. The big BMWs had interiors not much grander than a 2002. E12s and BMW's other new '70s models were plainer and starker than their '60s counterparts, as well as Daimler-Benz rivals. One can afford to be functional when living in a niche.

From the outside e12s could be differentiated by observing the chrome trunk lid model badge, with an equivalent badge on the front grille if a 520i or higher version was at hand. Why did the 520/520i have a flat hood pressing, but the 525/528 have a power bulge? That's because the I6 variants had a huge Pur-O-Lator air cleaner box for the M30's dual carbs, and this box needed hood clearance. Why was there a small cutout in the hood sound-deadening pad towards the radiator? Otherwise the engine-driven cooling fan would cut into the pad when the hood was shut.

Modern and functional: if it isn't there, it doesn't need to be there. That's why the e12 range didn't have a 518 until 1974. The e12 was hunting the Daimler-Benz Compact. Given there was no MB 180, BMW didn't bother to do a 518. The old 1800 had been the top-selling variant in the New Class era, but BMW was taking the e12 upmarket, so the product planners said no thank you to the 518, initially. There was a MB 200 and a BMW 520, a MB 250 and a 525, etc.; the pieces of the puzzle seemed to fit just fine.

BMW 2.5CS, 1502 & 518—Unbeatable Gas Mileage!

The new e21 3 series was coming out in mid-1975. This bigger, more refined 2002 replacement would offer a BMW 318. BMW reasoned the new 318 would look after 1800 trade-ins. However, BMW changed its mind when the 1973–74 fuel crisis struck. As with the earlier Suez Crisis, the oil squeeze made buyers search out smaller-engined cars. BMW obliged with not one, but three Econobimmers. There was the 1974–75 BMW 2.5CS coupe, the 1975–77 1502 and the new 518.

These 3 new versions had smaller or detuned engines fitted to BMW e9, 02 and e12 shells featuring decontented trim. All 3 versions were successful in sales, which shows that intelligent BMW buyers knew the value of economy. However, they achieved most of their success in West Germany and continental European markets. Buyers outside Europe have never been happy buying stripped-out Bimmers. The Karmann-built 2.5CS had its usual 3-liter replaced by the 2500's motor. Introduced in June 1974, the 2.5CS went on to sell 844 copies before the e9 was discontinued in 1975.

The 1502 used a detuned 75 bhp version of the 1602's 85 bhp 1.6 liter M10. As the cheapest BMW car one could buy, the 1502 notched up 72,632 sales before it was deleted in 1977. This 02 was sold alongside the new e21 3 series, and its popularity led BMW to introduce an e21 315 equivalent after the 1502's demise. However, the longest-lived of the economodels was the 518. Even after the fuel crisis the 518's popularity saw it become a permanent fixture. In truth it didn't offer the best overall gas mileage in the e12 fleet, its 1.8 M10 had to work hard for a living, but there were other savings.

The 518's 1,766 cc engine size and 90 bhp rating put it in a category attracting lower road tax, insurance and company car cost. The 1.8 liter M10 made maximum power at a leisurely 5,500 rpm, and with its 8.6 CR was the only Euro e12 capable of running on 91 octane gas, from the '76 MY. The 520–528 needed 98 octane premium grade. The 518 had the same Solex 38 PDSI downdraft carb as used on the 1600–2. Buying a 518 limited the number of options available; for example, a 4-speed stick shift was mandatory. Automatic, or the close-ratio 5-speed available on the 520/520i, were unavailable. A 518 couldn't be optioned with a/c, plus it was the only e12 that didn't come with a rear armrest!

It may have sounded like a sub-compact miser pack special, but the 518 was a logical choice for budget buyers. BMW rightly reasoned that anyone in the 1974 slump who really wanted a/c and automatic could easily have risen to a 520. Restricting the 518's spec cut down on unnecessary production line variation. One item the 518 had that other e12s didn't was a manual choke. Some like the idea of pulling out the choke, manually enriching the engine on startup, and pushing the choke home once the motor had warmed up. This reliable system is favored over carbs with automatic chokes in cold climates.

When pollution controls started coming, enthusiasts sought out the manual choke, because they knew it was the only way to overcome the fiendishly bad drivability of carb cars that tried to meet emissions regs. Before starting a new 518, the driver would pull out the choke, a pull-out knob below the instrument binnacle, where the hazard warning light switch would be on 520–528s. The "low gas" warning light in the instrument cluster would come on, since it did double duty for low gas and choke operation on the 518.

Size was another reason for choosing a 518 over a 318. The e21 3 series didn't offer comfy seating for four, and came with the inconvenience of a 2-door only format. The West German public seemed to have a higher regard for the 518 than the 1973–74 2002 Turbo. Their love of excellent machinery and true high performance has always been matched by a concern for the environment and the need to conserve. The public's mood was that the 2002 Turbo's front spoiler mirror turbo script was a bit of overkill. Given the auto climate of the time it was their right to question the necessity of a small high-speed hovercraft, which could gobble up several liters of premium if its turbo motor was unleashed.

In the end the figures speak for themselves: 1,672 2002 Turbos against 125,000 e12 518s. There was a temporary Autobahn limit of 100 kph, and a complete ban on Sunday driving for the whole of December 1973. Indeed, there were moments when one could dance on the Autobahn during those times with complete impunity.[7] Dr. Joachim Zahn, president of Daimler-Benz, stated in the aftermath that having a blanket Autobahn speed limit under 140 kph would be an economic and social disaster. If anything it would have resulted in a complete waste of the Autobahn network as traffic slowed to a crawl to conserve oil.[8]

A need to conserve oil imports saw Britain introduce a blanket speed limit on its motorways in 1973 ... of just 50 mph! This was lifted back to 1967's 70 mph in 1974, but not before BMW Concessionaires GB put out an advertisement stating the gasoline consumption of the 2002tii, 520 and 3.0Si at 50 mph. In a reworking of the "Unbeatable BMW" ad slogan, the line proclaimed, "At 50 mph BMW is Unbeatable," as well as "Unbeatable performance, unbelievable economy." The oil crunch crystallized the need to be able to maintain good cruising speeds, 80–90 mph, with low gas consumption.

BMW didn't make a diesel in the '70s, but its sports niche seemed to insulate it from the 1974 car industry slump. While big car makers like VW and Opel suffered and specialists with gas-guzzling V-8s like ISO and Jensen closed, BMW hugged the middle ground and prospered. Indeed, right into the '80s BMW said it chose to steer clear of the V-8s and V-12s of rivals, feeling that the injected big six was all the enthusiast required for power, smoothness and economy. This argument was driven home during the spring of 1974 with the release of BMW's largest and most luxurious limousine of the modern era, the e3 3.3L.

The efficiency of the long-wheelbase 3.3L was plain to see when compared with the MB 600. According to Autocar figures for automatic-equipped cars, the BMW recorded 0–60 mph in 9.9 seconds, a top speed of 124 mph and overall fuel consumption of 17.7 mpg. The 6.3-liter MB 600 had respective figures of 9.7 seconds, 130 mph and 11.6 mpg. BMW's limousine achieved 95 percent of the V-8 Mercedes' performance with 3 liters less displacement and a handy fuel efficiency saving. There was also the BMW 3.3Li, with fuel injection, which took power from 190 to 197 bhp.[9]

The 3.3L/Li came with automatic as standard, but BMW's 4-speed manual could be selected to bring greater performance and extra mpgs. Even in the aftermath of a fuel crisis, the Bavarians were challenging the Swabians for the title of best luxo sedan on the planet! BMW could afford to be bullish, their bookkeeper only used red ink in the second half of 1974, the only time the company has been in the red since the rebirth brought by the 1500. However, there was a price for good design and success: high prices for consumers. In the

In 1978, San Diego, California–based company Tfa (Toys for Adults) created a soft toy version of the U.S. e12 528i, in association with artist Margie Smith (courtesy Ulrich Thieme, http://www.e12.de).

new world luxury car hierarchy one could safely assume that the only pricier rival to BMW would be a Benz.

A BMW 528 cost more than a Rover P6 3500, a Volvo 164TE or even a Jaguar XJ6; the only higher plane was a MB 280E. The public weren't fazed; they understood why the 528 cost more. The 528 cost more because it was a BMW. However, in North America BMW tried to be more accessible. The Munich concern remembered what happened when they brought out the e3: not much! To combat slow sales both the 2500 and 2800 were replaced by a competitively priced edition using the 2.8 liter M30. BMW called it the Bavaria, and this e3 variant was a hit, just like the 1600–2 was in the 1967 MY.

Exports Ahoy! The 1975 U.S. 530i Arrives

Americans appreciate value for money, so BMW priced their first U.S. e12 appropriately. It was 1975, the year of the mini-yacht. In the wake of the fuel crisis it was wise and fashionable to go small. A V-8-powered Mustang II Ghia looked like a MB 450SLC if one squinted. What about the new AMC Pacer? Small truly was never this wide! Then there was the new Cadillac Seville, derived from the Chevy Nova, to get Mercedes conquest sales in the new "international size" luxury sedan class. Cadillac was pleased; the 5.7-liter Seville priced out higher than their full-size 8.2-liter Deville, which lent new meaning to the term "value added." Still, the MB S class was $20,000, the Seville only $13,700, and Cadillac almost matched Daimler-Benz sales with the Seville alone, so it must have been a bargain.

BMW was breaking a few U.S. records of its own. The 1974 MY saw the 02/e3/e9 American total jump to 15,000 units. If one was to select a BMW rival to the Seville and MB 280S, it would be the e3 Bavaria sedan. However, by 1975 the Bavaria was replaced by the U.S. e12 530i, technically. In Europe the e3 was a size up from the e12, and in its home market the e3 was replaced by the new e23 7 series range in 1977. In America the size distinction between the e3 and e12 was negligible. The mere 3-inch length difference between Euro spec e3 and e12 hardly amounted to a hill of beans.

In the U.S. the 530i was considered the new Bavaria; the newcomer even used the 3 liter I6. This was the only M30 I6 used in North America from 1972 to 1977. The e3 continued in America as the 3.0Si. The 3.0Si was a Bavaria loaded with formerly optional accessories, and came with the same super-smog 3-liter used in the new 530i. With its list price of $13,800, U.S. Bimmer fans had two alternatives to a Seville: drive away in a stock standard 3.0Si, or tick option boxes to bring the 530i's price up. Naturally the Seville didn't offer a manual gearbox.

BMW had garnered a good reputation amongst small sports sedan fans with the 2002, and some celebrities drove BMWs too. Jackie Onassis had a green automatic 1974 Bavaria and Henry Winkler ("The Fonz") owned a blue 733i. However, if one wasn't a weekend autocrosser, or not a celebrity, BMW was still a mystery. In 1975 BMW brought its Batmobile CSL to America to take part in IMSA racing. Some U.S. newspapers mistakenly reported on the two cars driven by Hans Stuck Jr./Ronnie Peterson and Brian Redman/Sam Posey as coming from the British Motor Works! From that point on BMW made sure Bavarian Motor Works was writ large across the racers' windshields.

In deference to the lack of brand recognition in the U.S., BMW introduced the 1975

530i at just $9,097 on the east coast. This 4-speed manual sports sedan had the new 3-liter M30 ecomotor. For 1975 BMW was forced to revise its emissions strategy for the U.S. Matters had moved on from the 1969 MY, when the e3 made its U.S. debut with an engine sans smog gear. BMW had designed into the first M30 a special triple hemispherical combustion chamber. By having one hemisphere around the intake, exhaust valves and spark plug, the engineers created a thorough burn swirl action.

The initial 2.5 and 2.8 I6s matched their European spec outputs, while passing U.S. pollution dictates using a leaner idle mixture. For the 1972 MY, BMW replaced the Bavaria's 2.8 with a lower CR 3-liter, since emissions law was starting to bite. The upside was that the 3-liter could now use leaded regular; previously the 2.8 needed premium gas. Premium 99 octane gas, muscle cars and their premium fuel motors were becoming as extinct as the dodo. The low CR dual carb M30 continued through 1974 when BMW and Honda embarked on maverick motors. One had to be a maverick to meet 1975 emissions dictates without a catalytic converter.

BMW studied the 2-way cats available at the time and didn't like what they saw. Placing this fancy filter in one's exhaust system brought as much benefit as a banana up the tailpipe. Apart from being restrictive, it made the engine hard to tune so that it could pass smog tests and ensure survival of the cat. Short-lived cats also tied the owner to a strict diet of unleaded, lest the cat should get poisoned by lead! Many gas stations used to like displaying a low-leaded regular price, only for the motorist to arrive and discover that the unleaded price was exorbitant. Most owners of new cars by the mid–'70s could only use unleaded, so they had zero choice.

Honda grabbed headlines with their stratified 3-valve-per-cylinder CVCC engine. The Civic's segmented combustion chamber had a small part with a rich mixture; the rest used a lean fuel mixture. Emissions and drivability were licked on leaded regular. BMW's 530i achieved this using thermal reactors. Munich's solution was to place two thermal reactor chambers on the exhaust manifold. This was combined with established tricks like exhaust gas recirculation (EGR) and an air pump. EGR channeled exhaust gases back into the intake side. The air pump, a.k.a. back pressure Meister, put air into the exhaust ports to lean out the fuel mix. It was a means of cutting pollution by having a hot combustion chamber mixture, which went through the thermal reactors before exiting the 530i's exhaust.

BMW could be proud of the result. The 530i using Bosch L-Jetronic fuel injection made more power than 1974's 3-liter Bavaria did on carbs. In 1975 a net power rating of 176 bhp (SAE) at 5,500 rpm was nothing to be sniffed at. The 1975 base-engined Corvette had 165 bhp, and as a 4-speed car it was slower than the BMW 530i 4-speed, in spite of a 2.7-liter displacement advantage. The 530i's 176 horses also looked spry next to the Caddy Seville's 350 (5.7 liters) Olds-derived 170 horses, another fuel injected engine like the 530i. However, the 530i did have electronic-tuned port fuel injection years before Detroit. The Bavarians also had a decided advantage over Daimler-Benz.

The MB 280S was rated at 160 bhp in Europe, but only 120 bhp in America. In contrast, the U.S. spec 530i was the most powerful and fastest e12 anywhere. The European spec 528 had 165 bhp, claimed top speed of 198 kph and 0–100 kph in 9.5 seconds. Manufacturer figures for the 530i were 200 kph and 9.3 seconds. At a time when European power outputs were getting lost in translation, the 530i was delivering authentic BMW to U.S. patrons. As with the Bavaria 3.0Si a high percentage of buyers chose their 530i with manual transmission. Seventy percent of 1975–78 530i owners surveyed chose the manual 4-speed, according to *Road & Track*. However, the life of a car lover is never an easy one.

No car is perfect, and even the 530i had its faults. Lift the hood on a 530i and a bewildering array of fuel injection and smog gear plumbing greet the eye. The 530i may have had great drivability, but the pollution controls muted the 3-liter's response unless the gas pedal was floored. The thermal reactor route involved retarded ignition timing, especially so for Californian 530is, which worked against crisp engine response. The 530i's rich fuel mix and retarded spark also spelled bad gas mileage. In spite of using cheaper leaded regular the 530i, even in 49-state tune, drank like a fish. An auto oxymoron, the 530i was a gas-guzzling compact.

Consumers Union feared that Jaguar, BMW and Rolls Royce might have to leave the U.S., since their cars fell so far short of the new auto fleet gas mileage boosting CAFE standard.[10] Of equal concern was the fact the 530i, and other thermal reactor-equipped Bimmers of 1975–79, were getting a little hot under the collar. The reactors were doing their job, glowing in the dark of night, but their close proximity to the aluminum cylinder head precipitated cracking of same. Cracked heads were a problem BMW didn't anticipate to the degree the problem occurred. In *Road & Track*'s survey, 7 percent of surveyed '76 MY 530i owners suffered cracked heads.

BMW decided, eventually, that it was wise to keep U.S. owners happy and extended warranty support beyond the usual 12 months/12,000 miles. If an owner experienced cylinder head cracking, even if it was outside the normal warranty period, he was entitled to a new head at no charge. In addition, BMW redesigned the M30's head with different and wider coolant passages (13 mm vs. 9 mm) for 1980. Look for the two-digit head casting stamp; you want it to say "80" or higher. BMW had completely dumped thermal reactors by the 1980 MY, so the cracked head problem ceased to be an issue anyway.

The 530i also had the dubious honor of being fitted with extended 5 mph bumpers. Insurance companies wishing to avoid payouts for low-speed fender benders pressured the U.S. government to get tough on car bumpers. As Consumers Union observed, the stricter law was to protect the car, not its occupants! The 5 mph bumpers were rubber-clad aluminum bars, sitting on hydraulic rams, with the body-to-bumper gap filled with rubber and concertina side trim. The bumpers took the e12's length to 190 inches and added 200 lbs! Normally the e12's front turn signal lamps were on the bumper, but these were eliminated on the 530i.

The U.S. e12s had large side marker lights, amber at the front and red at the rear. Side markers had been mandatory on cars sold in the U.S. since the 1970 MY. As per other '70s imports, the side markers and 5 mph bumpers looked tacked on, rather than designed in as per domestic designs. U.S. e12s also had an extra centrally placed dash instrument pod, with warning lights for seat belt usage, thermal reactor service, and EGR inspection. Attempt to drive without a belt and a warning buzzer (no soft chimes in the '70s) plus the warning light told the driver to do the right thing. Interestingly, Porsche and Volvo chose to share their 5 mph bumpers with the whole world. They did look decidedly chunky on the Volvo. The Swedes also thought the seat belt warning lamp and buzzer were worth including for all world markets.

America wasn't the only place BMW was making changes for a safer and greener world. In 1975, the final year for the 520i with Kugelfischer injection, BMW also discontinued

By the 1980 MY the U.S. 528i had gained a manual 5-speed as standard equipment, and lost 110 lbs. Weight-saving measures dropped the curb weight to 3,180 lbs. (courtesy Adam Wilson).

the Euro spec 3.0Si with Bosch D-Jetronic. Emissions and service ease saw the 520i switch to Bosch K-Jetronic and the 3.0Si changed to Bosch L-Jetronic. Visually the 520i looked as it did in 1975, but the '76 model had a different heart. The latest injected 2-liter was a new version of the M10, designed for lower octane gas and to be used in the e21 320i. The K in K-jet stood for Konstant or continuous mechanical injection.

Emissions-aware K-jet was part of a reworked lower CR I4, down to 9.3 to one from 9.5, making 125 bhp instead of 130 ponies. The 520i was slightly slower according to official figures: top speed was 113 mph, not 114 mph, and 0–60 mph had risen to 10.8 from 10.5 seconds. Similarly the 1976 3.0Si dropped 5 horses, 195 versus 200 bhp, with 0–60 mph worsening from 7.4 to 7.6 seconds. The upside was that K and L-jet were easier to deal with, and less prone to ECU-fooling vacuum leaks which affected the intake manifold vacuum pressure sensing D-jet.

BMW also made a smooth change concerning automatic transmissions, by switching to the ZF 3HP22 unit in 1976–77. This modern unit used clutches rather than old-fashioned brake bands, which were known to stretch with age. The 3HP22 was lighter, more compact and featured a Simpson planetary gearset. BMW would use this autobox on all its cars from 1977 to 1982. The only deviation was on the BMW 635CSi/735i and turbo 745i, which used a strengthened version to cope with their 224 and 280 lbs./ft. torque.

The 6 series tried out the new box in 1976; the 5 series waited until 1977. Previously the 5 series used different autos depending on engine size. 1976 also saw the 518 get a different carb: the Solex DIDTA 32/32 downdraft unit. This item came with automatic choke, and the 1.8 liter M10 experienced a CR drop, from 8.6 to 8.3 to one. Horsepower stayed constant, torque suffered a bit, but claimed performance was unaffected. As usual the 1.8 liter only had half the number of crankshaft counterweights compared to the 2-liter, 4 versus 8.

1977–81— BMW e12 Series II

Of greater import were the changes slated for the 1977–79 model years. Over the road in Stuttgart, Daimler-Benz was replacing the W114 with the much-revised W123 Compact. The latest mini–Merc had styling to match the W116 S class, a new-look dashboard and various mechanical amendments. BMW responded with the series II e12, which had new frontal styling to blend the e12 in with other new '70s Bimmers. As started by the BMW Turbo gullwing sports car, the latest Bimmers had raised kidney grilles, tapered into the nose and integrated into a narrow raised hood power band.

The 1977 e12s also took on the e23 7 series style rear lamps. The rear lamps were now larger and more visible compared to early e12s. The new taillights necessitated the movement of the gas tank filler from the rear deck to the side of the rear fender. Inside BMW gave the e12 adjustable dash vents, two at the center and one each at the outer ends. They are popular e12 retrofit items. The e12 dash molding was also slightly altered so that the part with the 3 rotary HVAC controls came further forward. This alteration was to fit in with the changes to the dash arrangement on e12s with a/c.

The 5 series cars with a/c no longer had separate controls. The main rotary temp dial now had a red segment and a blue segment. To turn on the a/c one twisted the temp dial into the blue section, and used the main knurled ring to control fan speed. The car stereo was repositioned in a more user-friendly place just under the HVAC controls. Previously the radio/cassette player on e12s with a/c sat low on the transmission tunnel, and was pretty much blocked by the shifter. The other main change for 1977 concerned the introduction of the Solex 4A1 carb.

The Solex 4A1 was now used on the 525 and 528. Horsepower rose to 150 and 170 bhp respectively, and drivability was also improved. In place of the previous 2 × 2bbl Zeniths, the single 4bbl Solex was an easier creature to deal with. On the cosmetic front 1977 saw the flat shiny chrome hubcap for the e12's steel rims become slightly dished. The revised hubcap design was short-lived, as were the 1977–78 black plaque mounted trunk-lid model i.d. badges. For 1978 the e12 adopted the steel rim pattern with small chrome/roundel center cap seen on the 1974 MY 2002, plus e21 3 series and low spec e23 7 series, where the lug nuts were exposed.

In 1977–78 BMW finally reordered its Euro e12 range to match their tradition of having one injected version as the top model. This practice also involved the top version being manual only, with a lower tuned carb variant acting as a special automatic model. Thus, for 1973 the 3.0Si and 520i were the most powerful e3 and e12 versions, with a 520A as the automatic e12. The order was confused in 1974–77, when the M30 big six-powered 525 and 528 arrived as range toppers. Now BMW anointed the 2.8-liter e12 as the true top e12 by giving it Bosch L-Jetronic fuel injection.

The 528i had a claimed top speed of 129 mph and upgrades to keep its 184 bhp in check. It was the only e12 variant delivered with 195/70 14-inch VR tires as standard, plus there were larger 11-inch front vented disks. The 518 and 525 were also upgraded to 11-inch front disks for 1977, but their front rotors were solid. The L in L-jet stood for Luft, which means air. The electronic injection used a vanemeter, which operated on the amount of air aspirated. The vanemeter was a box with a moving door. The more power required, the more air was needed to go with the extra fuel. The vanemeter door would open wider to admit greater amounts of air.

The position of the vanemeter door was relayed via a potentiometer to the engine management computer (in the glove box), which worked out how long to leave the injectors open. This system can't be chipped for more power. There is no removable EPROM chip containing fuel/ignition maps that the computer's CPU can utilize. Bosch K-jet and L-jet came out in 1973, second generation fuel injection after the world's first electronic system Bosch D-jet came out in 1968. The 1978 520 didn't offer Bosch K-jet; it didn't even offer the M10! The M10-powered 520/520i were axed at the close of the 1977 MY.

Now, according to the words of a BMW e21 ad, even in the economical 2-liter class one could take the farsighted step up to six cylinders. BMW had introduced a new engine family, one that is still with us, albeit much modified. For years fans had loved the power and smoothness of the big six; now the time had come for BMW's baby six! The new M60 small six was released under BMW's engine chief Karlheinz Lange. The e21 3 series was larger and heavier than the 02 family it replaced. The new small six would give the e21 greater refinement, plus a way to get more power without using a turbo.

After the 2002 Turbo it was BMW's intention to improve performance with larger displacement naturally-aspirated I6s. To this end the first new 6-cylinder e21s were the 320/6 and 323i. The injected 2.3 liter 323i motor wasn't used in the 5 series, but the smaller six was. It was a 122 bhp straight six with cast-iron block, aluminum SOHC head, and a new development for modern Bimmers, a toothed rubber belt for the camshaft. The cambelt was part of the M60's tremendous refinement. In the 3 and 5 series the 2-liter M60 soon gained a reputation for being the smoothest six in the world.

Unfortunately the early small sixes also had a reputation for cracked heads. This wasn't thermal reactor related; it was just that the original head design could develop cracks, sometimes at low mileage. A well-cared-for engine would need a new head at the 100,000 mile mark. There were usually several cracks so the head couldn't be patched up. BMW released a revised design when introducing a 2.5-liter version for the 1986 MY, so a buyer today should check the head date stamp to make sure it says "85" or later. The baby six needs regular inspection of the cooling system, and regular coolant changes. The rubber cambelt must be replaced every 30,000 miles; if it snaps, your motor will come to a dead standstill.

There was no need to worry about carburetion, since the 520/6 used the reliable Solex 4A1. It was easy to tell if one was piloting a new 520/6, because there was a 520 chrome badge on the front grille. The previous 520/4 didn't have this item. E12s from the 1978 MY also had new chrome side mirrors mounted in the corner of the window, rather than on the door as previously. One complaint about the 520/6's performance was its pokey power delivery. The M60 baby six lacked the torque of the old M10. The problem couldn't be disposed of by ordering the close ratio 5-speed, since this option was taken away from 2-liter e12s when the 2.0 M10 was discontinued at the end of the '77 MY. One could order the CR gearbox on the 525/528i, but the 520/6 was limited to just four on the floor.

Standard equipment of all I6 e12s for the 1979 MY was transistorized ignition. No more contact breaker points subject to wear and tear. The steering column of 1979 MY e12s received the nicer-feeling, chunky column stalks found on the e23 7 series. The lamp in the instrument binnacle that used to cover low gas tank level now did brake pad wear. If the pads got too thin the light would come on, thanks to a sensor fitted to the disk brake. The warning light for being low on gas was now placed at the low end of the gas gauge's scale.

BMW also decided to remove the chrome from the dashboard's wood trim panel. The chrome could glint distractingly if caught by the sun at a certain angle. In 1979, it was also the year of the BMW 518, and BMW acknowledged the model's popularity by making automatic and a/c available options. It was also a good time to introduce a new version of the e12 for North America. BMW got to work on a replacement for the 530i. The 1979 U.S. spec 528i was a test model for a new gas mileage maximizing, pollution control approach that would be introduced on the U.S. 320i/633CSi/733i for the 1980 MY.

It was the end of the road for thermal reactors. Better apparatus was at hand with the 3-way catalytic converter and Bosch Lambda sond oxygen sensor used by Saab and Volvo. The 3-way cat could control carbon monoxide, hydrocarbons and nitrogen oxide. The oxygen sensor sniffed exhaust gases and sent a signal back to the ECU to keep the air/fuel mixture at the optimal stoichiometric ratio. This pollution control method allowed the 530i's air pump, EGR and thermal reactors to be dumped; it also allowed a leaner fuel mix and more advanced ignition timing.

The changes implied that the new 528i wasn't just more frugal, it was also quicker and more responsive. Even with the displacement drop the 528i turned in a 0–60 mph time of 8.2 seconds and a top speed of 125 mph, with 3rd gear good for 100 mph. Both *Road & Track* and *Car & Driver* achieved near identical figures, so there was no doubt the mechanical amendments had been positive. The 528i was the quickest-model BMW sold in America at the time. Power and torque were down on the 530i, 169 bhp at 5,500 rpm/170 lbs./ft. at 4,500 rpm, but the 528i made more efficient use of its M30 I6.

The U.S. 528i was EPA rated at 20.5 mpg overall, and this figure got better when BMW introduced an overdrive (0.81 for fifth) 5-speeder as standard equipment on the 1980 U.S. 528i. In the wake of the gas crunch of 1979, BMW made overdrive 5-speeders available on all e12s from the 520 up. It was also possible to choose a close ratio 5-speed, but not on the U.S. 528i. The Euro heavy duty suspension option was also unavailable, but one could specify a limited slip differential. Most thinking with the U.S. e12 was directed at gas mileage and it's notable that the 528i's final drive was 3.45:1, rather than the original 530i's 3.64 ratio.

In such oil-conscious times BMW put the e12 on a diet, trimming weight wherever it could: less sound insulation, thinner glass and sheet metal in places, different radiator hoses. The only diet downside was a tendency for the differential to tear away from its trunk floor mounting in some cases. It's a symptom that doesn't affect pre–1979 e12s. Going back specifically to the U.S. market, the 528i was reliable and well liked, preferred to the 530i. BMW settled into a pattern of importing 6,000 to 7,000 5 series cars per year, and by the time the e12 was discontinued at the end of the '81 MY, nearly 50,000 U.S. e12s had been sold.

For 1980 BMW replaced the e12's analogue clock, located in the central dial of the HVAC controls, with a red L.E.D. digital unit. It was a modern upgrade at the time, but collectors today prefer the classier analogue example. Similarly for the 1980 MY, BMW changed the e12's side mirrors to large black plastic casings, which became standard issue on the e21 and e23 too. This style of mirror lived on into the e32 7 series era, but wasn't as attractive as earlier chrome equivalents. Moving the e12's seat belt buckles onto the seat track for 1980 was unquestionably all to the good.

3

The e12 5 Series Motorsport Creations and Tuner Versions

Alpina and the e12

What is a tuner and why is one needed? It is a company specializing in improvements for a certain make, or makes, of automobile. Such companies exist because some people can't find the exact model they are looking for. Tuners dealing with BMWs service a niche demand within a niche, and one of the oldest and best known is Alpina. Burkhard Bovensiepen was a trailblazer with his Bavarian Buchloe concern when he created a hop-up kit for the BMW 1500 in 1965. The kit consisted of a pair of Weber 2bbl sidedraft carbs, custom intake manifold and oversize oil-bathed air filter.

BMW 1500 owners loved the hop-up kit, since it gave them the go of the latest BMW 1800 without having to trade in. BMW liked Alpina too; impressed with the company's quality, they chose to honor the standard BMW warranty even after the car was modified. BMW also took an interest in Alpina's work since such improvements could be applied to future regular production BMWs. Indeed, the well-known turbine spoke alloys available on the e12 for the 1974 MY, also used on many other Bimmers, was patterned off Alpina's design. Right from the start, if one owned an e12, Alpina had something to upgrade it.

It was possible to upgrade the 520/520i with one of Alpina's established A1, A2, A3, A4, A4S or A5 M10-based power plants. These engines offered between 120 and 170 bhp using Weber carbs, gas flowed head, sports cam and treated crank. Add a sports exhaust, firmer suspension, front spoiler, rims and body decals from the Alpina catalogue to create a unique 5 series. Alpina even had a special version of the 520i injection motor yielding 155 bhp. It had 10 to one CR and produced 0–100 kph in 8.8 when fitted. This was engine tuning similar to the 160-horse 520i from the house of Reppekus. Alpina kept on using Kugelfischer mechanical injection even after BMW had stopped.

Start with an I6 e12 and one could choose Alpina's B2 3-liter motor. The B2 was a triple carb M30 I6 that made 230 bhp. The A1–A4S series was often fitted to the BMW 2002, the B2 featured on the e3 sedan and e9 coupe. The injected 2.8-liter B6 engine was also available in the e12 5 series. The B6 engine made 200 bhp and became closely associated with the e21 3 series. Even with the B6 the improvement on a normal 528 was appreciable, The Alpina 528 B6 did 0–100 kph in 7.6 seconds with a top speed of 212 kph, the B2

In 1979 the e12-based 155 mph Alpina B7 sedan became the fastest 4-door production car in the world ... then came the Alpina B7S (courtesy Ulrich Thieme, http://www.e12.de).

version taking those stats onto 6.9 seconds and 228 kph. Nifty in the '70s, but Alpina was concerned with the bigger picture.

By the late 1970s Alpina had made the transition from tuner to car manufacturer, realizing that even in Europe all new cars, standard or modified, would have to meet pollution, noise and safety dictates. These were not BMWs, they were Alpinas, complete haute couture creations sold as unique variants in their own right. Alpina would still sell engine, suspension and cosmetic upgrades on an individual retrofit basis for existing cars, but their heart was now in creating zero-mile turnkey modified new cars. One could select the Alpina B6, a 2.8-liter injected 200 bhp e21 3 series, or the Alpina B8. The B8 was an interesting predecessor of the very popular 245 bhp e28 based Alpina B9 of the '80s. The e12-based B8 used a warmed-over 240 bhp version of BMW's injected 3.2-liter M30.

The naturally aspirated B8 was the Alpina e12 often seen in right-hand-drive markets, where it was often called the Alpina 533i. It offered Alpina's special suspension, 16-inch alloys, cross-drilled vented rotors, belt-driven differential oil cooler etc., combined with a clean modified engine that used Bosch fuel injection, after the toxic B2 era. A much spicier Alpina offering was available in West Germany and on the Continent, namely the B7 sedan and coupe. Why were these cars for Europe alone? The reason was turbocharging. The B7's turbo/exhaust manifold would get in the way of the steering mechanism of right-hand-drive cars.

The Alpina B7 was based on the e12; the B7 coupe used the e24 platform. Central to both was a custom 3-liter turbo BMW M30 I6. With the planet concerned with pollution

Top: The Alpina B7S upped the ante by replacing the B7's 300 bhp turbo 3-liter I6 with a 330 bhp 3.5-liter turbo upgrade. *Bottom:* The special touches to the e12 B7S included a transmission-tunnel-located turbo boost control knob bearing Alpina's logo. ZF made a custom ZF S5-40 box for the B7S. ZF have long since sold all items for S5-40 for Alpina and Tom Walkinshaw Racing (courtesy Ulrich Thieme, http://www.e12.de).

and economy, Alpina's Dr. Fritz Indra felt a blown six was the sensible solution. Turbos are rather muffler-like in nature, hushing up an exhaust system, which was great for noise pollution testing. Alpina also sought to better Porsche's 930, which also made 300 bhp, but required 3.3 liters. To achieve the target, Alpina used a KKK K27 turbo blowing as hard as 12 psi, at which point a bypass valve stepped in.

The turbo was blowing through racing-style Pierburg/Zenith DL mechanical fuel injection. There may have been no black box with the injection, but there was with the ignition. In a world first for a road car the Alpina B7 used electronic Hartig ignition, making the spark at the right moment. This was crucial for reliability and power. In spite of an intercooler, there would be times when the turbo 3-liter would be making under 300 bhp. Turbo motors already have to deal with hot exhaust gases, and on a warm day sometimes not even an intercooler is enough. In these cases the Hartig ignition system optimally retarded ignition timing.

In other respects the B7 sedan looked much like its naturally aspirated B8 counterpart, with 16-inch rims, 7 inches wide at the front, 8 inches at the rear, special Bilstein tuned dampers, Alpina's wild art decals and that differential oil cooler which wasn't mere frippery. However, the B7 did have one visible party trick, an adjustable turbo boost dial bearing Alpina's famous logo. This was placed on the transmission tunnel; turn it in the right direction, stir the close ratio 5-speeder and your destiny would be 155 mph. Thus, the e12 B7 was the fastest 1979 4-door sedan in the world. Alpina also claimed 0–100 mph in 13.7 seconds.

At U.S. $31,500 not many B7 sedans were to be seen, but that didn't worry Alpina. The 149 brand-new B7 cars the company produced suited its scale of business, and there was always the next step. In the 1979 MY, BMW made available its 3.5 liter M30 for the first time in a production model (BMW 635CSi), giving Alpina scope to improve the B7. The Alpina B7S ran from November 1981 to May 1982 as a 3.5-liter 330 bhp replacement for the B7 sedan. The new version used slightly higher boost, 12.5 psi, with changes aimed at reducing dreaded turbo lag.

With a claimed top end of 162 mph, plus slightly better standing-start acceleration, the B7S was better and, at DM 85,000, it was DM 10,000 pricier than the B7, but its true value would never be revealed at a traffic light Grand Prix. No, any car with a tall 2.93 final drive is more concerned with easy cruising at 130 mph, and that's the reason 60 Alpina patrons bought the B7S, and that 60 covered both the sedan and coupe combined! However, if Alpina was the way to the future, the GS Tuning 530 was an example of traditional tuning. No black boxes, just black tire lines left behind as the driver dropped the clutch during a smoking start.

GS Tuning 530

The figures were impressive, a top speed verified by *Automotor und Sport* to be 238 kph. *Modern Motor* magazine recorded 0–100 kph in 6.2 seconds in damp conditions. The GS Tuning 530 was named after founder Gerhard Schnedier and used a 240 bhp 3-liter triple carb M30 I6 redlined at 7,200 rpm. The model started in 1974 and used a BMW 525 as a base with e3 3.0Si upgrades. In 1974, GS Tuning also prepared a 2002 that finished

A different kind of hot 5 series, a fire brigade series 2 1978 e12 520. BMW also supplied vehicles to the police and ambulance medical services. Note the absence of chrome from the B pillars and bumpers (courtesy Ulrich Thieme, http://www.e12.de).

2nd in the ETCC, behind a Zakspeed Ford Escort. Starting with a 525 implied no power steering, which helped towards the GS Tuning 530's low weight of 1,315 kilos. Like the BMW 1800/2000TI, the GS Tuning 530 used Solex sidedraft carbs, in this case 3 × 2bbl Solex 45 PPH rather than 2 × 2bbl Solex 40 PHH as on the older I4 cars. An engine oil cooler and 304-degree sports cam were also present.

As with the 1800/2000TI, the GS Tuning 530 was perfectly well behaved when tooling along at low rpm, and as with any Bimmer it was safe to explore its high limits. At a time when the e12 525 was sold with solid front and rear disks, the GS Tuning 530 was improved with the 4 wheel vented rotors of the 3.0Si. The 3.0Si also bestowed its optional LSD, and some of its suspension parts were used with Bilstein shocks on the GS Tuning 530. In place of the 525's 5-inch-wide steel rims were Mahle anodized 7-inch-wide alloys, plus a pick 'n' mix front grille badge. GS Tuning created a badge using the five from 525, and the three zero from the e3's 3.0 trunk lid badge.

BMW gave its blessing to the work of GS Tuning and its technical director Dieter Basche, but after the fuel crisis, European car regs, etc., the market didn't welcome a specialist. The GS Tuning 530 showed the way things were; the smog-controlled U.S. 530i showed how things had become. In this formal, ordered market, there was no room for free

A dual Stromberg M10 is an odd sight on a 1978 e12. The 115 bhp I4 was last inserted in 520s before the summer of 1977. It seems BMW kept using this motor for emergency services cars (courtesy Ulrich Thieme, http://www.e12.de).

radicals, unless one lived in California. The land of the "smog Nazis" might have seemed an unlikely location for a BMW tuner. Almost all the U.S. speed shops dealing with U.S. cars, like Royal Pontiac and Mr. Norm's Grand Spaulding Dodge, had been legislated and insurance-premiumed out of business.

Hardy & Beck

U.S. tuners in the late '70s were mostly focused on improving the handling of imported makes. IPD of Oregon and Volvo springs to mind. Alpina's U.S. agents were Miller & Norburn; Dietel Enterprises, which created a 745i-powered Alpina e21; and Alpina/West. Alpina/West was run by Allen Hardy and Hans Beck, a pair who started a BMW repair shop in Berkeley, California, in 1974. As Alpina/West they fitted Alpina gear to U.S. Bim mers, which meant rims, suspension, body kit, seats, and rosewood shifter, but M10/M30 Alpina upgrades were disallowed due to pollution regs.

It didn't take long before complaints surfaced. Alpina's parts were not fine tuned to U.S. spec BMWs, or U.S. driving conditions. They didn't consider the effect of the 5-mph

Top: **In the guise of Alpina/West, H&B was a U.S. West Coast Alpina agent. An Alpina/West 530i is shown at Sears Point.** ***Above:*** **The H&B 528i was 100 percent Hardy & Beck. The Alpina connection was severed, and H&B became the first U.S. tuner to offer a complete range of turnkey modified Bimmers, based on the e21/e12/e24/e23 variants (courtesy H&B, http://www.hbspecialists.com/).**

bumpers and different ride height compared to Euro spec, or the patchwork quality of many U.S. roads. And those Alpina seats were rather snug. In true American entrepreneurial style, Hardy and Beck saw the shortfall and started fitting the cars with some of their components. Eventually friction occurred between Alpina and Alpina/West, with the former accusing the latter of passing off their wares as genuine Alpina merchandise.

Even though the crime never actually occurred, the writing was on the wall and the

Top: The H&B 528i had outright performance equal to a U.S. spec Ferrari 308 GTB of the same vintage ... with 5-seat comfort (courtesy H&B, http://www.hbspecialists.com/). ***Above:*** Like Miller & Norburn, H&B offered soundly engineered turbo kits. On the big six, that meant 250 bhp (SAE net) (courtesy Allen Hardy, http://www.hbspecialists.com/).

two entities parted. The positive upshot was a company name change to Hardy & Beck, and 1980 cars that were 100 percent H&B. H&B had packages for the original 3/5/6/7 series; indeed, H&B even predated Dinan in having a complete modified car for customers to buy. Gone were Alpina's wacky racer decals, and in came discreet pinstriping and cartoon-like "H&B" script on the front spoiler. By 1980–81 a fully equipped H&B 528i would cost $7,166 more than a normal 528i, taking the tab to around 28 grand.

The H&B experience included a CK53 chassis set which had special Bilstein shocks. Back in their Alpina agent days, Bilstein had offered to create custom shocks for H&B that matched the weight properties of U.S. Bimmers. These went with shorter, stiffer springs and thicker adjustable sway bars, 26 mm front and 19 mm rear. H&B were now using their own design alloy wheels, 16 × 7 inches front and 16 × 8 inches rear. They were 3-piece modular items based on a BBS design, with a unique H&B center. They were turbine in style, but with rounder spokes than Alpina's 16-inchers.

H&B rims tested out as being much stronger than the average modular. They were wrapped in the same footwear as an Alpina B7: Pirelli P7, VR rated 205/55 fronts and 225/50 rears. This all helped the H&B 528i generate 0.78g on the skidpad. As with any tuner special, ride comfort was affected, but some like it firm! However, the car was certainly faster, 5 mph faster. H&B incorporated their own free flow exhaust manifold which allowed the Bosch Lambda sond oxygen sensor to be retained so that everything was emissions legal. Combined with the H&B front and rear spoiler, this contributed to the extra scat.

With a top speed of 130 mph and 0–60 mph in 7.8 seconds, the H&B 528i was on a par with a U.S. 2-valve Ferrari 308 GTB, and that's what it was: a 4-door Ferrari! The interior had somewhat more space and comfort thanks to large Scheel 560 front buckets. The 1980 528i's standard overdrive 5-speed allowed the improved audio to be enjoyed. One could listen to Blondie, The Knack or other New Wave sounds on the Blaupunkt 3001 radio/cassette deck with additional KLH woofers and tweeters.

The professionalism of Hardy & Beck Performance Inc. was plain to see. By 1980 H&B had 50 selected dealers, an extensive spare parts inventory and after-sales service. There was an established local supply chain of companies that helped make parts that went into H&B automobiles, plus even a receptionist's desk made out of the front quarter of a BMW 2002!

Motorsport GmbH—The First M Cars

Why go to a tuner for a fast five, when BMW offered a program of improvements via their Motorsport division? BMW Motorsport GmbH was formed in 1972 on the watch of BMW's chief salesman Bob Lutz. "Win on Sunday, sell on Monday" was the old adage. The idea was to formalize the competition department which had been overseeing BMW's racing e9 CS coupes. There would be a positive spinoff for sales if this branch of BMW was involved with road cars. Motorsport oversaw the development of the BMW 3.0CSL, an essential homologation special.

Motorsport was also involved with the BMW 2002 Turbo, with Adolf Fischer responsible for test assembling the 170 bhp engine. The 2002 Turbo was a belated tribute to the car that won the 1969 ETCC. Both Bimmers sported Motorsport's natty tri-color livery,

BMW's Paul Rosche, a.k.a. "Camshaft Paul," handled the M530's racing engine as per South African "Modified Saloons" category regulations. This involved using 3 × 2bbl Solex 40/36 carbs and a racing profile camshaft (courtesy Ulrich Thieme, http://www.e12.de).

because tigers do come with stripes. However, Motorsport didn't actually build these cars. The CSL was done by Karmann, and the blown 2002 on the regular assembly line, but Motorsport did build e12s. For special patrons they were willing to build custom 5 series cars. Motorsport brought in completed cars from Dingolfing and added stuff from the BMW parts catalogue in hand-built fashion. There was lots to choose from: Scheel bucket seats (the 3.0CSL had Scheels), HD suspension with Bilsteins, Motorsport striping. Vented disks were used on the e3 sedan, and these could be added, as well as any of BMW's big sixes.

Two common choices were the 180 bhp 3-liter dual carb using Zenith carburetion from the 3.0S, and the 200 bhp 3-liter Bosch D-jet injected 3.0Si version. Just such a car was created in 1974 for Jonathan Sieff, former racer and by then the current owner of BMW's UK agent BMW Concessionaires GB. His choice was an e12 with a 3.0CSL spec motor, but why stop there? When a U.S. businessman complained that his 1988 M6's 256 bhp I6 was a bit weak, Motorsport supplied the parts necessary to take the big six to 325 bhp!

Custom e12s made their way out of Motorsport's doors, but the very first formally released "M" cars went to South Africa. BMW Suid Afrik was involved in a 5 series racing car program, much like the e9 CSL's ETCC exploits. Two racing 5 series cars were built, in style and substance 4-door CSL equivalents. There was more similarity in that Jochen Neerpasch and Martin Braungart saw to the development of the South African 5 series racers. These two individuals had defected from Ford West Germany to BMW, where they helped the Bavarians win the 1973 ETCC using the famous 3.0CSL Batmobile.

Schnitzer racing prepared one of the South African racers, with the second patterned off the first in South Africa itself. The M530 sedan racers triumphed on the track. In the period from the middle of 1976 to 1978 the two-car team achieved a run of 15 consecutive victories! To allow the racers to compete, BMW South Africa offered 216 road cars to the public in 1976; it was a homologation special. Although these roadgoing M530s were assembled by BMW South Africa, they were the very car Motorsport had been making for special patrons at home, with one exception: they were right-hand drive!

The M530 had the Motorsport front and rear spoilers designed for the e12. The front spoiler was unique in that it was an all-in-one spoiler/bumper with the e12 front turn signal lamps built in. Measures were taken to reduce weight. Aluminum and thin steel body panels were used; the trunk lid support hinges and footwell pedals were drilled. There was a special cutout in the trunk to place the battery in the interests of better weight distribution. Even the rear bench seat adhered to a weight-saving foam base. In the cockpit one was greeted by a pair of blue cloth Scheel buckets, with the driver stirring a close ratio 5-speeder, the usual Getrag dogleg box found in 5 and 6 series cars.

The 5-speed interfaced with a tuned version of the e3 3.0S's dual carb motor through a lightened flywheel. Power was 197 bhp at 6,000 rpm, with 204 lbs./ft. at 4,300 rpm. M530s were supplied in white, silver, light blue or dark gray, with Motorsport decals and a standard LSD. Over in West Germany, Motorsport decided to formalize their e12 modification program with a 1978 catalogue conversion model for purchasers of new 525/528 e12s. This car was simply called 533i, since it used the 197 bhp Bosch L-jet 3,210 cc I6 from the BMW 633CSi/733i.

Using the series 2 e12 body (1977–81), this M533i had the familiar e12 Motorsport upgrades done since 1974. There was the CR gearbox, LSD, Bilstein HD suspension and Motorsport's 380 mm 3-spoke steering wheel, as seen on the BMW M1. Seat choices were ASS or Recaros on this small run of 100 to 200 cars. There was a practice in West Germany in the '70s whereby affluent owners left off the model i.d. badging of their powerful machines. The German environmental movement was quite a force, and examples of conspicuous consumption were frowned upon. Thus, Motorsport delivered their 533i *sans* badging in 1978 and 1979.

By the close of the '70s there was a mood change from discreet to overt. The e12 was reaching the end of its currency, and something was needed to maintain buyer interest until the new Five could arrive. In addition, BMW was just starting to exploit the marketing power of the Motorsport entity. The M1 had come out in 1978, achieving icon status quickly, and it was time to spread the sizzle to BMW's normal ranges. So it was that BMW revealed the e12 M535i at the 1979 Frankfurt autoshow, and in the wake of the second gas crunch, no less! Production of the left-hand drive M535i started in April 1980, but BMW was displaying the car earlier.

The new 3.5 liter e12 was pictured and called 535i in BMW's 5 series brochure dated January 1980. The early nature of this depicted car was shown by the presence of 1978–79 chrome side mirrors, rather than the large black plastic equivalents found on later M535is. With the M535i, Motorsport took partly completed cars to their works, where they strengthened the front and rear bulkheads, finishing the rest of the car by hand. It actually states

The 216 road cars offered by BMW SA were assembled in South Africa. The 1976 M530 was the first Motorsport car formally made available to the public (courtesy Klaus Wiehl).

"M535i" on the car's build plate. Motorsport GmbH ended up creating 1,410 e12 M535i sedans.

Power for the M535i came from the early big-bore, short-stroke 3.5 liter M30 shared with the BMW 635CSi/735i. This 3,453 cc engine had 9.3 to one CR and made 218 bhp at 5,200 rpm, and 224 lbs./ft. at 4,000 rpm. All three cars were provided with an engine oil cooler as standard equipment. The M535i was only fitted with a close ratio 5-speed box, and featured the chassis upgrades found on earlier Motorsport Fives, except with smaller rims. Previous Motorsport e12s all used 14 × 7-inch BBS/Mahle basket-weave rims, but the M535i's rims were only 6.5 inches wide.

Motorsport also made right-hand drive M535i cars for the UK market. At first, only 200 RHD cars were going to the UK, but popularity of the M535i in the British Isles saw that number rise to 450. *Autocar* magazine tested an M535i and found it could do 0–60 mph in 7.1 seconds, with a top speed of 139 mph. The car's identity varied somewhat, because BMW Motorsport wasn't a big part of the enthusiast's lexicon yet. In German and UK advertising it was called M535i, but simply 535i in UK price lists.

A special chrome front grille badge was done for the M535i, as per all I6 e12s during 1978–81, which read 535i. An "M" badge for the other side of the front grille was available. It was also possible to order a new M535i without front and rear spoilers, or with the spoilers, but no badging, or with or without striping. Individual cars were varied, but like the 1978–81 Euro spec 528i and earlier Motorsport converted e12s, they all had 195/70 VR rated 14-inch tires. The M535i also used the same brakes as the Euro 528i, except that the front disks were 3 mm thicker.

Originally only 200 e12 M535is were earmarked for the UK, but its popularity saw 450 right-hand-drive M535i e12s eventually reach UK shores (courtesy Andreas Gattingers and *Auto-Classic*).

To achieve the 10 mph speed advantage over the 528i, the final drive was made taller, 3.07:1 versus 3.45:1. The close ratio 5-speed and the extra power and torque of the 3.5 liter M30 meant things were lively between gears. In fact, apart from the M1, the M535i was the fastest car BMW made in 1980–81. The 1979 635CSi had the same engine, CR gearbox and 3.07:1 final drive, but carried a 200-lb. weight penalty compared to the Five. 1980 also saw the debut of the 252 bhp turbocharged 745i, with blown 3.2 I6. However, the 745i was auto only; it could almost match the M535i's top speed, but trailed slightly in standing-start acceleration.

One structural issue that popped up on the M535i was a tendency for the differential to tear away from its mounting, a problem related to BMW's e12 weight-loss program. A repair kit was released for the M535i to correct the problem. Other woes included final oversteer and wind noise. The M535i was to be handled with care on the limit, lest the rear end should suddenly let go! More power can sometimes mean more trouble.

European Car magazine experienced the wild breakaway on their "Project Barnyard Bimmer" in the early '90s. This restored and modified 1977 U.S. 530i had a 300 bhp Metric Mechanic 4-liter M30 2-valve I6. The chassis was upgraded with after-market springs and shocks and wide 16-inch Hartge rims with Yokohama tires. Even so, the prodigious torque of the MM 3900 Hi Flo ST (Surface Turbulence) motor was enough to generate a bucketload

Not officially available in the U.S. at the time, but where there was a gray market there was a way. A trickle of Euro M535is made it into North America in the 1980s (courtesy Adam Wilson and www.firstfives.org/).

of tire smoke in second gear, even in dry conditions, which was fun.[1] Less amusing was a fast-track scenario where the breakaway limit lurked.

Jay Jones discovered a pendulum effect: the 530i's tail would swing out, grip, swing the other way, grip, swing once again, etc. The e12 needs an experienced driver, one that can judiciously jab the throttle to balance out the nose heaviness of this generation of Bimmers, yet feather the gas pedal to drive around the limit when necessary. Only skilled pilots need enquire within. If said pilots remembered to bring ear plugs, they would certainly come in handy.

BMW's boxy shapes of the '60s and '70s tended to generate wind roar around the front pillars. At 140 mph, an e12 M535i was a loud place to be. Still, it was some consolation that one bid farewell to a 1980 Corvette L82 4-speed at 130 mph; one would be deaf, but victorious. South Africa is a nation that takes victory in sport seriously, but it is also a place of low-gasoline octane and high altitude, so the people like torque. No surprise then that this right-hand-drive market should get the M535i.

South Africa's import tax law encouraged local assembly, so M535i CKD kits were sent out to the BMW Suid Afrik Rosslyn factory where 240 M535is were made. However,

Among the special interior touches added to this 528i Turbo are e34 540i power/heated leather front seats and extra wood appliqué (courtesy Zane Coker and Max Earey, http://www.featurecars.net/).

there were a few differences. This M535i came with the Motorsport 14 × 7-inch rims and an overdrive 5 speed, plus it came with a/c, power windows and door locks as standard equipment.

Curiously, the South African e12 M535i wasn't available with the Euro M535i front/rear spoilers, or even Motorsport livery. It was a most stealthy vehicle, and one attuned to the low-octane gas of the country. The 3.5 liter M30 was retuned to make 214 bhp and 229 lbs./ft. of twist. It was also the final M535i to be built, with production running from February 1981 to July 1981.

Opposite, top: **The M535i typified BMW's performance philosophy at the time: go faster with unblown larger displacement sixes (courtesy Christian Hartmann).** ***Opposite, bottom:*** **Zane Coker's modified 1980 e12 528i Turbo was featured in the June 2006 issue of *Performance BMW.* This is an extreme blown e12 that uses an e26 M1-based 4-liter block, and has been known to sniff nitrous (courtesy Zane Coker and Max Earey, http://home.att.net/~Nastroma/index.html).**

4

The 5 Series' Second Coming

The e28 Chassis

The Bavarians Strike Back with High Tech

Two decades of success since the 1961 BMW 1500 had passed. Pundits' praise had been unrelenting, but the time had come for a new generation. This role fell to the e28 5 series, the second draft of BMW's middle child. The Bavarians thought that after 9 years their shoebox sedan could use a shine. The world was expecting BMW to think outside the box, but BMW had other ideas. The Munich men were still happy with the box; a box was still a safe place to be and a quiet place for deep thinking. The end result wasn't a new car as such, but the single biggest reworking of an auto design seen in history.

BMW wasn't a large company, and it had launched several all-new ranges in the '70s, so this was a time for consolidation. Pennies were counted while the Munich moguls pondered the future. Open the front doors on an e28 and witness the same raised circular monocoque pressing about the B pillar base. There were also the same sheet metal cutouts behind the bumper as on the e12, but there was method to this madness because the e28's effectiveness made a clean sheet design unnecessary. Right out of the box, as it were, the e28 became an ETCC champ.

Rulebook changes had ushered in the new Group A era in the European Touring Car Championship, and with it the appearance of cars closer to the machinery one could actually buy. In 1982 the BMW Italia-prepared 240 bhp e28 528i helped Italian racer Umberto Grano earn the ETCC driver's title. It was the usual success for BMW in racing, following in the winning tire tracks of the 3.0CSL, but the e28 brought something new. The e28 was about things away from the track, just exactly where one has to be to get mainstream sales.

It was the '80s, when the microchip was increasingly dominating life. To be a winner a company had to be on the cutting edge. These were the years when BMW became positively associated with high tech, and much of the electronic wizardry and driver aids were introduced on the e28. Technology was linked to speed, but the flip side is better economy. The latter was very important in Europe. The world had gone through a second oil shock in 1979 and gasoline gluttony was no longer rewarded.

The e28 represented a thoroughly reworked 5 series designed for the 1980s, with much emphasis on fuel efficiency. Daimler-Benz had done much the same with their W116 to W126 S class transition. MPGs mattered to the Bavarians, especially since, unlike their Stutt-

The new e28 5 series featured a Bosch Motronic engine management system, if a 1982 U.S. 528e was at hand (courtesy Kitt Scott).

gart rivals, they had no diesels in the cupboard. BMW was ready to go beyond mere overdrive boxes and painting 1981 e12 tachs with green and red segments. The Munich men were ready for total efficiency with a fresh four-car range that commenced production in June 1981.

In keeping with recent BMW success, the e28 was a sales smash hit from the start. Buyers knew the new one was coming and had put off their 5 series purchases until the e28 arrived. Secondly, BMW got a head start on its rivals Daimler-Benz and Audi. Mercedes' last major revision of its 200–280E range had been the 1976 makeover of the W123. Audi had yet to release its aero 100; in Ingolstadt they were still retailing the boxy 1977–82 four- and five-cylinder 100/5000. It was a timely moment for the latest BMW 518/520i/525i/528i variants to make their appearance.

BMW was on the march to offer fuel injection across the board, starting said policy with the revised 1980 728i–745i. Now it was the 5 series' turn ... almost. The e28 range started with the 518, which didn't have injection. The littlest Five soldiered on with the rugged 1.8-liter M10 I4. The 1,766 cc motor still made 90 horses, but now featured transistorized ignition and, like the final e12 518, since October 1980 used the Solex 2B4 carb. CR had risen to 9.5 to one, making 98 octane gas mandatory, which explained why the 90 horses now arrived at 5,500 rpm and not the previous 5,800 rpm.

Surprisingly, of all the e28s it was the 518 that was worth trumpeting because of its I4's motorsport connection. The 518 was the only e28 using the old M10, and this engine

Good for 115 mph and 0–60 mph in 10.5 seconds, the 520i was starting to lose out to more aero-wise 2-liter rivals in top speed. The model weighed 1,220 kilos (courtesy Stephan Becker).

was still making waves in racing. The M10 had been very successful in Formula 2, powering chassis that claimed 7 European titles between 1973 and 1983 in modified DOHC form. Even greater publicity was earned in 1983 when Nelson Piquet became the first Formula 1 champ in a BMW-powered car. Renault may have been first at the 1.5-liter F1 turbo base camp, but it was Brabham/BMW that reached the mountain's pinnacle first. The championship winning car was the BT 52 designed by Brabham stalwart South African Gordon Murray. Paul Rosche and BMW Motorsport took care of the 1.5-liter DOHC 16-valve turbo 4-cylinder.

The humble I4 embarrassed Renault's turbo V6, as well as BMW's test rig. In GP qualifying trim the turbo four, using up to 2.9 metric bar boost, produced 1,300 bhp, a feat beyond the test rig's 1,280 bhp scale! With 1,300 horses and 11,000 rpm, it was no problem for the engineers and the little four bearing the words "BMW M Power" on the exhaust side cam cover. Eight hundred ponies was a sensible figure for the actual race, and while the KKK turbocharger was blowing, Bosch DME (Digital Motor Electronics) was keeping microprocessor tabs on the optimal fuel mix and ignition timing. Bosch DME was another item available on the e28 from the start, if one was driving a 1982 MY U.S. 528e. The earlier M530s were built from manual 525 CKD base cars, with many converted to full touring car race spec by privateers.

All that was left for the racer to do was steer and pray — pray that the engine didn't expire, or the car run out of gas, prior to race completion. Such were the joys of turbo F1 life once refueling was banned at the end of the 1983 racing season. Turbo F1 engines were more fragile than the once default normally aspirated 3-liter Cosworth DFV V8, but BMW had proved a point. A winning F1 turbo motor could be based on a production block and the company reaped the benefits when it came to advertising the e28 and e30. An extra bonus occurred in 1983 when Dieter Quester snatched the ETCC driver's title using a BMW 635CSi.

Such racing success seemed to imbue the e28 518 with extra vigor. At 102 mph and with a 0–62 mph time of 14 seconds, it was 2 mph faster and 0.8 quicker than the e12 518. Not the kind of pace that gets the heart racing, but it was the thought that counted. The 518 was once again manual only, with a choice of 4-speed or optional 5-speed overdrive. However, the 518 could be optioned up with leather and sports suspension!

E28, More Engineering Changes Than Meet the Eye

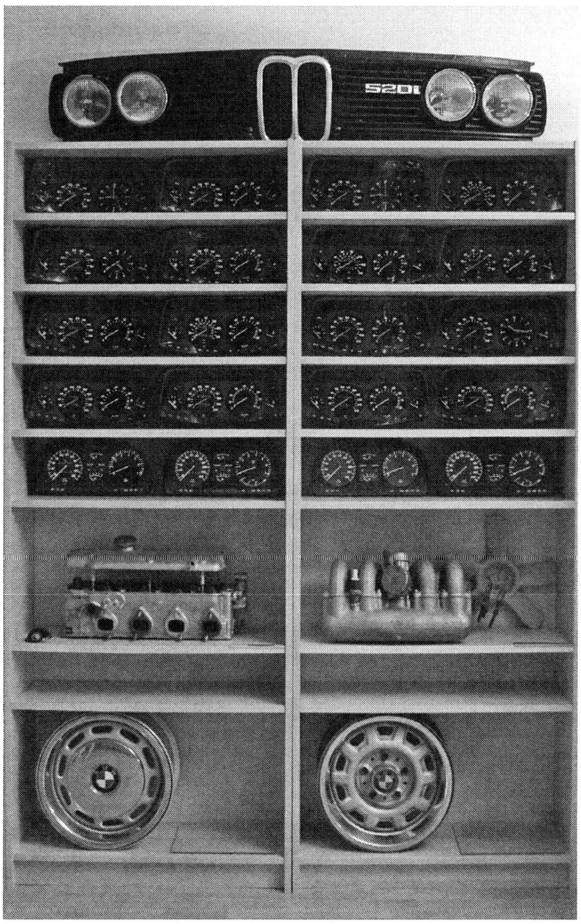

The early '80s were a difficult time for BMW. The company had many stylistic icons on the shelf, but how to incorporate such stuff in the aero '80s? (courtesy Ulrich Thieme, http://www.e12.de).

Matters were improved somewhat going into the 1985 MY when the 518 was replaced by the 105 bhp 518i. This Bosch L-jet injected variant used the same engine introduced by the e30 318i in 1983. To get an automatic the 520i was the first port of call. F1 connection aside, the lure of the silky-smooth 2-liter I6 was hard to ignore, and made the 518i's M10 seem tractor-like. For the first time since 1977, the 520 with baby six now had fuel injection.

The e28 520i started with Bosch K-jct and 125 bhp, just likc thc 1976–77 520i I4, but the e28 520i had an intake manifold just like the 323i. Even though the 520i now had a CR of 9.8 to one, versus 9.2:1 on the e12 520/6, the baby six's all or nothing behavior was still in evidence. Road tests put the new 520i equal to the Kugelfischer injected 130 bhp e12 520i for outright performance — top speed 115 mph; 0–60 mph 10.5 seconds — but the six lacked torque.

Steps were taken to improve the 520i, for 1983 there was a switch from Bosch K-jet to electronic Bosch L-jet.

On this right-hand-drive 1984 BMW 520i with 4-speed auto and a/c, BMW's move back to slider vent controls is visible. The a/c could be turned on in any mode (heat and vent) by depressing the snowflake button, which illuminated blue in the on position (photograph by author).

The e21 323i style intake manifold was ditched because that car was out of production. The 520i now used the same shape intake manifold as the e30 320i/323i, all three cars using Bosch L-jet. Longer and narrower intake manifold pipes, plus altered cam timing, tried to eke out extra low-speed torque; power output stayed at 125 horses. Another benefit of having L-jet was that the 520i joined the e28 525i/528i in having fuel cut off down to 1,200 rpm on a closed throttle.

Take the foot off the gas pedal and fuel to the motor was shut off until 1,200 rpm was reached. Why waste gas when coasting downhill? The 520i gained an extra 4 horses going into the 1986 MY, and yet this was a model that always majored in smoothness. The 520i's great refinement, plus the lure of having an injected I6 Bimmer in the 2-liter class, kept the 520i as the volume-selling Euro variant. However, dreams of true Bimmer performance still lay with the M30-powered cars. The 525i was a new variant, representing the first time a 2.5 liter 5 series had received fuel injection.

The carb e12 525 had 9:1 CR, but the new 525i boasted higher 9.6 to one CR and Bosch L-jet. Even the new e28 528i still had just a 9.3:1 CR. However, the 525i remained at the 150 bhp level, another one of those West German market fiscal tax cutoff points. Both the e28 525i/528i had greater efficiency since their 1,200 rpm fuel cutoff resumption point was much lower than the 3,700 rpm level used by the e12 528i. The e28 525i/528i also shared a new style intake manifold. This torque scavenging design had the "2.5/2.8" i.d. insignia on the casting.

A 1984 Australian spec 528i Executive 4-speed automatic. The '80s "Executive" versions of Bimmers sold in this market denoted a model with a higher level of luxury features (courtesy Remy Davison).

The end of e12 M535i production implied that range-topper status now fell to the 528i, which had two standard fog lamps at the front and rear. Previously only one rear fog lamp was present. The 528i was also the only initial e28 to get a standard 5-speed stick shift. As per the e12 it was an overdrive box with 0.81 fifth; the e28 528i's 3.45 final drive and 184 bhp output were also unchanged, but performance was a mite better than the e12. Top speed was 1 mph up at 130 mph, with 0–62 mph 0.4 seconds quicker.

Swifter acceleration suggested that the e28's weight savings played a greater role in the mix than the new car's better aero stats. However, better aero did improve steady speed cruising gas mileage with the new 528i on 31.4 mpg at a constant 75 mph, versus 29.7 for the e12 version. BMW knew how key aerodynamics was for improving gas mileage and image in the '80s, but the company was sending mixed messages.

On the one hand BMW knew it had to improve its aero status quo, and they wanted the public to know they had done good work on the e28. However, at the same time BMW tried to downplay the importance of a low drag shape. The company advanced the line that it was still important for a BMW to look like a BMW, which was code for "Let's stay boxy." Skepticism surrounded this view, given that BMW was known as a forward-thinking concern. Out of 3 e12 replacement proposals, Munich management okayed the most conservative one.

Claus Luthe, chief stylist at BMW, said he was given an order to go old school. Even though rivals were cooking up ultramodern fare, BMW felt it was better to spend the money on other aspects, since cost and model cycle constraints were key factors. A total body makeover would be pricey, and would have to be applied to all model lines to keep things in synch. Such action was for a later date.

The e28 was a detailed reworking of the e12 shell to cut drag. The designers succeeded in slashing the drag coefficient (Cd) from 0.44 to 0.38 for the e28. Apart from the need to move through the air more easily, the changes were directed at improving high-speed handling and reducing wind noise. The idea was to reduce lift at the front and increase downforce at the rear. In spite of the e12's center section and doors being carried over, the changes to nose and tail meant that all other body panels were new. The leading edge of the hood was carried slightly forward and downwards and the kidney grille, whilst still tapered into the hood, was now a bit squatter. This was the last new Bimmer brought out with a reverse slope shark grille.

The front turn signals were no longer on the bumper as per the e12; they were now blended into a new lower fairing/spoiler complex. This area also had integrated front fog lamps, when specified; previously the front fogs were exposed and disturbed airflow on the e12. More noticeable were the changes at the back. The trunk line was raised, and the trunk lid and under bumper apron were squarer, to clean up airflow and increase downforce. Aero achievements are all about the little things. The 518/520i had a new take on steel slotted rims with hubcaps. The 14 × 5.5-inch steel rims had new circle perforations and a matte finish chrome hubcap that covered the lug nuts and sat flush. This new design looked like an '80s version of what BMW used on e12s during 1972–77.

The useful ZF 4HP22 (EH) Switchable 4-speed autobox on a 1986 M535i. Turn the dial and different shift programs changed the auto's behavior. This was not a gimmick (courtesy Gary Langton).

The M30 525i/528i cars without alloys had full diameter wheel covers which were worth 0.009 towards the e28's Cd figure. However, even in fuel-economy-conscious Europe, most folks tossed out the covers in favor of the optional alloys. What good is a Bimmer without some pizzazz? Such is the mentality when one gets beyond butter-and-egg German Ford Granadas and Opel Senators. Blockish though the e28 may still have seemed,

BMW's tinkering had made it number one among market rivals in the fall of 1981. At 0.38 the e28 was even ahead of the slippery-looking Citroen CX (Cd 0.39). However, the winds of change were blowing a gale in auto design.

The 1982 Ford Sierra and 1983 Audi 100 were two new European cars that took the drag factor down to a 0.30 level. Audi was so impressed by the achievement, they even had this figure etched into the rear C pillar window glass. Indeed, Audi, Ford and others used their Cd figures as a positive point in advertising, sometimes even at the expense of BMW. In 1984 Audi ran a comparison print ad featuring the Audi 100 2.1-liter I5 and the BMW 520i. Both cars had 125 bhp, but the 520i was 10 mph slower than the 125 mph Audi 100. Audi highlighted the difference by showing their car in the foreground ... with the poor 520i way off in the background.

Audi said a low drag factor allowed their 100 to get closest to achieving perpetual motion. Take the foot off the gas at speed and the Audi's pace didn't drop like a stone. The car didn't waste engine power pushing air out of the way. The irony was that a few years later the Audi 100/5000 got a bad rap in the U.S., as some automatic Audi 5000s increased their speed without driver involvement. The TV show *60 Minutes* ran the story of the Audi 5000s that surprised their owners, with negative effect on Audi North American sales.

BMW wasn't a company to rest on its laurels, or wait on a rival's misfortune. The Munich men had a growing test center outside Munich, with a new full-size wind tunnel that was ready in 1980, but not soon enough for the e28. The lion's share of the e28's aero work was done at the St. Cyr wind tunnel in Paris. In some ways BMW was even getting nostalgic over its past. The e28 was brought into line with the e23 7 series in terms of larger outboard low-beam headlights, and a body-colored stale air extraction slat for the rear C pillar. However, that stale air vent panel was also just like the one introduced on the revised '72 MY e3 sedans!

The e28 went from the e12's single central fresh-air hood grille, to having two hood grilles, one on the driver's side and one on the passenger side. Once again, this was just like the late '60s e3 sedan and e9 coupe. The e28's "new" taillights were also spookily reminiscent of those on the e3. Passersby and fellow road users may have thought a well-kept BMW Bavaria was at hand. To underline BMW's affection for old school, the e28 carried much chrome. The only chrome cut from e12 days was that on the central B pillar. This area was now blacked out, as on the 6 series, 7 series and soon-to-be-revealed second-generation e30 3 series. E28 door handles were also finished in black.

Family resemblance is important, resale value is key, for all this and more keeping things stable can be a good thing. Chrome on the bumpers, window surrounds and hubcaps made the e28 a chariot of bling, years before there ever was such a thing. Retention of rain gutters wasn't that modern, and neither was the absence of flush-mounted glass, but the e28 did have a wider version of the decade-old Bimmer raised-hood power band. Things weren't as dire as they seemed, because even this early on, prestige buyers had eyes for just two marques.

BMW and Mercedes were the equivalent of Pepsi and Coca-Cola. Other brands may have offered good cars, but badge magnetism meant buyers in this class were only ever going to choose between a Bimmer or a Merc. As long as the e28 5 series was visually in keeping with Stuttgart's machine, the W123, there was no problem. BMW boss Eberhard von Kuenheim even answered the critics at the outset, defending the e28's stately form: "For years,

In the new 5 series range the 2.8 liter 528i was the most admired version during the e28's early years. This 1987 MY UK 528i SE was featured in the May 2007 issue of *Total BMW* magazine (courtesy Derin Oloyede, http://www.bmwclassics.co.uk/).

the Press has been complaining that the industry must be mad to invest so much money in mere cosmetic changes, rather than technical progress. Here we spent money on a lot of technical improvements and you say we should have spent more on cosmetics!"[1]

In the U.S. the e28's stand against planned obsolescence was even stronger because BMW was prevented from introducing the European spec e28's larger outboard headlights. U.S. lighting law didn't permit unequal-sized lamps, so the U.S. e28s all had 4 equal-sized front lamps, just like an e12! It also wasn't possible to include the Euro e28's faired-in front spoiler turn signals and fog lamps. Once more U.S. spec 5 series cars had extended 5-mph bumpers, although they didn't protrude quite so badly as on the e12, plus the side marker lights looked better. The side markers were no longer mounted on the fender sheet metal; they were now discreet little squares integrated into the sides of the plastic bumper.

As a sign of the times, European (EEC) law caused the Euro spec e28s to get side marker lights of their own: small amber indicators on the front fenders behind the wheel wells. If the exterior seemed all too familiar, then the interior brought greater cheer with fresh thinking. The 5 series was the last of the BMW line to receive the new angled dashboard first seen on the 1972 BMW Turbo gullwing safety car. The famous BMW divided dash that placed major controls, HVAC, stereo, etc., on a molding angled towards the driver was

A most effective 2.8-liter I6, still producing 184 bhp, allowed the 528i to outpace all European rivals, including the Audi 200 Turbo and Rover 3500 SD1 (courtesy Derin Oloyede, http://www.bmwclassics.co.uk/).

an ergonomic sculpture that left the front passenger out in the cold, but underlined the fact that BMWs are cars for drivers.

In revising the Five's interior for the '80s, obvious changes were made. Wood trim was out, even on high-line versions, although there was a wood kit available for the e28, in the home market special options/accessories catalogue. Vinyl door tops and chrome strip trim were also absent, replaced by textured plastic that followed the tops of the doors and met up with the new dash. The new plastic capping also incorporated the ashtrays on the rear doors. There was an awful lot of plastic in the new car's interior, so BMW humanized surroundings using two-tone dashboards and material.

Cars with a light sand beige interior had the lower half of the dashboard colored to match. BMW 518/520is had simple vinyl door trims, but the 525i/528i had special material. The door trims were made of nylon flock featuring a fishbone pattern. A very obvious change from the e12, located in this area, was the mechanism for opening the door from the inside. Gone was the reach-through-the-armrest grab lever, replaced by flush-mounted flap levers as per the e23. The older mechanism had become associated with cases where occupants had mistakenly tried to open the doors while the car was on the move!

Comfort in the 5 series was much greater if occupants remained in the car when it was moving, and they had greater reason to do so, now that the e28 offered optional front center

When BMW took over the import/distribution of BMW cars in the UK (1980), they chose competitive pricing to boost sales. However, by the mid- to late '80s, BMWs were pricier than rivals. This loaded 528i SE with power roof, 4 power windows, cruise control, headlamp wash/wipe and automatic cost a small fortune new (courtesy Derin Oloyede, http://www.bmw classics.co.uk/).

armrests. Occupants were also feeling more revived thanks to the e28's four new adjustable dash vents. The vent apertures were well forward in the e28, providing better airflow control and the possibility of opening and closing individual vents via a knurled thumbwheel, to eliminate drafts where necessary.

At the helm were two new steering wheel designs. The standard wheel was a four-spoker with a very small flat boss, permitting an unobstructed view of the instruments and dashrail-mounted switches. This design was new to BMW and would soon be shared with the e30 3 series. Optional was a leather-covered 3-spoke rim of 380 mm diameter. A BMW is all about control and BMW made some odd changes concerning the Five's switchgear. HVAC controls were now via sliders, rather retrogressive after the e12's rotary controls.

The e28 was the first Bimmer to get this new panel controlling air distribution; it would subsequently be introduced on the e30 and '83 MY 6 series. The move was most likely done to appease the U.S. market, where the rotary controls caused confusion. Blower speed and air temp continued to be set using dials. BMW also decided to ditch the e12's pull-out knobs and push in/out switches for lighting, replacing them with toggle equivalents.

These toggles were generally regarded as being too small, making it too easy to overshoot desired positions.

An area of marked improvement involved the power window control buttons, now placed on the shifter surround. They intuitively suggested which button controlled which window. If only the same were true for the e28's power seat buttons. The e28 was the first Five to get power seats and BMW placed the controls on the handbrake housing surround between the front buckets. Black buttons with white graphics controlled the 10-way power seats; later models also had a 3-setting memory function for the driver's side.

Daimler-Benz solved the seat snafu via a three-dimensional seat controller. Play with the mini seat and the actual seat did likewise ... but the Bavarians wanted you to sweat a little! BMW claimed the e28 offered greater interior space than the e12. The new car may have lost a half inch from the wheelbase, but BMW said headroom increased by an inch, with 1.6 inches more rear legroom — greater rear legroom than the old e3 Bavaria, according to BMW. Given that the e12 center structure was carried over, the incremental gains were achieved through flatter seat squabs and thinner front seat backrests.

Although it took a keen eye to distinguish the difference, BMW had reshaped the Five's seats. They were now more deeply contoured, more bucket-like. For the adventurous, front sports seats were optional. BMW also made amendments to the 5 series' HVAC facility so that driver and passengers would be in optimal comfort. From the 520i on up, the e28 had an electronic heater which acted independently of engine rpm or vehicle speed. There were sensors in the footwell and on the heater itself. The e28 also featured a much revised a/c system, with a snowflake button.

Emphasizing the continued add-on nature of the Five's a/c, e28s without a/c had a console with a storage cubbyhole in front of the shifter as per the e12, a space under the radio sufficient for string-back driving gloves. However, e28s with a/c had a large rectangular molding added as part of the dash. This cornflakes-like box carried the stereo and HVAC controls, and was angled towards the driver at the same angle as the rest of the dash. Press the snowflake button and cool air came through the e28's vents. As part of the e28's development, engineers drove a black e12 528i with black interior 500 miles in one day during the height of a Texan summer. It has been rumored that some nefarious character in BMW's sales and marketing department disabled the power windows on that 528i, by removing the appropriate fuse from the fuse box, but this tale has never been verified. However, it can be confirmed that BMW fitted a slightly larger evaporator core and associated squirrel-cage blower. Behr a/c hardware was used once again, but the overall result was a worthwhile improvement over the e12. The new closer dash vents proved practical.

Another feature one requires on a long desert trek is cruise control. The e12 never offered this as a factory option; the Escort systems found on some cars were dealer-installed. The e28 went one better with the option of factory-fitted cruise, bringing with it an additional control stalk on the right-hand side of the steering column. BMW was also moving with the times concerning automatic transmission. This option was available on more Bimmers, and was being more frequently chosen by customers. BMW introduced a 4-speed autobox on the revised 1983 MY e23 7 series, and so began a phased changeover from the trusty ZF 3HP22 to the 4-speed ZF 4HP22.

The fourth gear in this box provided an overdrive ratio to cut rpm and noise, and thus boost fuel economy when cruising. The e28 received this 4-speed autobox for the 1984 MY,

Through manipulation of seating thickness, BMW gave the e28 1.6 inches more leg room than the e12. This was more rear space than the old e3 Bavaria, on paper (courtesy Derin Oloyede, http://www.bmwclassics.co.uk/).

and for 1985 got BMW's Switchable electro-hydraulic (EH) version of the ZF 4-speed auto as an option. For years a slushbox had no place in an enthusiast's car, never coming up with the correct gear at the right moment. The 1984 MY seemed a fitting moment for a 1984 Orwellian microchip brain to work out optimal shift points on the BMW 7 series. Now it was the e28's turn to be controlled!

On the auto shifter surround, the Switchable auto had a 3-position dial. There were "S" (Sport), "E" (Economy) and "3.2.1" (Manual Hold) settings. Select Sport and the auto kicked down more readily and held a lower gear for longer; choose Economy and the auto lived in the taller gears longer to stretch the MPGs and improve winter traction. The 3.2.1 setting cut out fourth, apt in stop-and-go urban motoring where there's little chance of cruising, and where the driver doesn't want the auto to hunt between ratios. A computer is superimposing its control over the automatic, hence electro-hydraulic.

Each auto mode represented a different computer program. The EH auto's microprocessor took in various inputs, using sensors, to calculate the right auto behavior. The computer knew which slot the auto shifter was in, which mode the 3-position dial was turned to, and whether kickdown had been engaged. It also observed engine load by considering rpm, air volume (at the airflow meter), gas pedal position (throttle butterfly), fuel pressure, valve open/close duration and the e28's actual speed. The result was a smart auto and the verdict was good. *Autocar* magazine tested a 1984 735i with the Switchable box and discerned appreciable behavior differences between modes.[2]

Both versions of the 4-speed auto also had 4th gear lock-up. When cruising in top, the engine and gearbox would connect solidly, like the flywheel and clutch in a manual car. This was to curtail the gas-mileage-hurting efficiency losses found in a conventional torque converter autobox, where engine power is transferred through moving vanes of fluid. In spite of the electronic trickery the ZF 4HP22 unit was a conventional auto; it has also proved less durable than the older 3HP22 box. In addition, being an overdrive 4-speeder, there was no accelerative advantage over the previous 3-speed. Porsche was offering a 4-speed auto with direct one-to-one 4th for improved flexibility.

The e28's Check Control panel couldn't tell you if the auto was about to give up the ghost, but it could inform on other matters. Low engine oil, coolant level or an emptying windshield washer container, burnt-out brake lights, license plate illuminators and low-beam headlights: if there was a problem the driver would be informed, actively. The Check Control panel was a regular on the 6 and 7 series, but with its e28 debut the driver got an instrument cluster warning light when something was wrong. Previously, the panel's test button had to be pressed before any inkling something was wrong could be given.

Once warned, the e28 driver pressed the panel's test button. This would show what the problem was, and would store it in the system's memory. On a subsequent journey, pressing the test button would see the problem area illuminated on the panel for 5 seconds. This was a useful device and one that could inform about low oil level even while on the move. However, even with the e28's larger dash there was no place for the device, so the Check Control panel was placed above the interior's rear view mirror. The new e30 3 series had its Check Control panel similarly positioned.

Continuing with the microchip mania was the introduction of BMW's onboard computer, a device introduced earlier as an option on the revised 1980 MY 7 series. Neatly placed to the right of the tach (on LHD cars), this car computer couldn't take on a Cray super computer, but it could provide information on average speed, fuel consumption, range remaining with what was left in the tank and an automatic warning if the outside air temp dropped to a level where black ice could form on the road.

The computer tied in with an also optional anti-theft alarm system. Punch in a code on the keypad and electrical power was reinstated, allowing the electric fuel pump to come online and permitting the car to start. The alarm system covered the doors, trunk and hood. Anyone trying to break in would trigger the alarm, sounding the car's horn at 30-second intervals. These were worthwhile options if one did long Autobahn trips, with occasions where the car had to be parked in high-risk urban areas, but expensive toys otherwise. There was some consolation from the fact the onboard computer was very accurate, confirmed by independent testing. In addition, the Check Control panel came as standard equipment on the 525i/528i.

Balanced against options that cost extra was a standard e28 feature that promised to save the owner money: meet the Service Interval indicator system, standard on all e28s, and a first on any Bimmer. No need for fixed mileage servicing regimens; the e28 introduced "valued mileage," considering engine revs, coolant temp, mileage and time. These inputs would go into an electronic driver's logbook, with the correct time for a service worked out by computer. Short trips, frequent starts and hard driving with several redline visits would

The 528e was a hit, or in the words of BMW N.A. supremo Jack Cook "some people may not have liked the label, but the dogs loved the dog food" (courtesy Kevin Ellis).

create short service intervals, while gentle freeway cruising with little urban stop-and-go would reward with longer intervals.

So commenced the modern BMW-speak of Service I and Service II inspections, as the indicator system guided the owner between alternate oil changes and inspections with greater prescribed checks. Right in the center of the e28's instrument binnacle was a series of 9 lights, 5 green, 1 yellow and 3 red. Start your e28 after a service and all 5 green lights would briefly greet, then extinguish. As more miles accrued, fewer green lights would appear on startup, then the yellow lamp would signify that a service appointment should be made. Procrastinate and the 3 red lights would progressively appear, letting the driver know that the need for service was going critical. The system was rigged up to go yellow if no service had been done within a 12-month period. BMW said most folks would go longer before needing a service; the prescribed interval up to that time had been 7,500 km. The U.S. EPA didn't like the sound of the S.I. indicator system, since U.S. pollution law dictated fixed service intervals so a vehicle got checked out regularly and didn't become an emissions enemy. However, the device was cleared for U.S. use for the 1983 MY.

A fair few owners took exception to the S.I. indicator system for a different reason: the lights went out too quickly. The device soon appeared on the e30 3 series too, as well as the revised 6 and 7 series of the 1983 MY, and there were several reports of the system seeking a service more frequently than the usual 7,500 km interval. What BMW referred to as its "Service Concept 2000" proved to be something of a nuisance. This was especially the case once the cars got to 5 or 6 years of age. Look behind the dash of an e28 5 series and there was no mechanical speedo drum, but an electronic equivalent and other modern marvels.

The S.I. indicator system was on a single printed circuit board with microchips and two AA batteries. These batteries helped keep the electronic logbook if the car's battery had been disconnected, and would store the data for a long period of time, up to four months. This was particularly key for the "time" factor input in the S.I. indicator's calculations, which was determined by a separate microprocessor. The trouble occurred when the buffer battery started to lose its charge. A soldering iron is required to remove the flat batteries and attach a fresh set, but this solution doesn't seem to work in the long run.

As a sensitive electronic device, the S.I. system seemed vulnerable to a fluctuation caused by the quick voltage dropoff in the discharging cells and replacement with a new set. The problem was very similar to those cases where a car's engine ECU gets fried when someone tries to jump-start the vehicle after a dead battery. As for the S.I. indicator system, the only solution is to replace the entire circuit board which the nickel cadmium batteries are attached to. On the plus side, many garages, not just BMW dealers, carry the service tool that resets the S.I. indicator's lights. Indeed, there are retailers that advertise this tool in the back of popular magazines like *European Car*.

Many BMW enthusiasts play it safe by sticking to a fixed service mileage interval. It was a sign of the times that a luxury car maker was pushing economy. It was in 1980 that BMW's slogan changed from "For The Joy Of Motoring" to "The Ultimate Driving Machine," but could it still be the ultimate driving machine on 3 cylinders? Not such a bizarre question, given that before 2007 came along, 1981 was the year that saw the price of gasoline reach its highest level, in inflation-adjusted real terms, for the U.S. motorist.

Diesel, variable displacement motors: these were the buzzwords at the start of the 1980s when the world energy picture was looking quite uncertain. Cadillac put a 6-liter V8-6-4 motor in production. Using state-of-the-art electronics and selective valve-train engagement, this engine spent some of its time in V6 and V4 mode to save gas. Unfortunately it spent too much time in V8 mode, was complex, and had reliability issues that saw it replaced by a new aluminum 4.1 liter V8 for 1982. BMW was also working on a variable displacement engine at the dawn of the '80s, based on a special e21 BMW 323i.

BMW's method was to shut off fuel to half the engine when not required, and to channel the hot exhaust gases from the 3 working cylinders to the 3 dormant cylinders using baffles. Keeping the dormant chambers warm would make their refiring easier when the load sensor sensed the driver needed full power, resuming fuel feed to all six cylinders. This wasn't far-fetched tech; fuel shutoff was used on the Bosch L-jet equipped BMW 525i/528i when said models were coasting, and baffles weren't exactly rocket science either.

The only fly in the ointment concerned compliance with the oxygen sensor of the 3-way cat fitted to U.S. Bimmers. However, this special 323i wasn't for sale anywhere; its job was to test the theory, and the theory proved valid. The modified 323i spent much of the time in 3-cylinder mode, with sprightly performance and real gasoline savings. The lessons learned from this and other studies would be put into practice for the '82 MY as the "eta"

With 121 bhp and 170 lbs./ft. in U.S. trim, the 2.7 liter eta six was the liveliest economy engine ever. A diesel never sounded this good, and the eta didn't mind starting in cold weather (courtesy Billy Isbell).

concept. It was a gas-mileage-improving strategy that combined established ideas with modern engine management to create a balance of performance and economy never seen before in a gasoline power plant.

Eta Means Economy

It all started out of necessity in Detroit. The Big Four's engineers discovered that mpg figures could be improved if an engine turned over slowly at high load. It was important after the first fuel crisis, and with the coming of CAFE, engineers worked long and hard to improve their fleet average and put a more appealing EPA mpg number on the window sticker. Such an overt economy drive was alien to a sporty company like BMW, but now they too were searching for extra CAFE credits, and their research confirmed the value of the turn slow/high load principle, and why it made for superior gas mileage.

The two reasons were lower frictional and pumping losses. High revs equal wasted energy, going towards making the moving parts of an internal combustion engine move against each other. Secondly, energy is also wasted when an engine tries to breathe through an almost closed throttle butterfly, just like a person finding it hard to inhale through a blocked nose. The latter was partly the reason why the variable displacement 323i produced such good gas mileage. By setting the test car to stay in 3-cylinder mode as much as possible, the throttle was mostly wide open as half the engine was put under high load to motivate the car.

With half the 323i's engine breathing freely through an open throttle butterfly, pumping losses were minimized. To optimize the whole deal, BMW worked out that the best way forward was to change up at 2,000 rpm using ¾ throttle. It produced the best gas savings, and avoided snail-pace progress, but one required the right package to pull it off. BMW had the car: it was called the 1982 528e. This model was North America's first taste of the e28. The car's name arose from a need to avoid nameplate confusion. In the '70s many were confused during downsizing when nameplates were swapped, often with a smaller car inheriting a name once used by a bigger car.

BMW bamboozled lots of people when they replaced the 530i with the 528i. What happened to the old car? Was the new model a size down? Hard to believe, given that BMW sold only four North American models at the time (320i/530i/633CSi/733i), but true. When BMW re-engined the U.S. e21 320i into a 1.8 liter car, it retained the 320i badge to avoid confusion in 1980. Fast forward to 1982 and the U.S. e12 528i was replaced by the e28 528e. The new car actually had a 2.7 liter engine, but the "e" part was for real. "E" stood for eta, the seventh letter in the Greek alphabet and the engineering symbol for efficiency.

The 2.7 liter motor was an inline six, based on the M60 baby six sold in Europe in 2 and 2.3 liter forms. A physically smaller and lighter block than the usual BMW M30 big six, the Bavarians bored and stroked the wee six so that it nearly had the displacement of the much-loved 528i. With dimensions of 84.1/81 mm yielding a displacement of 2,693 cc, the eta motor was a true breakthrough. The engineers had squeezed whatever they could from the block. It's also worth noting that this was the first time America had met BMW's baby six.

Compression ratio stood at 9 to one, much better than the U.S. 528i's 8.2:1. So far so good, but there was a fiendish catch: this was an economotor! BMW had taken its high-rpm baby six and turned it into a low-rpm engine maximized for fuel efficiency. For BMW worshippers the eta six carried frightening figures, namely 121 bhp (SAE) at 4,250 rpm. The redline was set at 4,750 rpm and suddenly BMW aficionados were crying in their lattes. It seemed Munich really wanted their car to top out at the speedo's 85 mph marking.

The low redline was to safeguard the soft, lightweight valve springs, another move to cut frictional losses. However, the good news was that this eta 2.7 made tons of torque, 170 lbs./ft. arrived at 3,250 rpm. BMW wasn't known for making such torque in this vicinity, and the proof of the pudding was most certainly in the eta's eating. The standard overdrive 5-speed (0.81 fifth), combined with the high-torque 2.7 and lightened e28 shell, produced welcome results. Top speed was 110–115 mph, meaning one could cruise in fifth at double the national speed limit.

Acceleration was respectable with 0–60 mph arriving in 10 seconds; *Car & Driver* got 9.5 seconds, eye-popping results compared to a diesel Seville and many other 0–50 mph fiends of the day. BMW didn't have to quote 0–50 mph like others to look fast. The best part was that the 528e felt fast; it was the torque that did it. The 528e liked to buzz along, and econowunder or not, its I6 engine was happy to rev, until it hit that low redline. At that point the driver was greeted by an abrupt fuel shutoff and it was game over, but there were sizeable compensations.

This 1988 Dinan M5 has Dinan 3-piece forged rims, 17 × 9-inch front/17 × 10-inch rear and Dinan Stage 4 suspension. Also boosting the M88/3 engine conversion are a Miller Mass Air Flow sensor, Perfect Power Piggy Back ECU controller and B&B stainless steel exhaust (courtesy Scottie Sharpe, http://bmwturbos.scottiesharpe.com/).

The whole eta point was to achieve great gas savings, and with EPA city/highway numbers of 22/32 mpg, BMW succeeded. The final 5-speed e12 528i was rated at 18 mpg city, and with the CAFE fleet target rising to the 27.5 mpg Holy Grail, there was method to the 528e's madness. It may have looked like a grown-up 2002, but the 528e was a vision of the future. Master its special driving technique, take advantage of that low-end torque, and the economic gains were there.

In 1982 a $24k automobile could be an economy car, because the world had grown up and the path to more mpgs was more sophisticated than Chevette Scooters without a back seat. The higher price tag bought the 528e owner a clear conscience and Bosch Digital Motor Electronics (DME). This was an engine management system umbrella that incorporated Bosch L-jet, plus electronic ignition. The system was first used by BMW on the 1980 Euro 732i; the eta Five was the second road car application. DME monitored engine rpm, chosen gear ratio, coolant temp and, for U.S. eta cars, exhaust gas content.

After considering all of the above, DME continuously retuned the engine, altering fuel mix and engine idle speed and choosing from 256 ignition advance angles that related to

The e28 524td was BMW's first diesel production car, and the world's fastest diesel sedan in 1983. It used a 115 bhp turbocharged I6 engine (courtesy Chris Hinkel).

different rpm and intake manifold vacuum. As the driver thought how to maximize the 528e's economy, so did the car! The 528e standard manual transmission format and torque were ideal to exploit the high load/low rpm technique. However, an automatic was also good at the 2,000 rpm, ¾ throttle shift shuffle.

Autoboxes like to change up early, unless driven with vigor. They tend to make the motor live in the lower portion of the tach. If the driver doesn't engage kickdown, a tall gear can be held while the engine labors at low rpm. An auto suited eta, and encouraged the gas-mileage-maximizing driving style. Thus, in Europe the eta concept found a home in the auto-only 525e.

Even more confusingly named, the 525e had a higher CR version of the 528e's 2.7-liter I6. Arriving fresh for the '83 MY, the 525e was BMW's tech answer to the Audi 100 CD 5-cylinder, a fuel-efficient car for the businessman of the '80s. BMW was going to prove in Europe that luxury motoring needn't carry a big gas penalty. The results were impressive, as an auto I6 it was nearly as frugal as the 518i 5-speed, and much swifter in real-world motoring. The power turned out to be 125 bhp (DIN) with max torque of 177 lbs./ft., the same torque as the new e28 528i, but at that limbo-low 3,250 rpm.

The 125 horses weren't to be snickered at, either; it was the same rating as the 520i, and in West Germany, car insurance class is based on horsepower. The 525e had punch; it

Normally limited to stock 11.6 psi boost pressure, this 2.4 turbodiesel has been modified with a cold air intake, external wastegate/manual boost controller and larger 12 × 11 × 4-inch intercooler (courtesy Chris Hinkel).

just chose to save it for the right moment. A large number of European buyers selected a 525i/528i with automatic. In spite of the marque's hi-po image many buyers chose an auto even during the e12 era. As an auto the 525e worked better than a 525i/528i with zombie shift. The 525e's huge 11-to-one CR, and low rpm design brief, made it the thinking man's automatic Bimmer.

This was a quirky car that could do cool things like 1,600 rpm at 60 mph, unusual for a BMW. However, quirky was for Citroen, not for BMW. The Bavarians were known for all-out firepower, and the 525e became regarded as an oddball. Whereas across the pond the 528e was the volume seller, in Europe it tended to be overlooked. The mood was summed up by UK's *What Car?* magazine in 1988: "...the 525e as a model is now obsolete and right up to its last build date was never one of the 'sexy' BMWs. Not like, say, the 528i, 635CSi or 325i."[3]

In the years since, the eta has developed a cult following among BMW enthusiasts, and its smooth refinement has become more appreciated in Europe. In North America the 528e was being enjoyed in the present. BMW 5 series sales doubled in 1982 and better things were on the way. Taking on board *Car & Driver*'s comments concerning how early the 528e threw in the towel, BMW's R&D boss Dr. Karlheinz Radermacher instituted a change to fit stiffer valve springs and increase the redline to 5,000 rpm for '83. Those searching for something extra could chip a 528e.

In the '90s aftermarket companies offered high-performance power chips for the eta's ECU. Swap the stock item with a superchip and enjoy the instant plug-and-play power trip. AutoThority provided for the 528e, and B.B.R. (Brodie Brittain Racing) had a Star Chip for the 525e. U.S. tuner Dinan even had a bolt-on package for eta cars. Dinan Performance Engineering's kit consisted of a special intake manifold, power chip and sports exhaust that raised the bidding from 121 to 158 bhp. In the UK the eta crank was used to get more from the BMW baby six.

Les Stannard of Stannard Motors offered conversions for owners of high-mile 320i/323i cars, using 84 mm Mahle pistons and the eta crank to get displacement out to 2.7 liters. As with Dinan a regular "i" cam could replace the eta's econocam, and with uprated valvegear 200–210 bhp was in the cards. Unfortunately the mods would mean gas mileage would go out the window. BMW effected more modest mods on their 525e. For 1986 the eta 2.7 was rerated from 125 bhp to 129 horses, even though CR had dropped to 10.2-to-one, plus the Switchable auto became an option.

In Europe there was a key economy area BMW didn't have a footprint in: diesel power. While the idea of an oil-burning 2002 was once heresy, needs move as the devil drives. As with eta the basis for BMW diesel would be their baby six. Engine man Karlheinz Lange oversaw the creation of a prototype turbodiesel as early as 1978. In 1979 construction of a new factory started, as part of a joint venture between BMW and diesel specialists Steyr-Daimler-Puch to build the new turbodiesel. BMW bought out Steyr in 1982, with engine production starting that year which included the engines of the 520i and 525e.

BMW's first oil-burner was the 1984 MY 524td. The Bavarians reasoned the square-rigged Five needed more of a publicity boost than the new e30 3 series, so they gave the 115 bhp 2.4 liter turbodiesel to the e28. The new motor used a Garrett T-3 turbo to make max power at 4,800 rpm with boost limited to 11.6 psi. Maximum torque was 155 lbs./ft. arriving at 2,400 rpm. To make the new diesel perform like a BMW, the first thing the company got rid of was compromise.

Others had rushed to convert gasoline engines to diesels in the wake of the fuel crisis, with mixed results. BMW gave their turbodiesel a new cylinder head, swirl-type combustion chamber and Bosch VE mechanical fuel injection. The result was a revelation: the world's first high-performance diesel! The 524td was the fastest diesel sedan in the world. Here was an oil-burner a BMW enthusiast could love, if only it had reached America sooner. There was a time when diesel was king in the U.S., when dealership patrons fought to be the lucky guy that got to take home the last Olds 260ci diesel Cutlass on the lot.

Daimler-Benz was there in those happy days; BMW was not. By the time the 524td arrived in America in early 1985 the diesel peak had passed, and it only lasted through to the close of the '86 MY. However, stateside the 524td did help BMW earn CAFE credits so that it could spice up its North American model lineup, and the e28 wasn't the only place to enjoy the new BMW turbodiesel. Steyr got a contract to supply Ford with the new state-of-the-art 2.4 turbodiesel. The 524td and Lincoln Continental Mark VII shared power plants. Ford decided to rely on foreign diesel expertise.

It's believed 200–500 BMW-Steyr powered Lincolns were sold while the 2.4 turbodiesel was on the Lincoln options list during the 1984 and '85 MYs. Most of those cars would

A UK spec Zinnober red 1985 528i, originally with 2-way sunroof and TRX metric alloys. The 1985 MY was the first year the 5 series changed to a flatter, plainer style of front seat head restraint (courtesy Peter Thorpe, http://forum.bmw5.co.uk).

have had the 4-speed auto, but a 5-speed stick was also available with evidence that at least one such car was so optioned. BMW was counting those mpgs with us, because in the lower half of the e28's rev counter, from the 525i upwards, was an econometer. As expected, BMW had something more refined than the usual green/yellow/red, good, bad and ugly vacuum gauge. This econometer told it like it was, at any given moment in time.

The e28 econometer considered the fuel flow of the engine's injector solenoids, and related this information to the car's speed taken from the speedo. Driving a car with a true gas mileage indicator does change behavior behind the wheel. A changed driving style commensurate with gas saving was the result. Plus, the e28 weight savings helped the new Five get more from every gallon.

The nature of the reductions showed a typical Teutonic thoroughness. Apart from obvious changes like thinner panels and glass, weight was pared from the rear semi-trailing arms, which were now seam-welded hollow units. E28 engine crankcases were thinner, but had more ribbing; sound-deadening material was deep-sixed, necessitating an additional muffler compared to e12 days. The e28 doors seemed much lighter to the touch compared to the hefty equivalents on early e12s.

The doors now clicked, rather than whumped shut. More noticeable was the new hood. Much, much thinner than the e12 version, it now flexed upon waxing. BMW's engineers had jettisoned the full-width, forward-opening e12 hood with counterbalance mechanism, in favor of a conventional hood supported by gas struts. Such reductions added to BMW's development costs, and anxious to show the press and public where the money went, the Bavarians provided an itemized weight saving list.

It was claimed the e28s were on average 90–100 kilos lither than their e12 predecessors, a claim verified by comparing the 1981 e12s with the 1982 e28s. The outgoing e12 520/528i had curb weights of 1310/1410 kg; for the new 520i/528i the figures were 1220/1320 kg. A sign of how hard BMW was trying to turn their cars into meringues was given by the change in badging. A 1972 BMW 520i trunk lid i.d. badge is a thick metal item, its 1982 equivalent a thin, plastic part.

In the e12/e21 era BMW stated its rust protection/paint process ran to 39 stages. With the e28/e30 models this was extended to 45 stages, but the anticorrosion warranty remained the same as it had been since the early '70s, 6 years. In spite of improvements in the paint process the e28s seem to have a corrosion trouble spot concerning the fresh air ventilation hood grille vent. On the e28 there are two vents, and rusting occurs where the hood's steelwork meets the body's firewall or bulkhead. When inspecting an e28 for sale, simply look down through the vent grille of a closed hood; depending on the state of deterioration, rust may be visible. Open the hood and inspect the rubber seals that cover the inside of the hood and seal it to the bulkhead, since these obscure the rust. Rust in this area has occurred on cars as young as 8–10 years in dry sunny climates, and can blemish what might otherwise be a mint car. It seems that the rubber seal adhesive gives way, allowing water to get trapped and rust out the sheet metal.

E28—BMW Goes Back to Suspension School

Suspension was one area where the new Five received a major makeover. A 1969 U.S. BMW 2500/2800 print ad claimed that BMW's suspension was speedier than even its excellent engine. The trouble was that for some the suspension was a little too speedy. BMW's semi-trailing arm rear suspension required expert attention. The grip limit was high, but the propensity to let go was sudden. Never before had the description "terminal oversteer" been so appropriate. When questioned over the 2002 Turbo's 170 bhp power output, BMW's Alex von Falkenhausen said that more was possible, but 170 bhp was the safe limit for drivers without a competition racing license.

Tire manufacturers were also displeased at the pressure their covers were placed under by BMW's suspension design. The European body ETRTO set a limit for suspension camber change, beyond which they wouldn't be held responsible for the behavior of their product. Thus, BMW set about Naderizing their suspension, commencing with the inclusion of the double pivot front suspension as seen on the e23 7 series. This system was fitted to all e28s and involved the front suspension's arms not meeting at a single point, the apex of an "A."

The benefit of having two pivot points was that a true pivot point nearer the wheel's turning axis was produced without getting in the way of the brake hardware. The double pivot front end cut brake dive, improved transient response and helped BMW achieve a

A UK '87 528i, bought with moonroof, a/c, TRX rims and OD 5 speed manual gearbox. Mods include pearl beige sport seats, CR 5 speeder, Alpina 16 in B9 rims and custom 6 branch tubular exhaust manifold (courtesy Jamie Myles).

small positive scrub radius. The e28 would run straight and brake evenly, even when the front wheels encountered two different surfaces. Mercedes used zero offset geometry to keep their W116 S class on course, but this setup relied on the steering box's not being worn.

BMW's double pivot front end paved the way for ABS on the 525i/528i, another first for a Five. On e28s not fitted with ABS, a diagonally split dual circuit braking system was present. Front disks on all e28s were 11.2 inches, 11 inches on the outgoing e12s, and the 528i's front rotors were now 25 mm thick, the same thickness as per the e12 M535i. In the e28 era both the 525i and 528i had vented front rotors, but the 518/520i class retained rear drums.

As introduced on the 1980 BMW 745i, the e28 525i/528i were available with ABS. These e28s also used 7-series-style high-pressure hydraulic pump-powered brakes. The conventional vacuum brake booster used on e12s continued on the e28 518/520i. The biggest e28 chassis change concerned the rear suspension, and this alteration was unique to the 5 series. The 528i was the first variant to receive the new hardware. Previously tuners had got around the semi-trailing arm limitations by using firmer shocks, stiffer springs and larger sway bars, tactics to limit suspension movement.

To improve traction in slippery conditions, some added a sack of potatoes to the trunk,

BMW's stylish e24 6 series. The 1983–89 e24s, like this 635CSi, use the e28's double pivot front/13-degree Trac-Link rear suspension (courtesy Robert Duckworth).

trying to press the rear wheels onto the road. On the new 528i the engineers reduced the trail angle of the rear suspension from the 518–525i's 20 degrees to 13 degrees. The Munich men also added a suspension helper called "Trac-Link." The drop from 20 to 13 degrees was to reduce camber change associated with BMW's traditional wild oversteer. Unfortunately this change in degree lowered the static roll center, worsening the car's ability to change direction. The engineers then raised the rear suspension pivot points to restore the static roll center, but higher pivot points would cause jacking up when cornering. The suspension would raise the car's body with a loss of control and traction as the wheels tucked under. Trac-Link was the fix. This additional link was added below the rear suspension outer pivot, allowing movement inwards of the semi-trailing arm to curb jacking up.

A benefit of the higher rear pivot points was an anti squat effect. Sway bars were smaller on the new Five, and more effective because they were mounted behind the suspension. BMW had nearly worked a chassis miracle. The double pivot front meant more bite, but the tails of e28 518–525is still behaved very e12-like. All eyes were on the 528i, to see if it could ward off BMW's wayward rear.

The 528i's rear suspension did give greater warning that oversteer was coming. It was better at letting one know when it was about to let go, but experience was still required to handle a 528i. So the Five still wasn't for the faint of heart, and traction remained limited when things got slippery. If there was rain, snow or ice around, there was little chance of using the 528i's class-leading power, even at low speed.

BMW South Africa's Glas sedan-based 2004. The BMW 1800SA/2000SA and revised 1804/2004 were assembled at Rosslyn between 1968 and 1975 (courtesy Ulrich Thieme, http://www.e12.de).

BMW applied the 528i's 13-degree Trac-Link rear end to all North American '83 MY 5 series cars, just to be on the safe side. Another layer of e28 refinement came with metric-sized rims and tires. The Michelin TRX system involved larger rolling stock, with the idea of designing an entire wheel/tire system in harmony for more grip and better ride comfort with low-profile tires. The new rims had an easy-to-clean pattern. The Alpina-style rims had spokes that were a magnet to brake dust, with said brake dust being the very devil to remove.

The old 14 × 6 turbines made it onto early e28s, but the new rim pattern with small outer spokes was soon more common, and also available in a conventional 14 × 6 format. For those wishing to go metric the TRX rims were 390 × 165 mm, which equated to 15.4 × 6.5 inches in the old money. After the 14-inch era, TRX provided larger rims which allowed bigger brakes to be fitted. Ford, Ferrari and Jaguar also tried TRX on for size; BMW wasn't alone. For regular e28s the associated tire footprint and profile were 200/60.

E28s up to and including the 525i used 200/60 HR tires, and the 528i used VR covers. Aluminum rims, metric and conventional, were optional equipment on most Euro 518–528i cars, even though the 528i still had VR tires, even with steel rims. Alloys cost extra, and tire replacement for the TRX was exorbitant. The compensation was spry slalom progress and good ride comfort, but Pirelli's P7 was still the grip king.

As the '80s progressed, system TRX fell out of favor. In light of the cost of the 15.4-

The Glas-based South African sedans were increasingly BMWized until they looked like 4-door 2002s. The upside-down e12 taillights were just 2 of the items from the BMW parts bin (courtesy Ulrich Thieme, http://www.e12.de).

inch metric tires, many owners substituted conventional rims and turned their TRX equivalents into tablestands, sculptures and other forms of modern art. Such Warholian rims were merely a stepping stone to widespread adoption of the 16-inch format from the mid–'80s. System TRX had run out of road, but one concept that still had a home in Munchen was the e24 6 series coupe.

The close 5/6 series relationship had been noted since the '70s. When the U.S. 1977 630CSi came out, borrowing the 530i's motor, critics questioned the coupe's conviction. Was BMW dressing up their 530i, doubling its price and selling on style? After the e9 CS coupe, the e24 seemed like a method actor short on motivation. BMW made adjustments and critics soon came around, but now there were fresh changes underpinning the masterpiece. In the 1977–82 timeframe the 6 series had shared its chassis with the e12 5 series; now the e24 was getting upgraded.

For 1983 the Munich masters decided to share the e28 improvements with their luxo 2-door. The 6 series got the S.I. indicator system, scaled down onboard computer and HVAC refinements to match the e28. More importantly the 6 series received both the double pivot front suspension and reduced camber semi-trailing arm rear suspension with Trac-Link. The e24 was an e28 underfoot.

It had never been so pleasurable to hang the big coupe's tail out. The e24's new self-control was on display in the '80s TV series *Moonlighting*, where private detectives David Addison and Madeleine Hayes guided their e24 6 series through Los Angeles in glamorous fashion. The grace under pressure displayed by the iconic coupe was partly supplied by an e28 chassis, helping Dave and Maddy out of a few sticky situations.

BMW South Africa — Unusual Bimmers

Some thought it was a good idea to stick with the e12, and that some resided in South Africa. BMW in South Africa dates back to the late '60s when a company called Praetor Monteerders started assembling Glas automobiles. This concern in Pretoria started putting together a version of the Glas 1700 sedan under license in 1968. By this stage BMW had already bought out Glas and his Dingolfing factory, and were supplying Praetor Monteerders with a BMWized Glas sedan in CKD (Completely Knocked Down) form.

The Glas was a prestige middle-class sedan, like a BMW 1800, but the Glas had Hans Glas's innovative I4 rubber cambelt engine. The cars assembled in South Africa carried BMW badging and used BMW's own 1.8- and 2-liter M10 I4s, plus gearboxes. The vehicles produced were called BMW 1800SA and 2000SA, the SA denoting South Africa. The cars assembled at the Rosslyn factory, a plant that would soon be associated with BMW South Africa, were also sold in Brazil.

In the early '70s BMW bought an increasing number of shares in Praetor Monteerders, and the BMW e3 2500/2800 was made available to the South African market. The reason why so much local assembly takes place in South Africa is the high import duties on cars. For the 1974 MY, local assembly of the Glas/BMW sedan continued, and the model was revised to make it even more BMW-like. The 1800SA and 2000SA were replaced by the facelifted BMW 1804 and 2004.

The Glas-derived cars neatly slotted in below the e3 sedans, and were looking a lot like 4-door 2002s. The BMW parts bin had been raided to give the old Glas sedans a typically BMW four circular headlamp grille complete with chrome kidney and black plastic surround slats. At the back BMW e12 5 series taillights were utilized; just the basic body shell and dashboard were visual reminders of Glas ancestry. BMW had plans to replace this locally-made model with its own 5 series.

In March 1974 local production of the e12 5 series commenced at the South African Rosslyn plant, and in April 1975 BMW AG took over full shareholding and control of Praetor Monteerders to create BMW Suid Afrik Pty. Ltd. Production of the BMW 1804 and 2004 ended during 1975. As with the 1804/2004, the e12s produced in South Africa were constructed from CKD kits. In 1978 the BMW e23 7 series was added to the local BMW South Africa production program, bolstering BMW South Africa's position as a local manufacturer of prestige vehicles.

Matters rolled along nicely until 1982, by which time 53,248 e12 5 series cars had been assembled in South Africa. The arrival of the European e28 range then presented BMW South Africa with a choice: tool up for the new 5 series, or prepare the way to produce the new upcoming e30 3 series. Lack of production space and budget meant the company had to decide between the two options, and BMW South Africa chose the new 3 series.

Is it an e12? Is it an e28? No, it's a BMW SA assembled e12/8 518i. The e12/8 was an e12 shell fitted with e28 hardware and interior trim (courtesy Ulrich Thieme, http://www.e12.de).

The South African market likes practical cars; it has long had a preference for 4-door rather than 2-door sedans. As a result the e21 3 series was never available in South Africa. However, the growing worldwide popularity of the 3 series and the fact the e30 would be available with 4 doors, while the e21 was 2-door only, meant this was an offer too good to refuse.

With over 60 percent of BMW world sales being accounted for by the 3 series by late 1982, BMW SA's expansion would have to include the new e30 3 series. However, for 1982 BMW South Africa started making a hybrid vehicle, the e12/8 5 series. In short this new model incorporated the mechanical and technical e28 upgrades into the old e12 5 series body shell. It looked like an e12, but this BMW SA model range included the e28's double pivot front suspension, 13-degree Trac-Link rear suspension, M10/M30 revised intake manifold and e28 dashboard complete with S.I. indicator system, plus Check Control panel.

On the cosmetic side, while the e12/8's interior blended in much from the e28, it retained e12-style door armrests with the old-fashioned reach-through-and-pull door-opening latches. In BMW AG's records the e12/8 is classified as an e28 when it comes to production totals, but in reality it's a unique vehicle. In enthusiast circles it has become known as the e12 series 3 (e12 series 1 = 1972–76, series 2 = 1977–81). The e12/8 5 series was also a sign of BMW SA's development from CKD assembler to full-fledged car maker, capable of doing special projects.

South Africa is a country of high summer temperatures, power-sapping altitude and long distances. The octane rating of gasoline can also be low in places. In this environment the low drag factor and weight savings of the e28 carried less significance; torque was much more key. This was a place where people liked big, powerful, naturally aspirated engines, and BMW SA became something of a test bed for high-performance Bimmers. Under the guidance of BMW SA boss Dr. Eberhard von Koerber, three classic M30 powered BMWs arose.

The first was the e12 M530 sedan with associated racing program. Then came an unusual variant in the form of the e12/8 M535i. Although the e12 M535i had been discontinued, BMW SA continued with what was a forerunner of the e28 M535i. The e12/8 M535i was built from September 1981 to May 1984. It embodied the series 3 upgrades of other e12/8 cars. The e12/8 was only replaced by BMW SA in April 1985, when the e28 entered local production.

As per its e12 predecessor the e12/8 M535i was manual only; overdrive and close ratio 5 speed sticks were available. The e12/8 M535i also featured the early e12 M535i's steering wheel and leather shift knob *sans* shift pattern diagram. However, the e12/8 M535i didn't have a body kit; it did utilize the e28's metric alloys, though. The Michelin TRX system was in evidence in the form of 390 × 165 mm rims with 200/60 VR rated 390 mm tires. BMW SA continued to fit the old big-bore, short-stroke 3,453 cc 3.5-liter big six producing 214 bhp and 229 lbs/ft in South African spec.

Suspension on the e12/8 M535i was the same as the M-Technic package used by the e28 M535i. A total of 1,416 e12/8 M535is were assembled by BMW SA. Dr. Koerber also had plans for the e23 7 series. The German-built 745i started in 1980 as an auto-only turbo 3.2-liter, 3.5-liter motivated from the '83 MY, big-six-powered Autobahn cruiser. The turbo would have clashed with a right-hand-drive e23's steering assembly, so BMW SA came up with their own 745i. This South African–assembled e23 used the 286 bhp 24-valve DOHC 3.5-liter I6 found in the Euro M635CSi.

The naturally aspirated BMW SA 745i was available with 4-speed Switchable auto, or a close ratio dogleg Getrag 5-speeder; the model lasted from 1984 to 1986. In 1985 BMW SA produced something seen before from tuners Alpina and Hartge, a 3 series with the M30 big six. The BMW SA e30 333i started as an after-work idea while a beer or two was had, on the subject of what to do with the e30 3 series.

The big-six-powered e30 used Alpina parts and was brought to fruition under the watch of Bernd Pischetsrieder, BMW SA boss at the time and BMW CEO in 1993–99. Due to the market's right-hand-drive nature and under-hood space constraints, the high-efficiency exhaust manifold was a headache, so the 333i couldn't be offered with factory a/c.

5

Fast Shoeboxes

The e28 Motorsport and Tuner Variants

Back to Buchloe—Alpina and the e28

Sometimes performance takes priority. BMW SA understood that, and so did the tuners working on the e28 5 series. Once again the daddy of them all was Alpina, and the Buchloe boys had come to grips with the e28's new suspension in a version called B9. The B9 package used a naturally aspirated 245 bhp version of BMW's 3,453 cc M30. It featured a 10.2-to-one CR and a 268-degree camshaft. Wheels and tires continued with 16 × 7-inch rims front and 16 × 8-inch rims rear, using Pirelli P7s.

The B9 sedan was a successor to the 3.2 liter B8, and production of the new car started in January 1983. *Auto Motor und Sport* managed 152 mph out of the e28 B9 with 0–62 mph in 6.9 seconds. If that wasn't enough, Alpina offered their turbo M30 I6 in the e28 chassis. The model was denoted B7; it had a 3.5-liter blown I6, but power had been dialed back to 300 horses. The 3.5-liter used to make 330 bhp, but Alpina was concentrating on torque with the e28 application. However, patrons were in for a longer wait than the B7's turbo lag, since the new B7 wasn't released until April 1984.

The Alpina turbos were for bahn storming, the naturally aspirated versions the practical choice and the only ones available in right-hand-drive form. Alpina's UK agent was Sytner BMW, started by Frank Sytner. Their range started with a warmed-up 528i. Their RHD "2.8 saloon" produced 192 bhp. Sytner also offered the B9 in RHD form, a converted version of the e28 528i. From 1985 to 1987 Sytner UK produced a B10 5 series based on the e28 platform. This car utilized the e28 535i, which had a Motronic-managed 3,430 cc version of the M30 I6 producing 260 bhp at 5,700 rpm and 237 lbs./ft. at 4,000 rpm.

Note that at the time Alpina didn't formally make right-hand-drive versions of their models, so it was up to national importing agents to bring in Alpina hardware and fit it to new cars. Sytner BMW produced 64 B9s and 25 B10s in the eighties.

Back to Berkeley with H&B

Hardy & Beck continued into the eighties with a formal name change to "H&B" at the start of 1982, when Allen Hardy bought out partner Hans Beck's share. However, there

NKN-353
ALPINA

ALPINA
ALPINA
OILSERVICE
INSPECTION
TEMP
ARR
SPEED
MPG
RANGE
EXIT
TIMER
DIST
CODE
START
STOP
LOCK
TIME

was no change concerning their quality work, which included a hemi combustion chamber conversion. This altered U.S. spec motors to a dome piston/high CR configuration, as per BMW's original design intentions. There was also a really useful turbo kit utilizing a Japanese IHI turbo, as per the 1986 Italian market Ferrari 208 GTB turbo, available during 1980–84. The system worked with the fact U.S. spec M30s already came with low CR.

H&B added an airflow venturi downstream of the throttle body, with an add-on computer module considering boost pressure and rpm to calculate enrichment. Enrichment was delivered by an injector upstream of the turbo. With 8 psi boost pressure one could expect 250 SAE bhp, when the turbo kit was fitted to a 3.2-liter I6. This made the H&B 528i/633CSi/733i turbo more powerful than a new Corvette, but there was a change in business as the 1980s progressed away from U.S. designed and made BMW-boosting hardware.

The impetus for change came from a strengthening U.S. dollar and "Reaganomics." With the value of the U.S. dollar rising it became more feasible to do a gray-market import and tinker with said automobile, and President Reagan supported your purchase. A "Capital Investment Tax Credit" allowed buyers of such luxury cars to claim an initial 10 percent off their tax returns, and an "Accelerated Depreciation Allowance" took care of the remaining 90 percent of the car's value over a 3-year period. Greed was good, so why not bring over that BMW M635CSi, M1 or 745i?

H&B could certainly arrange for an exotic BMW import, and even had two brand-new Euro e30 323is in California long before BMW North America delivered the 1984 MY e30 318i. The plain H&B 323i with subtle pinstriping looked purposeful sitting on its stock e30 perforated steel rims, and was a bargain next to the official U.S. 318i. The fun needn't have stopped there, since with tinkering a H&B 327s was possible. Based on the Euro 323i, this car had a machined-out 49-state-legal 2.7-liter baby six with 10.5 CR and 180 bhp.

Fully equipped with H&B rims, suspension and decals, the H&B 327s sprinted out the door for $30–35K at 1985 prices. H&B prepared body kit for the e28 and e30 and investigated power tuning the eta I6. Unfortunately the ECU remap turned out to be technically problematic given the technology of the day, and turning the low-rpm eta into a high-rpm screamer was cost prohibitive.

Prevailing economic winds handed the baton to BMW North America to juice up its own offerings, which it did, eventually bringing in the e28 M5 and e24 M6 officially. By the mid–'80s H&B got out of the tuning business, but continues to this day as a BMW and Mini service specialist. H&B is still in Berkeley, California, under the control of Allen Hardy.

Opposite, top: **A 245 bhp 3.5 liter Alpina B9. LHD examples for sale on mainland Europe were put together by Alpina themselves (courtesy Francois Gaignaux).** ***Opposite, bottom:*** **In keeping with the high spec of Alpinas, this B9 came with the e28 trip computer and ABS. Early e28s had the central position ABS warning lamp, which was replaced by a warning light with international symbol at the base of the instrument cluster on later e28s (courtesy Peter Thorpe).**

HARTGE
Kelleners
BÖHM GMBH
Hartge-Vertragshändler-BMW
Am Pfauenzehnt 23 — 4220 Dinslaken
Telefon (02134) 52094 + 70221
HARTGE

Go Hard— Go Hartge!—The Hartge H5

Not as well known outside West Germany until the '80s was the tuning company Hartge. Rolf and Herbert Hartge were brothers who owned a successful BMW dealership in Beckingen, and also went racing in Bimmers. Spotting a market gap for tuned BMWs, they formed Hartge GmbH in 1971, bringing their race expertise to the world of road cars. The Hartge factory was built in the Beckingen area, and Hartge has formally been recognized as a car maker since 1983. Just before that, Hartge offered a 3.5-liter conversion package for the e12 528i.

The Hartge 535i was available around the same time as BMW's e12 M535i and boasted slightly higher compression and horsepower, 10-to-one CR and 220 bhp. Next, with the arrival of the e28 5 series, Hartge produced a revised version of their enhanced 3.5 liter producing 240 bhp. This power plant was also available in the 6 series, the 7 series and even the little e21 3 series! Hartge offered complementary improvements involving body kit, BBS 16-inch basket-weave rims and Bilstein dampers as part of a lowered suspension.

The 3.5-liter 5 series was still referred to as Hartge 535i, and had claimed performance figures of 230 kph and 0–100 kph in 7 seconds. By the mid–'80s Hartge revised its naming system, calling the 3.5-liter 5 series H5s. This car still featured the same 240 bhp 3,453 cc I6, but performance claims had improved slightly to 232 kph with 0–100 kph in 6.7 seconds. The other change was the adoption of Hartge's own in-house style multi-spoke rim design. These were 16 × 7.5 inches at the front and 16 × 8.5 inches at the rear, with 205/55 front and 225/50 VR tires rear.

For Hartge patrons seeking more punch there was the H5sp. The difference between the two concerned the engine. According to Hartge literature dated 8/85 the H5s used the older big-bore 3.5, the H5sp had the newer 3.4-liter (3,430 cc) edition with Motronic fuel injection. The latter power plant provided greater tuning potential and an output of 254 bhp. Claimed performance for the H5sp involved a top speed of 242 kph with 0–100 kph in 6.6 seconds. In the UK, BMW dealer Birds became an agent for Hartge in 1986, and their association continues to the present.

Speed with Schnitzer's S5

Another big name in Germany for faster BMWs is AC Schnitzer. This is another company with great background in motor racing. Team Schnitzer was started in 1967 by brothers Josef and Herbert Schnitzer, and Josef Schnitzer won the 1966 German Touring Car Championship in a BMW 2000TI. In the '70s, half-brothers Charly and Dieter Lamm joined Team Schnitzer, with Charly as racetrack team manager. Schnitzer racing operations were conducted in Bavaria, but the tuning company was placed close to the Belgium and Netherlands border in the city of Aachen.

The license plate code for Aachen is AC, hence AC Schnitzer! The name AC Schnitzer also coincided with Schnitzer's signing a deal with big BMW dealer Kohl Automobile

Opposite: **Rolf and Herbert Hartge transferred their racing experience to a range of road cars that covered the e21, e12, e24 and e23 (courtesy Hartge, http://www.hartge.de).**

British buyers got to sample Hartge's wares, once UK BMW dealer Birds became the country's official agent during the mid–'80s. Hartge offered 2.7-liter and 3.5-liter upgrades for the e30 and e28, respectively (courtesy Hartge & Birds, http://www.birds.uk.com/).

GmbH, concerning the sale and distribution of tuned road cars. The change occurred in 1987, prior to which time Schnitzer GmbH had produced and handled some tuned road cars like the Schnitzer e21 323i Turbo. From 1987 on, Schnitzer and AC Schnitzer have operated independently. Team Schnitzer have been involved with the 5 series since the early days. They were contracted to build the first racing e12 M530 that was shipped over to South Africa to take part in that country's touring car racing.

Team Schnitzer have had a long association with the BMW factory in racing. As team manager, Charly Lamm has been involved with 5 series and M1 turbos with over 1,000 bhp. However, the road-going e28 5 series tuned by Schnitzer GmbH was a more modest affair. The 245-horse Schnitzer S5 was based on the e28 chassis and was very similar to the Alpina B9 and Hartge H5s, in using BMW's 3.5-liter big six. The e28 Schnitzer S5 was a turnkey formal catalogue model with lowered suspension, 16-inch BBS rims and top speed raised to 240 kph.

Tuners were having a field day with 3.5 liter e28s, since BMW wasn't making one. Since the demise of the e12 M535i, the 528i was the top Euro e28, and if one wanted more, then the tuners would provide. In the U.S. BMW North America made amends by offering the 3.2-liter 533i for the 1983 MY. It was a version to complement the 528e, and even though its 181 SAE ponies livened up festivities, one could see BMW was more focused on mainstream matters. The first sign this was about to change came at the 1984 Paris Auto Salon with the unveiling of the e28 M535i.

At the customer's request H&B could turn a U.S. Bimmer motor into what its designers originally intended. Out went the flat-top pistons, replaced with high-CR dome equivalents, as part of a hemispherical combustion chamber conversion (courtesy Allen Hardy, http://www.hbspecialists.com/).

Time to Trust Motorsport with the e28

BMW felt the need to spice up its road-car range; this was especially vital with the e28 reaching the midpoint of the model cycle. Rival Daimler-Benz had a brand-new midsize W124 rival for the Five waiting in the wings, and BMW knew the heat was on. Thus, BMW set about fitting 3.5 I6s to the e28, which was bad news for the tuners that had profited from such business, and for MB, whose 185 bhp W123 280E would soon be eating BMW's dust.

The e28 M535i wasn't a hand-built model, just part of BMW's plan to spread the "M" mystique further through its range. BMW Motorsport was run by Wolfgang-Peter Flohr at the time, and part of his team's duties were M versions of various Bimmers, as well as Motorsport body kit and suspension. The mid- to late '80s was when the M-Technic accessory tag started becoming prominent, as a sports suspension or rear spoiler one might order for an e30 320i. In the case of the e28 M535i, it may have carried an M logo badge on the front grille and rear trunk lid, but the car was actually assembled at the Dingolfing factory, which made regular Fives.

It wouldn't have been possible for Motorsport division to have made the e28 M535i; its planned production volume of 5,000 units per annum was simply too great. This was a

As with some other U.S. tuners, H&B offered a turbo kit for BMW's trusty M10 I4. The kit was directed at the e21 320i, BMW's best seller of the era (courtesy H&B, http://www.hbspecialists.com/).

popular variant, and everyone was agreed that the car was conspicuously good value for a Bimmer. With a top end of 140 mph and 0–60 mph in 7.2 seconds it was on a par with the earlier e12 M535i, and nearly as quick as the Alpina, Hartge and Schnitzer competition, but for much less money. Indeed, the technical similarity between the M535i and the tuner specials prompted the press question: What's the difference? A BMW PR mouthpiece replied, "About 5,000 pounds sterling."

It was left to the auto connoisseur to work out if the handcrafted exclusivity and 27 additional horses of the Alpina B9 was worth 5K extra, but Bimmer patrons weren't complaining. Accompanying the new M535i was a regular 535i. As of the middle of August 1985 the M535i cost a mere 550 pounds sterling more than the 17,950 pound sterling 535i. Given the additional equipment brought by the M edition, the choice favored the extrovert M535i. From the collector's viewpoint, wise was the individual who chose an M535i and kept it in mint original condition. The subsequent M badge cachet and the M535i's unique features have produced a goodly premium over regular e28s.

The new M535i's engine held no surprises. This was the smooth and surprisingly frugal 10-to-one CR 3,430 cc M30 I6 introduced in the revised 635CSi and 735i. Slightly smaller in displacement than the old 3.5, the new version made the same 218 bhp with slightly more torque. Max power and the 229 lbs/ft arrived at the same respective engine speeds as before, 5,200 rpm/4,000 rpm. Bosch Motronic fuel injection ensured even temperament in all circumstances. The latest M535i was all about swift, fuss-free, high-speed motoring. To that end standard fitment, market dependant, was the 5 speed overdrive box with the Switchable 4-speed auto and CR 5 speed as no-cost options.

BMW procured a nifty advertising stat where the new M535i had the same average gas mileage as a 1978 98 bhp BMW 318! The 27.2 imperial mpg figure was more a sign of advertising BMW's efficiency and technical progress, rather than an attempt to hook M535i buyers through economy figures. The budget-conscious were hardly part of the M535i's buyer demographic, and those interested in the new model didn't believe in hiding their light under a bushel. The M535i's body kit got one noticed on the street.

The M535i featured a 9-piece color-coded body kit, with the exception of the rear spoiler, which was left black. There were wheel arch extenders, side skirts and a rear bumper/apron unit, but most noticeable was the front spoiler complex. The front spoiler/bumper with integrated turn signals and fog lamps was a one-piece '80s version of the unit fitted to Motorsport e12s. All this body addendum wasn't just for show; it helped cut the e28's drag factor to 0.37, in spite of the car's big wheels and tires.

The M535i had the BMW look of the '80s, confident with the emphasis on high-performance driving. As the decade went on, dechroming BMWs was a popular customization trick; BMW acknowledged this trend with its "Shadowline" dechrome option. The e28 M535i came standard with part Shadowline, its side rub protector strips and rear lamp lens trims were dechromed, with the option of full Shadowline treatment for M535is with the metallic exterior colors Diamond Black, Delphin Gray and Salmon Silver.

The car's interior was livened up with an M three-spoke steering wheel and standard sport seats with Motorsport tricolor trim at the front and back. The tiller was a new M design compared to the M1 and e12 M car days, and e28 M535i seating was available in cloth or leather. The driver would appreciate the sport seat's bolstering as the M-Technic suspension was put to good use. As per tuner specials, Bilstein shocks, lowering springs and beefier sway bars were used to improve the e28's chassis. Stopping power came from the usual e28 11.2-inch vented front/solid rear disks, gripped by single-piston fist calipers.

Something different came in the form of the e28 M535i's metric alloys. They were the usual 390 × 165 mm size, but the full disk pattern with cooling slots was unique to this model, and early e28 M535is had black-trimmed roundel center caps. Later e28 M535is had silver center caps, but all used 220/55 VR rated Michelin TRX tires. All e28 M535i cars also came with ABS as standard equipment, and brake rotors that, like the e28 528i, were 25 mm thick. The completeness of control was topped off by a standard 25 percent LSD.

There was a slight deviation with the Rosslyn CKD assembled RHD South African spec cars. These e28 M535is weren't fitted with the M-Technic body kit, and later South African e28 M535is stopped using the model's special M-Technic alloys and switched to regular TRX rims. Sport seats were optional on the South African cars, but the front and rear M badges were standard issue. In all, 11,751 e28 M535i cars were built, and the M badge was gaining notoriety. Starting in the West German home market, the M badge became the hottest-selling aftermarket accessory, as owners of regular Bimmers added the M to make their rides stand out.

It seemed like everyone wanted an M car, but in some places not even all the tea in China would grant access to an M. In North America BMW introduced the e28 535i as a

1985 MY replacement for the U.S. 533i. The 535i's 3,430 cc I6 was shared with the U.S. 635CSi and 735i. The new motor made 182 bhp at 5,400 rpm and 214 lbs./ft. at 4,000 rpm. The 533i's 3.2 liter made 181 bhp at 6,000 rpm and 195 lbs./ft. at 4,000 rpm. The new engine lowered the U.S. Five's 0–60 time to 7.5 seconds, but the rest of the car looked like previous federalized 5-mph-bumpered Fives. All 3.5 liter North American spec Bimmers came with ABS as standard equipment, and BMW North America had something special up its sleeve in the form of the 1987 MY 535iS.

The 535iS was a 535i with a sports equipment package. The "iS" theme was first seen on the 1981 e21 320iS, and involved using the standard smog-approved engine in a car with more options included in the price. The 535iS came with sports suspension, the trunk lid M-Technic rear spoiler seen in Europe and a special front spoiler/5 mph bumper unit specifically for the North American market. Emissions regs meant improvements were focused on handling; the 218 bhp Euro 3.5-liter I6 wasn't smog legal in the U.S.

Range rationalization and national regulations were also responsible for Australia's missing out on the e28 M535i; it was simply too small a market to cater for. It wasn't until 1986's legislated sale of new cars in unleaded gas/cat converter form that Australia got BMW's 3.5-liter I6, and the 3.5 received was the U.S. spec 182 bhp version, a rather ho-hum car. Just prior to the industry's going unleaded, a special version of the Australian spec 184 bhp 528i was made available. BMW was featuring prominently in Australia's local touring car series at the time. Gentleman Jim Richards became the 1985 Australian Touring Car Champion in a JPS sponsored 635CSi run by Frank Gardner.

In 1984/85 Gardner's JPS outfit produced the BMW 528i Motor Sport, a converted 528i available for sale at BMW dealers across Australia. No changes were made to the engine, and the car came with the usual 528i overdrive 5-speed. The alterations involved front/rear spoiler, body striping decals, conventional Mahle alloys with Michelin XWX rubber, and useful sports equipment from BMW's e28 catalogue. BMW's own futuristic 3-spoke leather-faced steering wheel, sports springs/gas shocks, LSD and — like the Euro e28 M535i — the overdrive box came with a 3.25 final drive.

As the 528i Motor Sport driver was cosseted by the Recaro sport bucket, his left arm got a good workout, shifting cogs to keep the 2.8-liter motor on the boil. This engine was set up for top-end power, and when combined with the OD box, wide ratios and tall final drive, torque was in short supply. The problem was slightly amended when the 528i went to a shorter 3.45 final drive for the '85 MY. Even so, there is no replacement for displacement, the car needed that 3.5 motor.

The ultimate factory-made e28 5 series came in the form of the M5, and the e28 became the first Five to receive the hallowed M5 nameplate when the model made its international debut at the 1985 Amsterdam Motor Show. This car was powered by a 286 bhp derivative of the 4-valve DOHC 3,453 cc I6 first seen in the 1978 BMW M1; the power plant was coded M88. Attached to this motor was an overdrive 5-speed box. The Motorsport engineers had replaced the e28 M535i's *vin ordinaire* Getrag 265 OD 5 speeder with the Getrag 280/5 unit.

The e28 M5 was in every way a Motorsport mobile. The ultimate e28 was developed by Motorsport division, and basic 5 series bodies were sent from Dingolfing to the Motorsport facility in Garching, where the cars reached hand-built fruition. The whole deal was going to cost the Bimmer patron a pretty penny. By the time the M5 was listed in the UK

The e28 M535i was BMW's affordable in-house alternative to the pricey, but more powerful and exclusive, 3.5-liter tuner e28s. With the M535i one had the convenience of being able to take the car to any BMW dealer for servicing (courtesy Gary Langton).

in July 1986, a 535i cost £19,095, a M535i was going for £20,095 and the new M5 retailed at a huge 31,295 pounds sterling. All 70 RHD M5s allocated to the UK market were eagerly snapped up, so even from the start the M5's high price never put off buyers looking for the best of Bimmer.

On the surface there wasn't much to show for the money. The M5 looked like a 520i with a set of TRXs and front fogs costing a third as much; this was intentional. Motorsport wanted to create the ultimate street sleeper. There was a special front spoiler and aero engine bay undertray, both of which defied detection. The e28's normal side reversing mirrors were present in body-matching color-coded form, as were a pair of "M5" badges, on the front grille and rear trunk lid. The badges were a delete option and many M5 owners chose to go without in the interests of appearing discreet. The M5 didn't even come with a trunk lid spoiler, and all the e28's chrome was intact.

What the e28 M5 did bring to the party was speed, and since it was lighter than the M635CSi, there was lots of it. Zero to sixty was a bit over 6 seconds with top speed a bit over 150 mph (more with the M-Technic body kit), most unusual results for the period. To keep a tight rein on that rate of forward momentum Motorsport turfed out the regular weight-saving e28 front single-spot calipers, replacing them with proper 4-piston equiva-

The e28 M5 was the first 5 series to bear said nameplate, and used a Motronic version of the M1's 24-valve DOHC 3.5-liter I6 (courtesy Richard Stern http://www.bmw2002.co.uk).

lents. Front disk rotor size was now 11.8 inches. The e28 M5 used normal e28 rear disk brake rotors/calipers. ABS was a standard fitment to all e28 M5s, naturally.

A possible point of visual identification was the M5's wheel/tire combo. Early Euro spec M5s had TRXs in the usual pattern, but they were bigger. The metric rims measured 390 × 195 mm, while all metric rims fitted to other e28s were only 165 mm wide. Combined with 220/55 VR tires and an absence of the M535i's flared fenders, the front 3/4 look revealed big rubber. There was clearly something afoot with the M5, although the oddball expensive and inconvenient nature of the TRX world saw the M5 switch over to 16-inch cross-spoke rims. These 16 × 7.5-inch rims carried 225/50 VR tires, most commonly Pirelli P700s.

The M5's handling was excellent, modification of the normal e28 528i suspension being surprisingly mild given the extra 100 horses stabled in the engine bay. The M5 had shorter/stiffer progressive rate coil springs, custom valved Bilsteins, and 25 mm front/18 mm rear sway bars. In the interests of better weight distribution the battery now resided in a special trunk compartment. Indeed, the trunk was an area of special cosmetic note on e28 M5s due to its plushness. The trunk had deluxe wall-to-wall carpeting and a cargo net, and the battery was located on the right side. There was an early and late design for the battery compartment cover.

Early M5s didn't receive the cargo net as standard. They also didn't get the black trunk lid inner lining; this area was usually gray on e28s. Another e28 M5 badge of honor was its black headliner; other e28s had gray. M5s also did without the e28 tach econometer; its

Bosch ML-Motronic, 37 mm intake and 32 mm exhaust valves plus two 264-degree camshafts added up to 286 bhp and 251 lbs./ft. in standard form (courtesy Jamie Myles).

inclusion would have been laughable given the M5's raison d'etre. Instead the M logo existed in the lower half of the tach; plus, the M5 came with a 170 mph speedo. Later M5s came with decorative M5 rocker panel plates, and although some markets carried the M tri-color metal seating tags, they were absent from the German home market.

Some M5 owners saw no reason to hide their treasure. In some markets it was possible to order the M-Technic body kit and make the M5 look just like an e28 M535i. Exercising this option made the 16-inch cross-spoke rims a mandatory fitment. In South Africa there was no need to exercise the option, since all RHD South African M5s came with the M-Technic body kit. This made up for the absence of the kit on their e28 M535i. Ninety-six M5s were assembled at the Rosslyn factory from CKD kits for the South African market.

Further cosmetic differences distinguished South Africa's M5. Its M-Technic body kit was accompanied by full Shadowline. This BMW M5 came with "Highline" Nappa leather trim for seating, door panels, center console, glovebox door, headliner, sun visors, upper door trim and even the dashboard. The Motorsport tri-color metal seating tags were also present, but the South African M5 didn't have the black under trunk lid trim found on most M5s. The only option for this market M5 was a power sun roof.

Since the South African M5 was painted at Rosslyn, color choices were limited to Henna Red, Ice White, Cirrus Blue, Delphin Gray and Diamond Black, with the last three as metallic colors. However, North American M5s, as Henry Ford used to say, could come in any color you like, as long as it was black!

This no. 804 US e28 M5 has a turbo 4 liter I6, Dinan Stage IV suspension with 25 mm front/19 mm rear sway bars, BBS RS 3 piece rims and e34 M5 Nurburgring brake upgrades (courtesy Ken Hawkins).

For years the gray market had been nipping at the heels of BMW. Companies like Hardy & Beck had been importing 323is, 745is and M1s, federalizing same and making a handsome profit. Eventually BMW was shamed into action. In 1987 it released the 535iS, and for '88 there was the North American e28 M5, plus its M6 sibling. The latter two used detoxed M88 I6s. Each still had 24 valves and DOHC, but with a CR drop from 10.5 to 9.8, plus a 3 way-cat that implied unleaded only. This motor was coded S38. The M88 made 286 bhp at 6,500 rpm and 251 lbs./ft. at 4,500 rpm; the U.S. spec S38 produced 256 bhp and 243 lbs./ft. at the same respective rpm in SAE terms.

Both M88 and S38 3.5s had Bosch ML-Motronic injection, 37 mm intake/32 mm exhaust valves and two 264 degree cams, but the M88 used a single row timing chain, while the S38 had a double row. On the outside the North American S38 only had the "BMW M Power" cam cover inscription. The early M88 editions had the BMW roundel and "BMW" on the cam cover; later versions had the roundel plus "M Power."

When matched to the Getrag 280/5 box the S38 helped the heavier U.S. M5 to sixty in 6.7 seconds, with exclusivity. BMW North America promised there would only be 500 imported 1988 MY M5s, but in fact, 1,370 M5s made the Atlantic crossing, which devalued the car's collector value for Bimmer patrons. Such buyers were probably price-gouged by evil dealers well over recommended retail price to start with. However, the story had a happy ending, in the form of a class-action lawsuit settlement, giving owners a credit towards the purchase of a new BMW.

Sadly, having a 1973 Mustang Mach 1 and a Pinto isn't quite the same thing as owning a single 1970 Mustang Boss 302. The M5 was never cut out to be a collector car. Collector cars drop in value once the zero miles seal is broken, and the M5 was too much fun to be kept in storage. Acknowledging the poor surfacing of many U.S. roads, Motorsport omitted the Euro spec progressive rate coil springs from the U.S. M5's buildsheet, and made the curious addition of standard Nivomat self-leveling rear suspension.

The U.S. M5 looked like a 535iS, sharing the latter's front air dam and rear spoiler. The U.S. M5 also had full Shadowline, the usual front and rear M5 badging and 16-inch cross-spokers. This hot compact also retained the U.S. e28's four equal-sized headlamps, 5-mph bumpers and side marker lights. On the inside the U.S. M5 was loaded like its South African cousin, and featured late-model M5 touches.

North American M5s had the front and rear M tri-color seating tags, and M5 insignia rocker panel dress plates. The interior was in most cases tan leather, but sometimes black. The North American M5s were hand-built by Motorsport, and to get some economies of scale it was originally agreed to have the one black exterior/tan interior combo. However, Canadian dealers wanted buyers to have the option of a black leather interior. Thus, Canadian M5s could have either interior. Since U.S./Canadian M5s were built to one mechanical spec, it was technically possible for a U.S. dealer to order a car with black leather interior too!

Given under 50 North American M5s with black leather interior were produced, this is a rare spec. Tan or black, the leather extended to the center console, glovebox door and door pulls. An eight-speaker cassette/tuner stereo was also standard equipment. Only heated

The U.S. e28 M5 came with 16-inch rims, and so does this M5, but they are 16-inch Hartge rims with 225/50 tires front and 245/45 tires rear (courtesy Armando Mendoza).

Never before has such a little tag meant so much to so many. North America was the biggest taker of e28 M5s, even though the variant was only available for the one 1988 model year (courtesy James Nelson).

front seats were optional on the U.S. M5, and the Canadians got that feature as standard. Indeed, the e28 M5 was all about being a custom car. Just as important as speed was the way the M5 could be tailored to suit the tastes of the buyer.

Such custom ordering was truly seen on the Continent. An M5 didn't have to have sport buckets; regular e28 leather seats could be chosen. If the M5's normal exterior and interior color/trim range wasn't to the customer's liking, the entire regular e28 catalogue could be brought into play ... at extra charge. The 5 series option list had grown greatly since 1972; the M5 may even have been fitted with an auxiliary heater that could be programmed to come on at a certain time for a set period to pre-warm the interior prior to a journey.

The e28 M5 was much rarer than the e28 M535i: just 2,241 e28 M5s were constructed. Naturally the M5's media job was to fuel the ambitions of the hundreds of thousands of 518/520i owners, to reaffirm their faith in the marque and create the dream that one glorious day they might reach an M5 by trading up! BMW had no problem keeping patrons loyal; so even were the price and horsepower steps from the 518 upwards that it was easy to stay with a Five. As a 1982 e28 print ad stated, "For under 10,000 pounds sterling you can have BMW 5 series specially built for you.... Why not come in so we can measure you up?"

The only problem with Munich's plan was resale value. Yes, BMW residuals were more robust than those associated with Opel, Peugeot, Rover or Volvo, but not as sound as those of Daimler-Benz and Porsche. Into the 21st century BMW has closed the resale gap to Benz, but that is more likely linked to the latter's recent quality woes; even so, the gap still lingers. Plus, cars with the three-pointed star still carry higher price tickets than equivalent Bimmers. Thus, the long-running rivalry between the two continues, in Formula 1 and elsewhere. The e28 may have won some battles, but the auto war was still very much on.

6

The e34 5 Series

A Time to Be Bold

1982–86—The Hungry Years

BMW wasn't a company to show weakness, but 1982 through 1986 were trying times. This period saw the launch of the major new ranges known as the e28 5 series and e30 3 series. The market welcomed them, sales went up, they were judged an improvement over their predecessors, but there was a problem. BMW never bestowed a new "e" code on a reskinned car, but they were new in a qualified sense. Plus, new European machinery was putting a question mark over BMW's value added. Europe's Ford Sierra and the new GM J car were lighter and more aerodynamic than past models. When it came to acceleration, top speed and gas mileage, a new Opel Ascona 1.6 showed up a BMW 316.

The BMW niche was honey to competitors' bees. The 1983 MB W201 190 range was a direct response to the success of the 3 series, and a serious rival BMW could have done without. The midsize MB W124 mirrored the sporty 190 ... BMW was battling. BMW was no longer the automatic first stop for a sport sedan, and it all happened while BMW was busy being a good citizen. Whittling away weight, introducing electronic advancements and improving fuel economy wasn't sexy. At a time when BMW was earning kudos for Formula 1 success, the image of its road cars was in trouble.

There was no hot e28 until the 1985 MY, and the boldest small Bimmer of the era was the 323i cabrio, and even Baur did that open-top conversion. BMW's R&D department needed a shakeup. Chairman Eberhard von Kuenheim fired the conservative Karlheinz Radermacher from the position of R&D chief. In 1985 Radermacher's successor, Hans Hagen, was in turn replaced by Wolfgang Reitzle. Turmoil in a transitional phase, and the Bavarian funk, carried over to their other mainstay, motorcycles. After 60 years BMW's trusty air-cooled flat twin was being largely phased out over 1983/84. The new family was the K series, affectionately called the "Flying Brick," which offered a water-cooled I4.

Beemer bike fans were a mite miffed over the loss of their old friend, and industrial strike action was making matters harder for BMW. On May 14, 1984, the metal workers of

Opposite, top: **A very early UK spec 1989 520i SE 5-speed wearing the upgrade 15 × 7-inch basket weave alloys with 225/60 VR tires (courtesy Andy Ottaway).** ***Opposite, bottom:*** **The original 520i's 12-valve SOHC six made 129 bhp at 6,000 rpm and 128 lbs./ft. at 4,300 rpm, which pushed the 2-liter sedan up to 123 mph (courtesy Andy Ottaway).**

G383 KUA

West Germany engaged in strike action to gain a 35-hour working week. BMW had to close four days later. The strike had a bad effect on German industry and specifically affected BMW with its new K series. As Eberhard von Kuenheim said, "In the U.S. we have already lost the '84 motorcycle business to the Japanese."[1] When it rains, it pours in the Black Forest!

On the books BMW was still in the black in any given year, but it was hard going in the economic jungle. BMW could only charge premium prices in export markets, upon which it was greatly reliant. At home BMWs cost less than comparable Mercs. Adding insult to injury, MB models made full list price, and usually had a long waiting list. The electronic gizmos Bimmers packed were partly responsible for the e23 7 series' gaining a reputation for taking unscheduled Autobahn naps! The moral of the story is that no one ever loved a computer.

Fortunately for the Munchen men, tides turn and fortune changes. By the mid–'80s BMW realized that the Motorsport division was the one entity Ford, Opel and VW didn't have, and that they should use it. The revised and expanded 1986 e30 range was a step in the right direction, with the biggest news being the imminent arrival of the 1987 M3. This 200 bhp mini-brick was the exact image-making variant BMW needed. Successful as a road and race car, the M3 was a Ferrari 308 GTB wrapped up in 2002 clothing. Everyone wanted an M3; it made people want a BMW again.

So commenced a glorious high-image era where Bavarian engineers no longer relied on their slide rules to impress the public. BMW had discovered the lure of style and its name was the new 1987 e32 7 series, a larger, crisper-styled e23 replacement courtesy of Claus Luthe's pen. With expansive flat surfaces implying power, the '70s blobby heaviness of the e23 was banished. Suddenly the W126 MB S class looked tired and cumbersome. The e32 was BMW's first all-new design since the 1978 M1, and hot on its heels was the also all-new 1988 e34 5 series.

E34 5 Series—The New Guy

In a major break from the past, BMW jettisoned its reverse slope shark grille, overhangs were curtailed, wheels were closer to each corner and the typically tall Bimmer greenhouse was shortened. The e34 was in line with the upcoming 1991 e36 3 series and both cars were a size up on their forerunners. The e34 cast a shadow similar to yesteryear's e23 Seven, and the e36 was a latter-day e28 Five.

BMW had a recognized style, and breaking away from the formula was tough. The e34's release was delayed because earlier drafts were sent back by management, since they looked too similar to the old e28. However, when the e34 made its debut in May 1988 it did have some old Bimmer standbys. Claus Luthe couldn't leave out that famous C pillar and the four-headlamp grille, but it was a slimmer, flat grille now with a color-coded kidney. BMW's old headlamp wipers were no more; just a high pressure jet remained.

The slimmer grille was facilitated by compact ellipsoidal projector-type headlamps. The ellipsoidal tech applied to dipped beam and fog lamp operation, permitting greater area coverage and less dazzle. The e34 clean sheet allowed greater advances in aero matters. With a higher tail, a smaller front, and an accentuated wedge, it was enough to cut the drag factor to 0.30–0.32 for the initial 520i-M5. As part of the Five's new modernity, the A

Note the e34's onboard computer registering an outside air temp of -35F. The onboard computer's info could be relayed to a dot matrix text display in the main instrument binnacle, via the turn signal column stalk (courtesy James Hartline).

pillar was more laid-back, the front windshield and rear window were flush bonded, and the rain gutters were flush too now.

With a nod to U.S.–style windshield wipers, the e34's partially disappeared at rest. There was very little e34 chrome trim; bumpers and side mirror housings were color-coded. Hunched down on its most aggressive TRX tire option, in Diamond Metallic Black, with thick muscular C pillars and a broad powerful look, for all the changes the e34 was still clearly a BMW. Indeed, the e32/34 L-shaped taillights became a contemporary BMW styling icon.

It looked bigger, because it was bigger. The e34 had the numbers over the e28 in almost every regard, 3.9 inches longer, a couple of inches wider and 0.1 inch shorter for that sportier look. The new Five also had a 5.3-inch-longer wheelbase. There was a clear physical link between the latest 5 and 7 series cars. The e34 took part of its floorpan and suspension hardware from the e32 7 series. Original planning consisted of even closer family ties, but that was dropped since it would have made the Five too heavy. There was also a need to differentiate the characters of the e32 and e34. As things stood, one needed to go to the long wheelbase e32 "L" (an extra 4.5 inches) to put daylight between the new Fives and Sevens.

The e34 also introduced a new kind of hush all over the 5 series thanks to additional

Top: With independent figures of 0–60 mph in 7.4 seconds and top speed of 145 mph, the 535i was faster than all its sedan opposition. However, it was pricier than both the Jag XJ6 3.6 and MB 300E (courtesy Tony Hart). ***Bottom:*** The 1988–92 530i used a 188 bhp 3-liter 2-valve version of BMW's small six. A 1989 UK example is shown (courtesy Paul Sharp).

sound padding. The polar opposite of the lithe 2002, the e34 big bus had 112 lbs. of sound-deadening material, not just under the hood and in the doors, but in the A and C pillars too. E34 extravagance even extended to rubber mats residing under the rear bench seat. Noise-absorbent plush carpeting/headliner, hydraulic engine mounts and special driveline bushings created a dwelling quiet enough for a pharaoh to rest in. The icing on the cake involved preassembled door seals, the best way to get a good fit on the assembly line.

Given the e34's higher cruising and top speeds it was key that the new Five be as silent as an echo chamber. Even the 520i had a top speed of 123 mph, the same factory figure as the 1975 528. However, extra refinement brought a weight penalty. Comparing 520i with 520i, the new e34 was 396 lbs. heavier, which taxed existing engine reserves. That said, one reached any destination more safely since the e34 was designed to meet higher parameters. The impact speed of the BMW crash program was raised to 35 mph.

The e34 was a safer place to be, and the boys in the white lab coats had the figures to prove it. Claimed flexural and torsional rigidity were 43 percent and 70 percent better in the static state, with both aspects 30 percent improved in the dynamic state. The new Five made a very good showing in a 1990 34 mph offset crash test performed by the German TÜV and the University of Heidelberg's Institute for Legal Medicine and Injury Research, for motoring journal *Auto Motor und Sport.* In the test of 8 large family sedans the BMW 520i came first![2] Second and third places were occupied by the W124 MB 200 and Volvo 740, respectively. The remaining 5 cars often showed great signs of passenger safety cell deformation, calling into question the priority placed on safety by other European and Japanese manufacturers. As for the e34's bumpers, they were not just 5 mph units; BMW had created 9-mph bumpers! Concealed behind the color-coded e34 bumpers were hydraulic dampers and impact boxes. These items would fend off low-speed thumps *sans* cosmetic flaw. If a 9-mph crunch occurred, the impact boxes were replaceable, limiting repair costs.

Another cosmetic benefit of the new bumper system was that the European and U.S. 5 series cars now looked the same, except for the U.S. side marker lights, which were well integrated by this stage. It was ironic that even though the e34 was a bigger car than the old Five, the U.S. e34 was shorter than the U.S. e28, due to the much neater 9-mph bumpers. Despite the big bumper changes, there was but relatively little change to BMW's suspension, which was no bad thing.

There was a continuation of the double pivot MacPherson strut front suspension, and 13-degree semi-trailing arm rear suspension with Trac-Link. Slight refinements were made to the optional Nivomat self-leveling device, and there was an extra steel brace bar added to the rear semi-trailing arms to stiffen the structure. However, it was the different nature of the new Five itself that brought real handling change. Bolting the parts to a new larger, wider Five with longer wheelbase and 50/50 weight distribution completely altered 5 series chassis behavior. The e34 introduced a new word to BMW's vocabulary: understeer! The handling spectrum ranged from boring understeer to neutral when pushed. Work at it hard enough and oversteer would come, but there was so much warning and it was a hard task to master in the lower-powered 520i/525i.

Banished for good was the sudden fishtailing of old nose-heavy Fives, but BMW wasn't willing to depart from system TRX just yet. The e34 range started with larger wheels, nothing under 15 inches; 15 × 7-inch basket weave cast alloys with 225/60 VR tires were a popular option. However, lurking on European and UK option sheets were larger metric

Top: The U.S. e34 525i was a direct replacement for the e28 528e starter Five; there was no eta in e34. The license plate present shows the "Power Cat" mascot of Kansas State University's football team (courtesy Dick Schneiders). ***Bottom:*** This 1990 Canadian spec 525i differed little compared to U.S. e34s, save the use of metric speedo and presence of French on some info decals (courtesy Alan Smith).

This 1989 U.S. 535i has 17-inch Borbet rims, Eibach pro kit lowering springs and Bilstein dampers. BMW North America's sales target for the '89 MY was 85,000 units (courtesy Barry Kaplan).

TRX rims and Michelin tires. This pack hung around until the e34's 1995 demise in the 415 × 195 mm size, shod with Michelin TRX 240/45 tires. As shown on the e28 5 series, and other cars, system TRX gave a good ride but other tires offered greater grip.

One of the few chassis differences in the e34 range was the separate spring and shock mounting on the 525i and higher models. Dual elastic rear suspension mounts were also utilized on the 525i and all variants north. However, when it came to braking, all e34s were on safer ground, using larger rotors than the e28. Front brakes were 11.9 inch vented disks, with 11.8 inch solid rotors rearwards. As per the e28, BMW continued to use weight-saving fist calipers. Even with the powerful new 535i, one was assured that the driver would never run out of brakes, tires or road!

E34 Electronic Aids—Trust the Computer

Old-school Bimmer ergonomics had a better reputation than the company's handling, so this area was just lightly redrafted for the e34. The angled dash returned, sporting more curves than on the e28. The designers placed the dash outer vents on the wraparound window trim connecting dash and door trim, so that a side window demist function was possible. The revised onboard computer was now placed on the center console below the central dash vents. Since the computer's readout panel wasn't in the driver's direct sight, its info was relayed to the instrument binnacle.

This UK spec 525i SE 24-valve was probably the best-value variant of the Euro e34s, explaining its popularity. The 1991 525i SE 24v cost 24,200 pounds sterling on debut (courtesy Craig Reeves).

Yes, BMW had carried over the Check Control function to the e34, but it was easier to use and fully automatic now. No need to look up at an overhead panel; it was all now displayed under the tach and speedo using a LCD dot matrix text display. Tap the turn signal steering-column stalk and the onboard computer's info would also be relayed using the same LCD panel. Directly below the panel was BMW's usual S.I. indicator system of colored lights. The intelligent BMW econometer was there, too, at the base of the rev counter.

Was this the cockpit of a BMW 5 series, or the flight deck of the Starship *Enterprise*? It was tough to tell now that BMW had introduced an electronic odometer/tripmeter display, an item becoming common on this class of vehicle. The idea was to make it harder to fraudulently doctor a car's mileage and thus enhance its Blue Book value. If one was boldly going where no human had gone before, then one might as well get comfy. BMW made this easier to achieve by copying the Daimler-Benz 3D power seat controller, now placed at the leading edge of the seat squab.

Manipulate the seat-shaped control blocks and electric servo motors did your bidding, moving the corresponding seat sections to the desired configuration. BMW also worked in auto height adjustable front seat belts, and reverse mount rear belts. The reasoning behind the outboard buckle connectors was so that in an accident the rear occupants wouldn't collide into each other sideways, causing head injuries. Rear seating space was slightly up

The revised M50 2-liter I6 made a decent 150 bhp. When the Vanos version arrived, max bhp/torque stayed constant, but the 140 lbs./ft. was now produced at 4,200 rpm, not 4,700 rpm (courtesy Mario Papakyriacou).

on the e28, but the e34 was a car with a lot of padding. The space-wasting rear drive format was the driver's friend, but the enemy of lovers of rear leg room.

One may have been cramped in the back of a Five, but at least the temperature was amenable. BMW included a dual zone temperature control heater as standard equipment in the e34. Standard in many export markets like America and Australia was a/c, with set-and-forget climate control as an option. Due to the e34's larger interior this was the first Five to get a rear HVAC outlet vent. It sounded like the new Munichmobile was getting softer than marshmallows, since there were a number of high-tech electronic driver aids for easier balance and control.

A hot topic of the '80s was traction control and BMW offered it on the e34 as ASC (Automatic Stability Control). Working with sensors used by the ABS system, ASC looked out for grip loss and instantaneously manipulated the throttle. If the surface was slippery it wouldn't let the driver gun the throttle, but would only permit as much engine power as could safely be used without traction loss. The system was initially withheld from the North American market: BMW management was anxious to avoid an "Audi 5000 phantom throttle" incident until ASC could prove itself in Europe.

BMW could look upon cars like this 1995 525i and judge the e34, the second all-new Five since '72, to have been a commercial Garden of Eden (courtesy Mehrdad Zarifkar).

Around the time the Vanos baby sixes were introduced BMW upgraded ASC to ASC+T. This expanded device, not available on the outgoing M30 e34 535i, selectively applied each of the rear wheel brakes to stop a skid. The extra "T" stood for traction, and ASC+T was available on Vanos 525i models during 1992, and subsequently on the V-8 e34s. So later e34s had electronic throttle and brake control on the menu, with one important quality: the system could be completely turned off. BMWs are drivers' cars and the engineers recognized that there were times when the driver didn't wish to be countermanded.

ASC was first seen on the e32 7 series, and so was EDC (Electronic Damper Control). The little brother e34 was also available with EDC, a driver-switchable electronic ride firmness device with two settings, comfort and sport. Recognizing that not all BMW owners enjoy a glass-smooth West German Autobahn, the BMW engineers working with company Fichtel und Sachs gave those traversing Belgian cobbles or English B roads a fighting chance to retain their teeth fillings! Some found it hard to discern the character difference between the two modes, and press-on types preferred the firm setting, so the option's value was questionable.

Similarly questioned sentiments existed over the optional Servotronic system for the e34's recirculating ball steering. Rather than base power assistance on engine speed, Servotronic measured out help using road speed. The system met its goal of giving extra assistance at low speed for parking maneuvers, but the assistance seemed to hang around at higher speeds too, leaving the steering feeling too light during freeway cruising. Once again, informed parties chose to avoid the expense of Servotronic, since the e34's regular power steering was already very good.

The 525i SE had many of the features that came as standard equipment on the 535i, like sunroof, alloys, sports steering wheel, onboard computer and Blaupunkt Bremen stereo cassette deck. The SE's value was clear to see ... even in a fog (courtesy Ollie Juggins).

As per later e28s, the e34 used the ZF 4-speed auto, with the option of a switchable EH version with 3-mode shift program. The latter EH box was standard on the e34 535i, and the mode selector had changed. No longer the e28's dial, the e34 used three buttons next to the shift gate on the driver's side. As before there was Sport (S), Economy (E), and the manual hold 1-2-3 mode, now denoted "M." For the 1993 MY, a ZF 5 speed 5HP22 autobox was introduced on the baby-six-powered Vanos cars.

The 5-speed auto brought a new level of flexibility in this engine size class. With the 5-speed the M button was replaced with a snowflake symbol, signifying a winter shift program for slippery conditions. The 5-speed auto never made it onto the M30 engined e34 535i. Standard e34 gearbox was an overdrive 5-speed manual, with a close-ratio 5-speed optional in Europe.

A couple of extra items brought by the e34 were pressure control for the windshield wipers, and a vent fan timer. The first feature was on the top-end 530i/535i versions; with higher road speeds the wipers were pressed more firmly onto the windshield. With the second it was possible to turn the fresh air ventilation on via the onboard computer's timer setting, so that air was circulated and the car's interior temp lowered while parked.

Fresh air was also coming from the e34's tailpipe thanks to stricter European emissions regulations. Those EEC regulations were agreed on June 28, 1985, taking effect from October 1989 to October 1993. It all implied a detoxed catalytic converter future for the e34, cat converters for the home market and the ability to run unleaded gas without adjustment.

Top: A 1995 UK 520i SE in Arctic Grey metallic, with Shadowline and 15-inch BBS cross-spoke rims (courtesy Martin and http://www.bmwland.co.uk). ***Bottom:*** This loaded 520i SE has silver leather interior, walnut trim pack, front armrests and a full-size toolkit (courtesy Martin).

Yes, the 525tds was an outright performance match for the 520i, and offered superior in-gear acceleration times, but its diesel couldn't match the turbine smoothness of the Vanos 2-liter shown (courtesy of the owner).

The latest e34 520i still had the familiar 1,990 cc I6 with 129 bhp, but its CR was slashed down to just 8.8 to one! The same applied to the 525i, which also had 8.8 CR, but many changes had occurred since the e28. The e34 525i used a 2,494 cc version of the BMW baby six, not the M30 big six as in olden times. Power rating was also well up, with the new 525i making 170 bhp. Similar news applied to a new European variant called 530i. The e34 530i sported a 188 bhp 2,986 cc edition of BMW's baby six, with a higher CR of 9 to one. This left just one more step in early e34 days: the 535i.

The e34 535i used the rugged 3,430 cc version of BMW's big six, but differences were abound. As with other e34 variants Bosch DME was a standard fit, plus a CR drop. The BMW 3.5 liter was no longer rated at 218 bhp with 10-to-one CR. The detoxed 3.5, as seen in the e32 7 series, had 211 horses and a CR of 9 to one. However, performance figures were generally improved over the e28 era. A better drag coefficient meant that claimed top speeds were mighty high. The new 525i and 535i boasting claimed terminal velocities of 137 mph and 146 mph, respectively.

Factory acceleration times were also adequate in spite of the e34's greater girth, and those weren't the only gains. For the U.S. 1989 MY it was all gain, with the e34 receiving 2 model variants with the same power enjoyed by Europeans. The U.S. 525i was rated at 168 bhp and the 535i was on 208 bhp. These were SAE figures, equal to the DIN outputs quoted by BMW. North America would benefit now that Europe had made friends with the cat converter, and the U.S. 535i's 208 bhp was a big improvement over the 182 bhp of

Top: For active safety BMW introduced ASC+T around the time Vanos became available. A precursor to modern stability control systems, the e34's ASC+T curbed understeer and oversteer in crisis situations by selectively braking individual rear wheels (courtesy of the owner). ***Bottom:*** In spite of the German-style front license plate, this 1995 525i resides in Sunnyvale, California. Clear turn signal lens covers are a popular aftermarket accessory (courtesy Robert Kane).

Top: The 518i lived on into e34 days, right until this final e34 1995 MY 518i SE with revised M43 I4. These late-design BMW alloys were supposed to stop the tire from jumping off the rim during a blowout (courtesy Darren Kelly). ***Bottom:*** This 1996 UK e34 518i SE Touring shows that BMW's new I4 was feisty enough to deal with a wagon body. The e34 Touring continued in Europe until the e39 Touring made a '97 MY debut (courtesy Ray Coldwell).

the previous U.S. spec 3.5. There it was: 2 billion deutsche marks well spent. The 5 series sat smugly in its new e34 business suit, looking rather pleased with itself.

The DOHC 24 Valve M50 Baby Six (520i/525i)

However, there was room for improvement with the small 6-cylinder e34s, BMW's Euro volume sellers. The BMW 2/2.5 liter I6s may have been emissions ready, but they were adjusted at the expense of throttle response. BMW needed something more in tune with the emissions challenge at hand. The solution was the heavily revised 24 valve M50 baby six, making a mid–1990 debut in the German home market, a 1991 MY entrant for world markets.

The new DOHC M50 I6s had class-leading power outputs of 150 bhp and 192 bhp, for the 2-liter and 2.5-liter versions respectively. The M50 was tilted 33 rather than 30 degrees from the vertical to permit the bulkier cylinder head to clear the hood. More cams and more valvegear meant more noise. To put a sock in the I6's mouth, hushing stereo cams and quad valves, BMW employed a sound-dampening engine lid. It was a fake dress cam cover that sat over, but wasn't very well aligned with, the real cam cover. However, with the doubling of engine parts and the move to chain drive, there were extra decibels to dampen.

A German spec 520i Touring in Oxford green metallic with the M50B20 multivalve I6. At BMW, cargo took a backseat to handling with the e34 Touring (courtesy of the owner).

The 525i (1995 example shown) and 530i were the e34 wagons BMW sold in North America, the latter having made a 1994 MY debut. Four-liter and Motorsport e34 Tourings were available in Europe (courtesy Greg Flint).

The M50 was the state-of-the-art small six that was expected from BMW. It even had a plastic breathing straw! The intake manifold was plastic, and its construction method promised better breathing. The whole idea was maximum return from low-octane unleaded, and that required high tech. As put into practice by Saab, the new M50 had one ignition coil per cylinder; it also had Bosch sequential fuel injection (DME 3.1). Having a knock sensor was crucial when having CRs at 10.5 for the 520i and 10 to one for the 525i.

A much sprightlier performance was provided by the latest 520i/525i, and it was almost a pure power gain because BMW had kept the weight gain to a minimum. The use of plastic plus a hollow cam and crank kept the weight rise to just 26 lbs. over the 2-valve motors. The new 24-valve sixes bettered every number in the book, nearly an unqualified improvement. Nearly, because tardy as the 2-valvers were, they had an edge in refinement. They were a hard act to follow, given the 2-valve 2-liter was said to have refinement equal to a V-12.

As compensation, the new 520i and 525i were as fast as V-12s ... almost! Comparing BMW factory-claimed top speeds the 520i was up from 203 to 211 kph, with the 525i racing up from 221 to 230 kph. Not bad, given no rise in displacement, but there was still a problem: an absence of low-speed torque. Especially in a heavyweight shell like the e34 there was no replacement for displacement, until BMW brought out Vanos. For the 1993 MY BMW introduced variable valve intake timing to the baby six.

L261 SUM
525ix

HYV311 GP

As with Honda's Vtec, one gets a cam for every occasion: one for mid-range torque, another for top-end power. In the Bimmer iteration there was hydramechanical adjustment of the intake camshaft by as much as 2.5 degrees, with such adjustment presided over by the engine's DME ECU. There were no claimed power increases for the 520i/525i, but their compression ratios were increased to 11 to one for the 520i and 10.5 to one for the 525i. The Vanos 525i combined with the new 5-speed auto set yet another new benchmark for complete, economical, sporty executive motoring in the 2 to 3 liter class.

When studying the e34 engine bay, there is a quick way to check whether the baby six at hand has Vanos. Vanos I6s have a protrusion at the front of the cylinder head, which accommodates the Vanos hardware. Bear that in mind the next time a plaid-wearing used car salesman tries to hoodwink you! With Vanos the writing was on the wall for the 530i, a logical if somewhat slow-selling e34 variant. The unloved 188 bhp 530i was dropped when the first 192 bhp 525i was introduced. The 3-liter seemed redundant, but the 535i continued apace.

M40—A New Generation of I4s

At the lower end of the range it seemed the Bavarians couldn't run away from the 518i nameplate. Combining an 1,800 cc engine with the large e34 body may have seemed like a joke, but BMW was serious. What started as a reaction to the OPEC oil embargo would resurface in the e34 with a new four-pot motor. BMW had pensioned off the ancient M10, replacing it with the lighter and thermodynamically more efficient M40. BMW's Karlheinz Lange came up with 1.6- and 1.8-liter M40s, which were introduced in the 1988 e30 3 series. Now for the 1991 MY the 1.8-liter version would appear in the e34 5 series.

Things started off with a 115 bhp M40 with a cast-iron block, alloy head and cambelt drive. The 2-valve-per-cylinder configuration contributed to the torquey nature of the I4; it didn't feel at any disadvantage to the departed 129 bhp 520i. This was the e34 to test the character of the owner. Could he live with a Bimmer without the credibility of an inline 6? Would she exercise the badge delete option when getting the 518i?

Those able to look past the image deficit got themselves a bargain. No shortcuts of any note were taken with the 518i's interior; this was a viable budget entry to the world of 5 series motoring. The 518i was the only e34 to use rear drum brakes, but ABS was still available, and braking performance was fine. As a package the 518i worked, so it was the fleet buyer's friend. Given a choice between a 518i and a loaded Ford Scorpio/Granada or Opel Omega/Vauxhall Carlton, the answer was child's play: the blue-and-white roundel ran out a winner every time!

Benefit from badge cachet, and the 518i's ability to run on a lower-octane gas than other Fives, all got even better during 1994 when BMW introduced the revised M43 I4 to the 518i. It was still on 1.8 liters, but now featuring lifelong chain cam drive. Torque was slightly up, from 122 to 124 lbs./ft. The revisions were first seen on the e36 family and

Opposite, top: **BMW's all-wheel-drive "iX" system combined with the e34 Touring body was a practical combo that predated the SUV. BMW's e30 and e34 iX models only used the 2.5 liter I6 (courtesy Mark Hoy).** ***Opposite, bottom:*** **BMW marketed the new 530i V-8 as a direct replacement for the outgoing 535i I6, with a 7 bhp advantage. Here we see the 530i in a South African setting (courtesy Duncan Meyer).**

Enjoy the 540i's 295 lbs./ft. at the track. A front spoiler with brake cooling ducts and rear vented disks were further trackside advantages the 540i enjoyed over the 530i V-8 (courtesy Dave Brennan and Jack Puryear).

included individual control intake manifold (ICIM) to eke out more go from the small four. Power output for the 1.8-liter I4 stayed at 115 bhp.

BMW factory figures for the 518i 5-speed manual (automatic was unavailable) involved 0–62 mph in 12.4 seconds and a top speed of 121 mph. This was no M5, but at least one could pretend to be in that exalted chariot while cruising at a genuine 100 mph in the humble 518i! For 1995 BMW extended the practical nature of the 518i even further through a wagon Touring variant. Indeed it was in that Touring body that BMW dabbled with an alternative fuel source in 1995. BMW released the BMW 316g Compact and 518g, model variants that ran on Compressed Natural Gas (CNG).

With CNG the driver uses more of it than he would gasoline, but in some parts of the world it's cheaper, so the motorist cuts overall cost. CNG is very clean-burning, but its convenience depends upon how established its distribution is in any given country, and it also works better with larger engine sizes. A more common alternative in Europe is diesel, and BMW was really picking up the pace in that area after a slow start. In the '90s they not only offered more diesel models, but were more proactive in selling their diesel engines to other manufacturers.

Top: With 286 bhp and 4 liters of displacement, the 540i V-8 auto got close to the M5 3.6 on paper, and even closer in real-world driving. ***Bottom:*** The new Nikasil 3- and 4-liter V-8 of the '90s was BMW's second postwar V-8 design, and like its '50s counterpart it was all alloy too (courtesy Lee Ridgway).

E34 Touring in a Diesel?

Open the hood on an Opel Omega or Range Rover and be greeted by the sight of a BMW diesel engine! A diesel e34 was around from the start of e34 life in the form of the 115 bhp 524td, a carryover from the e28 days. For the 1992 MY the 524td was replaced by two new versions called 525td and 525tds. As the names suggested, these cars had enlarged 2.5 liter I6s, courtesy of a longer stroke. The new M51 turbodiesels had improved torque: the 525td produced 115 bhp, but the intercooled 525tds came with 143 bhp.

Diesel motoring had come a long way in performance and refinement. BMW diesels had an encapsulated engine compartment, so that the e34 diesel interior was just as hushed as its gasoline counterpart. The mechanical refinement of the latest turbodiesels, their mile-stretching economy and high torque output were quickly making them the "thinking man's" 5 series. Given high European gasoline prices and the pokey power delivery of the 520i/525i, it was becoming difficult to overlook BMW's turbodiesels.

A greatly expanded model range is what the e34 was about. The 5 series was a niche player no more. There were diesels and there could even be wagons. BMW started on the sports wagon trail in 1971 when launching the 1600–2000tii Touring range, a Michelotti-styled hatchback version of the 2002. The hatchback was discontinued in 1974, not having been the commercial success BMW had hoped for. However, things turned around completely with the 1988 e30 3 series based Touring.

The e30 Touring hit a home run for BMW. The range was quickly expanded to embrace BMW's full line of 3 series engines. The new Touring was a good fit for BMW's demographic profile. Those who had dutifully bought BMW 2-door sedans needed something that could cope with a small family. The Touring was the answer, and it allowed Bimmer fans to stay loyal to the marque. On a larger scale, the subsequent 5 series Touring stopped defections to the Daimler-Benz T series wagon camp. For those who said they would never own a station wagon, BMW's e34 Touring was an acceptable compromise.

Thus, in the 1992 MY, BMW released the initial 520i and 525i Tourings. These wagons weren't heavy load-luggers in the fashion of a faux wood-paneled Ford Country Squire 351 or a Volvo 740 wagon. The emphasis was on style, a sedan driving experience, good looks with practicality. The e34 Touring didn't adhere to the "boxy is best" template, and the independent rear suspension didn't bless the style wagon with a perfectly flat load floor.

It was no workhorse, but BMW did wagonize the e34. The floor was raised an inch so that it was level with the loading lip. Carpeting in said load area was of coarser grade than that found in the passenger compartment. The 60/40 split folding rear seats allowed long items to be stowed while part of the rear bench was still inhabited. Optional split nets from the rear seats could attach to the Touring's ceiling to secure random small objects. The seat back bolster came with a privacy security load cover.

The Touring featured a reinforced e34 roof, and when fitted with optional luggage racks, further extended the wagon's cargo capacity. How much could an e34 Touring carry? With the rear bench folded, the e34 Touring was good for 51.2 cu. ft. This was much less than prestige rivals, especially the MB T's 76.8 cu ft, but it was a BMW, after all. The Touring offered the best ride comfort/handling class compromise; indeed, since Touring development was later than the e34 sedan, sentiment existed that the engineers had done a better job on the Touring.

Chassis changes were modest, but once again the Bavarians got things just right. Front springs were stiffer and so too were the rear shocks; larger diameter sway bars were used as well. There was also cosmetic harmony, as physical changes to the e34 concerned the B pillar rearwards. The designers created a gently rising swage line, and included larger versions of the e34's "L"-shape rear lamps to balance out the greater rear bulk and glass area. The result was a seamless wagon that thought it was a sedan.

Little touches to keep the family happy on a vacation trip covered a 10-speaker stereo with speakers hidden in the rear ceiling and a concealed radio antenna. Radio antenna wires, doing double duty as car alarm sensors, were placed within the rear side window glass. To maintain clear rear vision BMW used one rear window wiper, with a nozzle spray aimed into the wind so that the mist spray evenly covered the glass. In a move harking back to U.S. wagons of old, the e34 Touring possessed a split tailgate.

Open the entire rear tailgate, or just the rear glass window to access that toothbrush at night while camping: with the e34 Touring, the choice was yours, and there were electric servo motors to make light work of either task. Another possible aperture was an optional 4-way panoramic dual steel sunroof, a gadget fetishist's dream come true complete with a one-touch batten-down-the-hatches shut-up-shop facility. Officially called the Double-Lever Sliding Sunroof, the large dual panel device had a complexity that would have instilled fear into any Bimmer product liability czar.

The two tilt-and-slide sunroofs were enough to scare small kids and moderate-sized pets, as the power-assisted panels whirred to make the wagon a virtual convertible. Engine playlist options were regular 5 series fare. When the Touring went to the U.S. it started out in 525i form, with the 530i V-8 variant added for the 1994 MY.

With the V-8 version one could race to the golf course! The 530i Touring was the hottest 5 series wagon BMW North America offered. Europe received more potent versions although it was the turbodiesels that made the most sense in that part of the globe. A vehicle with all-wheel drive could also be useful in Northern Europe, during winter when the hills were covered with snow: all-wheel drive gave a car the surefootedness of a mountain goat. Audi proved this successfully in the '80s with its Quattro concept.

On All Fours—525iX

The 1980 Audi Quattro turbo coupe elevated the marque. A championship-winning vehicle that rewrote the rally rulebook, four wheels driven—good; two wheels driven—bad! Audi quickly capitalized on the Quattro coupe's attraction by bringing out Quattro all-wheel drive variants of all its model ranges. The public really dug the Quattro idea, leading other European brands like Alfa Romeo and Daimler-Benz to introduce all-wheel drive on some of their cars. Mindful of the Quattro's performance image, BMW weighed in on proceedings with the 1986 325iX, an Audi 90 Quattro rival, but the story started years earlier.

BMW started developing an all-wheel drive 3 series in 1980. Much re-engineering work had to be done to convert the baby-six-powered rear-drive 3 series into an all-wheel drive high-performance car. The result was a drivable pre-production version denoted 325i/4 in 1984, eventually being released as the 325iX. The engineering lessons learned from this exercise were transferred to the 5 series when the 525iX was launched for 1991. Powered by BMW's 24-valve 2.5-liter I6 (no other engine was offered), the 525iX featured permanent all-wheel drive with a rearward-biased 36/64 torque split.

It should be emphasized that unlike the 325iX, the 525iX wasn't offered as one of BMW's racer variants. This was just a sober middle-level e34 with traction benefits. The center differential had a viscous coupling designed by FF Developments and ZF, which used an electromagnetic multi-plate clutch. At the back of the 525iX resided a rear differential with electrohydraulic lock. There was a propshaft to the front axle differential utilizing chain drive; the e30 3 series had used a rubber-toothed belt. As with the e30 3 series, the engine sump was modified to integrate with the front differential and driveshafts.

There was computer control of the power spread carried out by the center and rear differentials, shifting what the I6 could produce from front to back and side to side on the rear axle. The 525iX models had uniquely shaped and styled 16 × 7.5-inch alloy rims that wouldn't fit on a regular 525i because the more deeply dished iX rims would clash with front suspension struts. Naturally, all this 4 × 4 hardware made the 525iX heavier than a normal 525i, by precisely 90 kilos. Performance figures suffered: for sedans, top speed dropped from 143 to 137 mph, and the 0–62 mph time rose up from 8.6 to 9.5 seconds.

The 525iX was also more expensive and thirstier than its two-wheel-drive counterpart. A 525i used 9 liters of gas per 100 km; the 525iX used 9.6 liters. However, in spite of the above, there was one cogent reason to purchase a 525iX: control! Independent testing confirmed that both in the dry and the wet, especially the wet, the 525iX showed clear advantages in putting its 192 horses onto the road and ease with which the driver could press on at the limit. The grip limit was a safer place to be in the iX, with BMW setting the car up to preserve BMW's typical final oversteer.

The designers had created a safe and entertaining automobile with the 525iX, very useful in ice and light snow where 2-wheel-drive vehicles would normally steer themselves into the nearest ditch. It was no longer necessary to give up an executive sedan and turn to a trusty MB G-wagon or Range Rover when the going got mushy. The practical benefits of iX were even available in the 525i Touring, and BMW's all-wheel drive system permitted regular functioning of the e34's ABS system. However, sometimes good products fall upon deaf ears.

The 325iX and 525iX never made it onto the BMW bestseller list. The public didn't seem to think that the iX price premium was worth it; for them, the regular 325i/525i sufficed. BMW and Daimler-Benz discovered that the Quattro cachet only shone at Audi. Stuttgart pulled the plug on their MB 4-matic model. In the sophisticated luxo segment, marques become associated with a set of qualities, and the market seldom rewards when a manufacturer plays against type. For BMW it would seem that even in the nineties, drivers still dreamt of getting sideways in a 2002!

M60 e34 530i/540i — Back to the V-8s

BMW is well known for its excellent engines, with power, economy, and smoothness ahead of the rest. In the 1950s the company's highest-profile engine was an all-aluminum V-8 designed by Alfred Boning. This unit was made in 2.6- to 3.2-liter sizes with an in-block oil cooler, and was the world's first volume-produced all-alloy V-8. However, there were areas of weakness: the in-block oil cooler wasn't that great, and it was a heavy engine. As an OHV design it didn't incorporate the hemispherical nature of the 1,971 cc OHV Fritz Fiedler I6 found in the classic BMW 328.

With dual carbs and 160 horses the BMW 507 3.2-liter was no match for the 3-liter I6-powered MB 300SL Gullwing with direct fuel injection and 240 bhp. As a grand tourer the 507's V-8 was friendly enough, but the Bavarians could do better. That better came in 1968 when BMW returned to the luxo segment and introduced 2.5/2.8 liter versions of its big six for the e3 sedan and e9 coupe. This engine was the head of the class, being durable, economical and, most importantly, powerful!

BMW made a better six than Daimler-Benz, or anyone else at the time. BMW's big six also served well through the '70s when the fuel crisis made the MB V-8s and Jag V-12 seem too extravagant. U.S. luxury V-8s also looked uneasy as they lost cubic inches and power with each passing year in the name of emissions control and better gas mileage. In 1981 BMW was pleased to declare that they would be sticking with a six for the foreseeable future, but that wasn't the whole story.

The BMW 2.5–3.3-liter I6, especially when teamed with a manual gearbox, delivered performance commensurate with a V-8 or V-12 automatic, but behind the scenes BMW too was trying to go large. BMW saw the MB 3.5/4.5 V-8 and wanted one too. So they joined a couple of M10 1.8-liter I4s at the crankshaft and voila! However, a 3.6-liter V-8 was on the small side, given the big six was up to 3.3 liters by 1974, so the engineers put together two 2-liter M10s. Unfortunately there were technical problems joining two M10s of this size, so the idea was canned.

BMW's thoughts then turned to creating a V-12 from its new 2–2.3-liter baby sixes. Destination for the supermotor was the upcoming e23 7 series, with its target being the MB 450SEL 6.9; BMW had always liked to dream big. So BMW made a 4.5-liter V-12 and put it in a manual-transmission e23, where it did 0–62 mph in 7.4 seconds, with a top speed over 140 mph. This was slightly swifter than the 6.9 liter Mercedes.

The public were invited to see this 275 bhp V-12 at the 1979 Frankfurt auto show, but BMW wasn't going to build it. Blame it on the high price of a barrel of oil, or the fact the M30 was up to 3.5 liters and 218 bhp by 1978; it seemed like now (1980) was not the time for a V-12 power plant. Instead, BMW put a KKK turbo on their 3.3-liter I6 (3,210 cc) to create the automatic 1980 745i turbo. It's still called 745i since, in racing regs, multiplying by 1.4 (3.2 × 1.4) gives an effective, normally aspirated displacement of 4.5 liters. Turbocharging also gave the 745i 252 bhp at 5,200 rpm and 280 lbs./ft. at 2,600 rpm.

Outright performance was unaffected by the change from 4.5-liter V-12 to 3.2-liter turbo I6, but there was some irony in the fact that the 745i was starting just as the MB 450SEL 6.9 was finishing. For the '83 MY BMW upped the ante even more by replacing the 745i's 3.2 with the then-current 3.5 liter. The turbo 3.5 made the same power, but max torque now arrived at 2,200 rpm, and even peak power was now produced at an even more accessible 4,900 rpm.

Accessible was the word: large or small, there were sixes for all. Those on a budget could enjoy the greatness of the mini 320i I6, while captains of industry had their chauffeur-driven 745is. Then there was the M635CSi whose 286 bhp 24-valve engine just happened to make the same power as the MB 6.9-liter V-8. The world was content with BMW sixes. Sadly, no truth stands forever, and a new state of play was revealed when *Consumer Reports* assembled 4 luxury players in 1990 in a showcase of the past, present and future.[3]

The past was obviously the Lincoln Continental, with all the soft luxury and silence offered for those who didn't want to know there was a road under them. It was ambling along in an unfussed manner. Present champ had to be the e34 BMW 535i, with revised emissions-friendly 208 bhp I6, but the future came in the form of two V-8 Japanese rivals. The newcomers were fast-rising stars known as the Infiniti Q45 and Lexus LS 400. The closest the Japanese had come to unseating the Germans was the V-6 Honda/Acura Legend, but these competitors from Nissan and Toyota were much more serious.

Nissan and Toyota had beaten BMW at its own game, being a supreme niche market player, if one could call 181,129 cars sold into May 1993 a niche. The Japanese saw a middle ground between the Continental and 535i. They knew 30-to-45-year-old U.S. buyers didn't want to drive the Lincolns and Cadillacs their parents and grandparents had owned, but they also knew that for many the high-sport Autobahn-bred Bimmer and Merc driving performance characteristics held little sway. This was still 55-mph America, and a company that offered a well-built V-8 luxury sedan filled with power assists/trimmings, and a nameplate that rhymed with success, would be suitably rewarded.

While the Infiniti benchmarked itself closer to BMW and Benz standards of driver involvement, Lexus took the comfortable scenic route and enjoyed longer-lasting sales success because of it. The LS 400 was well finished, comfortable and silent; most importantly, it was reliable. That was the clincher. Toyota had reinvented the series 62 Caddy Deville for a new generation. Worryingly for the Germans the LS 400 was like the 1975 Caddy Seville in its ability to appear from nowhere and take conquest sales.

The BMW 535i could still hang with the V-8 newbies. In comparing automatic cars the Bimmer matched the LS 400's 7.9-second 0–60 mph time, and wasn't far behind the Q45's 7.1 seconds.[4] Considering the Lexus and Infiniti had much more powerful and bigger DOHC V-8s, 4 and 4.5 liters respectively, the SOHC I6 BMW hadn't done too badly, but fashion was against it. The 535i was the Hudson Hornet of the early '90s, an I6 car in a market that just wanted to hear V-8s!

Daimler-Benz wasn't doing much better; its I6 300E was looking decidedly meek. The Japanese were happy for the 300E to inherit the Earth, as long as their cars were first to reach the drive-in burger joint. U.S. luxury brands were also caught napping with yesteryear's V-8s. Soon everyone joined the V-8 party, since the days of high gas prices, when everyone thought the V-8 would become extinct, were over. As David Benson of the *Daily Express* wrote in 1987, "Big is Beautiful—again."[5] So the message went out: Send us some decent V-8s. Ford readied its new modular V-8, Cadillac finally gave the Allante an engine to be proud of in the Northstar 4.6 V-8. Daimler-Benz launched a midsize 400E fit for J.R. Ewing and BMW prepared its own V-8.

BMW acceded to demands for larger power plants, but started at the top. In the final hours of the greed-is-good '80s the Bavarians released their V-12 based on joined baby sixes. All hailed the mighty 300 bhp 5 liter V-12 in the 750i/iL and 850i coupe, until the 1990 recession removed the wind from the proverbial sails. Below decks, BMW was working on some sharp V-8s to fill the chasm between the 192 bhp 24-valve 2.5 I6 and the 300 bhp 5.0 V-12. Thus, for the 1993 MY, BMW let the world meet the re-engined e32 730i/740i, powered by 218/286 bhp 3- and 4-liter V-8s respectively.

The new V-8s, designated M60, replaced the M30 3.5 I6. The 2/2.3-liter baby sixes used to be called M60, but by now all past 12-valve baby sixes were simply denoted M20. The V-8s weren't exactly all-new; they were created by joining two M40 I4s at the crankshaft. Audi did much the same when melding two 1.8-liter VW Golf GTi I4 motors to make one 3.6 liter V-8. What made the BMW V-8 special was that it used the DOHC 4-valve-per-cylinder head as seen on 318iS variants, and it was an all-aluminum motor. The construction medium gave a link to the all-alloy V-8 BMW made in the 1950s.

Aluminum was where similarity to the '50s V-8 ended. This Bavarian V-8 was technically equivalent to the modern Infiniti and Lexus V-8s. As with the M50 I6, the M60 V-8s used a plastic intake manifold, plus a noise-absorbent cosmetic engine cover. The early '90s was the start of the period where car makers wanted to make their engines look like neat household appliances. Wires and piping were all tucked away as shrouds descended, lest the poor consumer should accidentally see a mechanical component under the hood.

Bosch HFM Motronic 3.3 with knock sensors was running the V-8 show, permitting the 3-liter to have a 10.5 CR. The 4-liter had 10-to-one CR. Power and torque peaks were produced at 5,800 rpm and 4,500 rpm respectively. Max torque for the 3-liter was 214 lbs./ft., and the 4-liter had 295 lbs./ft. The 4-liter even had an edge on the Infiniti's power and torque, even though it was 500 cc down on displacement. Technical qualities extended to Nikasil bores and sintered connecting rods that weighed 538 grams, a 17 percent weight saving over conventional rods.

The M60 V-8's cams had built-in balancing of masses. During the V-8's development, use of a noncylindrical cam cured a bad sound effect displayed in the 2,500–3,000 rpm range. A chain drive rather than a cambelt was used on both V-8s. R&D boss during the V-8 project was Dr. Wolfgang Reitzle, with engine constructors Adolf Fischer and Reinhard Hoffmann. Differences between the 530i/540i V-8s were minor, badging and displacement aside. The 540i came out in 5-speed auto-only form. The 530i could have either a 5-speed auto or manual gearbox. The latter was a unique combination in this market sector, and BMW North America did offer the stick-shift 530i V-8. That was something the Japanese didn't have.

In the interests of matching horsepower with stoppability, the 540i had a front spoiler with brake cooling ducts. The 540i also had rear-vented disk brakes. For the 1995 MY, BMW made a 6-speed manual available on the 540i; in the U.S. this variant was part of a package that included front bucket seats and sports suspension. This was a worthwhile improvement because the stock 540i setup basically amounted to a 525i with M-Technic suspension. Also for the 1995 MY, BMW created a 540i Touring to complement the existing 530i Touring; the 530i also gained rear-vented brakes that model year.

One thing the V-8s had from the start was a special winged kidney grille. Broader than the regular e34 kidney, it visually distinguished the V-8 on its mid–'93 MY Euro debut. The V-8s also brought better performance stats. With a factory top speed of 146 mph the manual 530i was identical in achievement to the outgoing 535i, and matched the I6 car's 7.7-second 0–62 mph time. The 540i was electronically limited to 149 mph and 0–62 mph was 6.8 seconds as an automatic. When the 540i 6-speed arrived the latter figure dropped to 5.7 seconds.

The 540i with 6-speed incurred a price-raising gas-guzzler tax in the U.S., with an EPA city number of 14 mpg that was fair of the feds. However, BMW had long since stopped worrying about CAFE. The V-8s had breathed new life into the e32 and e34 ranges. V-8 power had returned the marque to the luxo/sport winners circle. The V-8s would also give the German tuners something new to tinker with, and the e34 certainly showed that the tuners liked to tinker. For a number of firms the e34 was the first Five series chassis they formally got involved with.

7

The Flying Bus

The e34 Motorsport and Tuner Variants

Alpina's e34 B10

As Germany's most established Bimmer tuner, Alpina wasn't ready to give up on the old generation just yet. By 1990 the Buchloe boys had decades of experience with the M10 I4s and M30 I6s. It made sense to pool such knowledge to create the ultimate 5 series to that point, the e34 5 series-based Alpina B10 Bi Turbo. Bi signified two, naturally, and Alpina chose two turbos to overcome the dreaded turbo lag. Usually high power conversions use a large turbo to deliver plenty of boost, but such units need extra time to spool up, hence the accentuated lag.

Alpina employed two Garrett T-25 water-cooled turbos in series, with turbo boost in the 6–12 psi range and oil spray for the piston's underside. Matched and balanced by Alpina itself, their role was to make sure at least one turbo was supplying boost to the 7.2 CR 3,430 cc M30 I6 most of the time. At full tilt the 6-cylinder produced 360 bhp at 6,000 rpm, and more crucially 384 lbs./ft. at 4,000 rpm. Peak figures higher than Alpina's turbo e28, but the bare figures didn't indicate the more even power delivery provided by two small turbos.

UK Alpina patrons could take a trip down to Sytner BMW and collect the keys to the RHD normally aspirated 260 bhp Alpina B10, based on the e34 chassis (courtesy Alpina).

Zero to sixty took just 5.2 seconds, with an unlimited top speed of 180 mph and the quarter mile dispensed with in 13.2 seconds. Hot stuff for a large 4-door weighing 3,733 lbs., and with a 2-valve-per-cylinder I6 of under 3.5 liters. The ability of the M30's bottom end to take the boost strain was assured. A rechipped version of the Bosch Motronic M1.2 found on the regular 535i was also up to managing boost enrichment matters, but Alpina made its changes where

A 1993 (May build) Avus Blue metallic Alpina B10 Bi Turbo. This is car number 500 of the Bi Turbos, with the final 50 being special edition models. This car has the V-8-style winged kidney, powered seats made with water buffalo leather and Motorsport side mirrors (courtesy Alexander Wildemann).

necessary. CR was dropped using Mahle pistons, and a 6-branch set of headers made by Boysen let out exhaust gases expeditiously.

An engine bay switch allowed the owner to toggle between regular and premium unleaded operation, all part of Alpina's thorough development. Alpina B10 R&D costs had run to $3.2 million, Alpina's logo was still a crest shield with a twin choke carb and crank, but the firm had progressed greatly from hop-up kits for 1500/1800s. Alpina specially commissioned a super-duty 5-speed manual box for the Bi Turbo from Getrag. There was a stouter propshaft and Alpina's trademark belt-driven rear differential oil cooler, and a 29-gallon gas tank so one didn't get caught short!

Fichtel und Sachs self-leveling rear suspension kept camber change and any threatening oversteer in check. Front disks were upgraded to 13-inch rotors gripped by 4-piston calipers, and 11.8-inch disks with 2-pot calipers were used out back. All 4 disks were ventilated, and braking hardware was by Lucas/Girling. Stock e34 brakes used solid rear rotors and fist calipers all round. The Bi Turbo rode around on 17 × 8.5-inch rims with 235/45 front covers, and 17 × 9.5-inch rear hoops with 265/45 rubber. Michelin MXX tires were supplied.

It was quite a sight to see the Boysen exhaust manifold glowing orange as the engineers put the 3.4 twin turbo through its paces on the test rig, but what was one to do in a right-hand-drive market? As before, the Alpina turbo/mounting would clash with the steering mechanism. A normally aspirated e34 Alpina B10 with 260 bhp would have to suffice. As

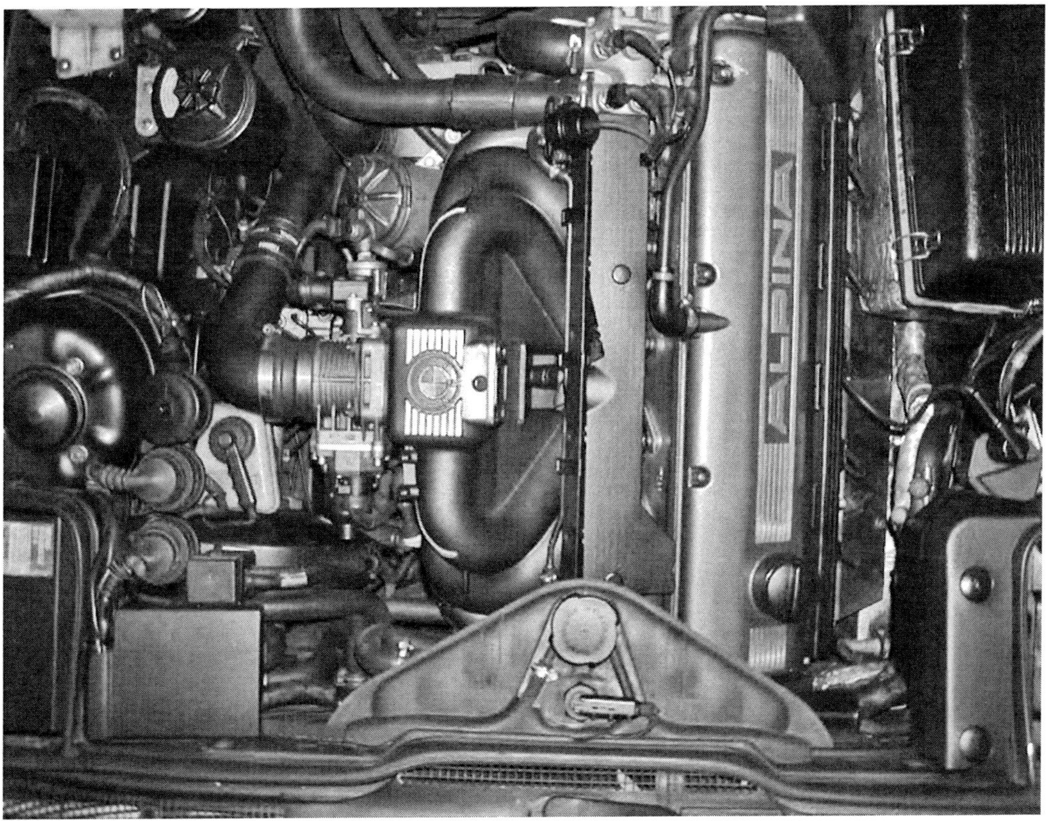

The old BMW 3.5-liter I6 with twin turbos/360 bhp, but flick an engine bay switch and the Bosch Motronic M1.2-managed engine could turn to regular unleaded (courtesy Alexander Wildemann).

familiar as Alpina's turbine spoke rims, the 260 horses were produced by the tried and tested 3,430 cc M30 I6. Top speed was a claimed 155 mph, with 0–60 mph a scant 6.3 seconds.

The 260 bhp B10 might have been an M5 alternative, since it had a similar mission statement. The Bi Turbo was a high-class competitor for the Lotus enhanced Opel/Vauxhall Omega/Carlton. These were stick-shift big sedans with turbo I6s, but at 180 mph it was only natural to trust Alpina more. However, why stop at 6 cylinders? Alpina made available an e34 5 series-based B10 4.0 V-8 using BMW's new all-alloy V-8 that made 315 bhp at 5,800 rpm.

Hartge's e34 H5 Range

Alpina left the baby sixes to its "C" group 3 series-based cars, but other tuners were more enlightened and decided to tune the very popular small block 525i. Hartge offered their 2.7 liter 220 bhp H27sp conversion on the 525i. This motor had been seen previously on the e30 3 series Hartge cars. As part of engine mods, the 2.5-liter's stroke was increased by 6 mm, from 84/75 mm to 84/81 mm dimensions for the 2.7-liter edition, using a new long stroke crankshaft in the process.

It wasn't all about forward thrust. Alpina's craftsmen could create a tailored interior to match the wishes of the Alpina patron (courtesy Alexander Wildemann).

Hartge continued to offer their H5sp M30 I6 (3.4-liter) 5 series upgrade, but also incorporated the new V-8 motors when they became available. The tuner offered larger displacement versions of the 3- and 4-liter V-8s. For those seeking more life from their 530i, there was the Hartge H5–3.6 with 270 bhp from its 3.6-liter V-8. The full powerhouse came in the form of a 340 bhp 4.7-liter Hartge H5-4.7. The latter was a step up for 540i owners, and matched the power output of the revised 3.8-liter e34 M5. As part of the Hartge V-8 package the owner received a newly cast Alusil block V-8.

One would do well to think of BMW Motorsport at this time, because they said no. Special requests were OK, up to a point. BMW Motorsport's chief in the early '90s, Karl-Heinz Kalbfell, said, "We can do anything, but we won't do everything."[1] The idea of a V-12 e34 M5 was ruled out, which was why it was handy to have Hartge. Hartge had no qualms about inserting BMW's V-12 into the e34. Hartge offered a bored and stroked 6-liter version of the V-12 displacing precisely 5,992 cc. Rated at 430 bhp and 450 lbs./ft., the Hartge H5-6.0 was a tire smoker for the record books. Hartge also offered the 6-liter on the e31 850i.

AC Schnitzer's First Five—e34 ACS5

The e34 was the first 5 series Schnitzer tuned as a road car under its new 1987 AC Schnitzer banner. Team Schnitzer did the racing, while AC Schnitzer did the tuning and sale of road cars. The range of performance-enhancing equipment for the e34 was wide, starting with the humble 2-valve M20 powered 525i. For this 170 bhp car AC Schnitzer offered their 200 bhp S5 2.7-liter long stroke pack. As with others, the 2.5's stroke was lengthened by 6 mm, and CR went up from 8.8 to 9.6 to one.

More extreme was the S5 3.0 motor for the M50-powered 525i, taking horsepower from 192 to 240 bhp. The improvement was achieved by boring and stroking the baby six out to 3 liters, turning the 2.5 into a 3.0 with 85.5/86 mm dimensions. There was also a slight CR rise from 10 to 10.5 to one for pre–Vanos M50s. The S5 3.0 package allowed the 525i 24v to achieve a top end of 250 kph, with 0–100 kph in 7.4 seconds. Years of racing experience with BMW's big six meant AC Schnitzer had something for e34 535i owners.

Still on the books was the Schnitzer cylinder head kit for BMW's 12-valve M30 3.5 I6. Targeted at the older Alpina B9, the kit also resulted in 245 bhp, with the stock M30's CR rising from 9 to 9.5 to one. The M30's standard 92/86 mm dimensions were kept. However, there was also the more elaborate 3.7 conversion for the M30 I6. Boring and stroking achieved the 3.7-liter size, with dimensions of 92.5/90 mm and CR raised to 9.8 to one. AC Schnitzer's claimed figures for the S5 3.7 involved a 260 kph terminal velocity, with 0–100 kph dispatched in 6.8 seconds.

The e34 was the third 5 series chassis to be handled by Hartge, and the tuner's fame was spreading beyond the German home market (courtesy Hartge, http://www.hartge.de).

Engine

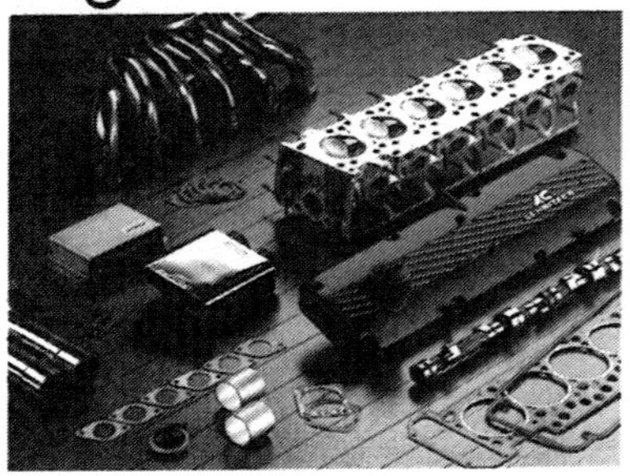

AC Schnitzer S5 cylinder head kit*
for BMW 535i catalyst **1112 34 05**
power increase: 25 kW / 34 hp
for cars with manual transmission
(recommended rear diff. ratio 3.73:1**)

consisting of:

AC Schnitzer cylinder head.	1112 32 02
AC Schnitzer camshaft	1131 32 03
AC Schnitzer gasket set	1112 32 04
AC Schnitzer exhaust manifold in stainless steel incl.	
AC Schnitzer connecting pipes 3 pieces	1811 32 20
AC Schnitzer control unit program	1214 32 06
AC Schnitzer valve cover	1112 32 10
AC Schnitzer exhaust tail pipe	1812 34 03

* in exchange only (max. 30.000 km)
** in exchange only

Optional:

AC Schnitzer sport exhaust **1812 34 52**

consisting of:

AC Schnitzer pre silencer	1812 34 27
AC Schnitzer rear silencer	1812 34 22

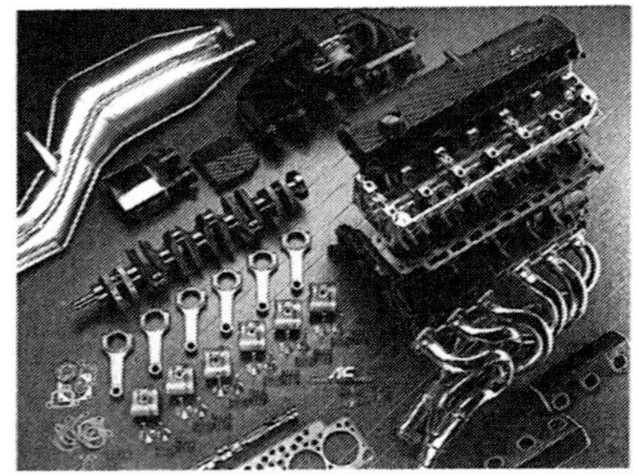

AC Schnitzer S5 3.7 engine kit* **1100 34 00**
for BMW 535i catalyst
power increase 37 kW / 51 hp

consisting of:

AC Schnitzer engine 3.7 ltr. incl. valve cover in AC Schnitzer design	1100 34 01
AC Schnitzer control unit program	1214 32 02
AC Schnitzer exhaust manifold	1811 32 20
AC Schnitzer metal catalyst converter	1812 32 65
AC Schnitzer exhaust tail pipe	1812 34 03
Cover for generator air routing	1362 32 13

* in exchange only (max. 30.000 km)

AC Schnitzer S5 cylinder head kit*
for BMW 540i catalyst **1112 34 01**
power increase 21 kW / 29 hp

consisting of:

AC Schnitzer special-camshafts (2 x inlet)	1131 34 03
AC Schnitzer intake	1371 34 10
AC Schnitzer special-airfilter insert	1372 34 10
AC Schnitzer sport exhaust system	1812 34 60
AC Schnitzer control unit program	1214 34 91
AC Schnitzer valve cover	1161 38 05

The ACS5 3.7 was a good match for Alpina's non-turbo B10. With an unrestricted top end, higher than BMW's limited 250 kph/155 mph, it could also outrun the M5. Thus, in Germany there were M5 alternatives which had the completeness associated with established tuning houses, that were considered fully fledged manufacturers by the German authorities. Engine conversions involved re-chipped ECUs, sports headers/exhaust system, dress-up cam covers with AC Schnitzer name tags, and metric engine size badging.

The ACS5 3.0 and 3.7 came with stylized "3.0" and "3.7" cam cover and airflow meter badges respectively in red. In red perhaps, but these engines were decidedly green. The S5 2.7 and S5 M30 cylinder head kit involved retention of the catalytic converter hardware found on German spec 525i/535i sedans. The S5 3.0 and S5 3.7 even incorporated special AC Schnitzer sports cats, with the 3.7's cat being made of metal rather than ceramic. All engine conversions were done on an exchange basis, which was normal practice with tuners where the donated engine could only have 30,000 kms at most. Such an ordered approach to modification was to be expected in a country with tough annual roadworthiness inspections.

Additions weren't ad hoc; the tuners were concerned with durability and emissions to the same degree as a regular automaker. Thus, it was hard to see where BMW's work stopped and AC Schnitzer's started. These cars were going on the Autobahn, so it had to work first time! AC Schnitzer's package for the e34 540i was similarly subtle. A cylinder head kit was available that took the 4-liter to an Alpina B10 4.0 matching 315 bhp, the same power as an e34 M5 3.6, no less.

The ACS5 540i had two high-lift intake cams, one for each bank of the DOHC V-8, plus a special intake manifold. The ECU was re-mapped and a sports exhaust system was thrown in for good measure. The "AC Schnitzer" badge sat neatly on both sides of the stock BMW V-8 noise-absorbing engine cover. To keep the balanced nature of the e34 intact, AC Schnitzer offered matching chassis alterations. There were no suspension kits for e34s with EDC, but they did have kits for cars with and without self-leveling rear suspension.

There was a 35-mm lowering job available on regular e34s, 20 mm on M5 3.6s. The e34 M5 3.8 was off limits because that car came with EDC standard. Sway bar kit measurements were 26 mm at the front and 19 mm at the rear. The hardware was given the acid test at the old Nürburgring, where development work was carried out in association with Bilstein and Eibach, the big names in the world of shocks and springs respectively. In making contact with the road, custom AC Schnitzer rims in the 15- to 18-inch size range were available.

In the huge range of rims AC Schnitzer made available, one heavy-duty winter 15-inch model existed. This rim design was coated with protective anthracite paint. Out of the range there was just one specially designed set for BMW's 525iX all-wheel drive variants. These rims were denoted "Racing wheels type II" and came in just the 17-inch size. Top rim offered by AC Schnitzer was an 18-inch forged model, 8.5 inches wide for the front and 10 inches wide at the back.

For the full racer-on-the-road experience, AC Schnitzer put together a matched set called S5 silhouette, with the term silhouette coming from the world of racing. In silhouette

***Opposite:* The past and the future met under the hood of an e34 thanks to AC Schnitzer. The tuner continued work with the M30 I6; see the cylinder head kit and 3.7-liter conversion. The new M60 V-8 was also catered to (courtesy AC Schnitzer, http://www.ac-schnitzer.de/en/).**

Top: Hold onto the AC Schnitzer 3-spoke leather sports wheel for dear life, because the 3.7-liter's 262 bhp could still hang the tail out in spite of the silhouette pack. ***Bottom:*** Apart from special 17-inch rims, the silhouette pack involved a 30 mm lowering job and AC Schnitzer's adjustable 26 mm front/19 mm rear sway bars (courtesy AC Schnitzer, http://www.ac-schnitzer.de/en/).

spec the ACS5 looked every inch the fully fledged touring car racer. There was a special body kit with bigger front spoiler, rear wing and those all important "bubble" arches. Those special arches accommodated huge wheels and tires. Three-piece 17-inch rims, 9 inches wide at the front and 11 inches wide at the rear, were wrapped in ZR-rated rubber. As part of the staggered wheel setup, front tires were sized 255/40, with the rears being 275/35.

The ACS5 silhouette package also featured a single-arm windshield wiper system, capable of clearing more of the windshield than a conventional setup; Daimler-Benz was gloating, no doubt. With all this emphasis on sport, AC Schnitzer didn't forget about luxo matters. The catalogue of interior items one could order to personalize the e34 5 series was immense. How about a 12-piece wood kit available in brown or anthracite using walnut root wood? There was additional matching wood trim for the gear shifter surround, and the same color wood for the steering wheel boss, depending upon the steering wheel selected from the catalogue.

The special aluminum shifter knob was also available with wood or leather. Aluminum pedals and a very nice driver's footrest, with AC Schnitzer insignia embossed, were just the thing for those hard-charging moments. Even AC Schnitzer velvet floor mats, with emblem on front mats, were possible underfoot. Exclusivity has always cost a pretty penny. The connoisseur appreciates detail, and even automatic cars weren't forgotten. Replacing the stock T-bar e34 automatic handle was a like-shaped item, complete with detent lever, made in matching walnut root wood in brown or anthracite with a high-gloss lacquer and the AC Schnitzer insignia sitting atop in contrasting white.

Fun with MK-Motorsport

German tuners invariably have a motorsport background, with lessons from the track applied to road cars. It is also true that for many outfits the first Five tackled was the e34. Both qualities applied to MK-Motorsport. The company with the snazzy stylized logo and distinctive block-pattern aluminum rims had a racing background. Specifically it all went back to a wild, wide-fendered 1976 Group 2 sedan racer that MK-Motorsport claims was the most powerful BMW 1602 in Europe!

Formally established in July 1978, MK-Motorsport is headed by company director and racer Michael Krankenberg. The company was even associated with a Group B victory at Le Mans in 1986 using a BMW M1. In the 1980s, body kit, uprated suspension, and wheel/tire packages were available for the e28 5 series, e24 6 series and e23 7 series. However, business was focused on the e30 3 series in terms of suspension, plus hotting up the 323i's baby six with the usual 200 bhp 2.7-liter long-stroke conversion at the top of the tree.

In 1988 MK-Motorsport's operation moved to its current Otigheim location. The e34 was the first opportunity for the company to seriously consider the 5 series. Some tuners cater for old models with spare parts supply, to keep older examples of their work rolling along, and some scale down the tuning options for older platforms. In the case of MK-Motorsport the e34 is still catered for, with some of the later M50-based engine packages retrospectively applied. Simplest on the list is an exhaust upgrade.

Even on the earliest 2-valve 520i/525is, MK-Motorsport offers front and rear mufflers to get extra horses. This even covers the 530i/540i V-8s, and M5 for the rear section muffler.

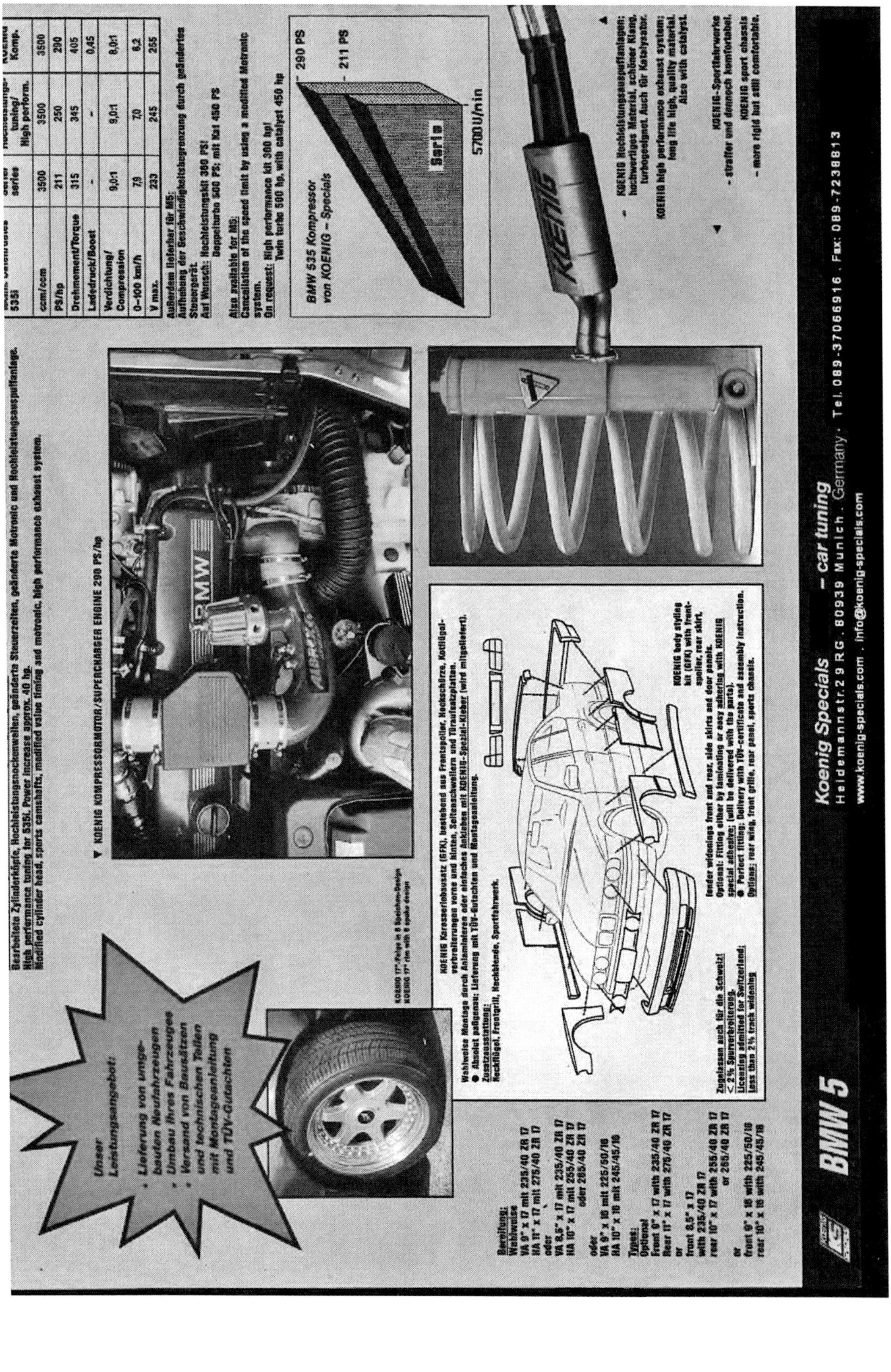
Bearbeitete Zylinderköpfe, Hochleistungsnockenwellen, geänderte Steuerzeiten, geänderte Motronic und Hochleistungsauspuffanlage.
High performance tuning for 535i. Power increase approx. 40 hp.
Modified cylinder head, sports camshafts, modified value timing and motronic, high performance exhaust system.
535i
Serie/series
Hochleistungs-tuning/High perform.
KOENIG Komp.
ccm/ccm 3500 3500 3500
PS/hp 211 250 290
Drehmoment/Torque 315 345 405
Ladedruck/Boost - - 0,45
Verdichtung/Compression 9,0:1 9,0:1 8,0:1
0–100 km/h 7,9 7,0 6,2
V max. 233 245 255
Außerdem lieferbar für M5:
Aufhebung der Geschwindigkeitsbegrenzung durch geändertes Steuergerät.
Auf Wunsch: Hochleistungskit 380 PS! Doppelturbo 500 PS; mit Kat 450 PS
Also available for M5:
Cancellation of the speed limit by using a modified Motronic system.
On request: High performance kit 380 hp! Twin turbo 500 hp, with catalyst 450 hp
Unser Leistungsangebot:
Lieferung von umgebauten Neufahrzeugen
Umbau Ihres Fahrzeuges
Versand von Bausätzen und technischen Teilen mit Montageanleitung und TÜV-Gutachten
KOENIG KOMPRESSORMOTOR/SUPERCHARGER ENGINE 290 PS/hp
BMW 535 Kompressor von KOENIG – Specials
290 PS
211 PS
Serie
5700 U/min
KOENIG Karosseriebausatz (GFK), bestehend aus Frontspoiler, Heckschürze, Kotflügelverbreiterungen vorne und hinten, Seitenschwellern und Türaufsatzplatten.
Wahlweise Montage durch Anlaminieren oder einfaches Ankleben mit KOENIG-Spezial-Kleber (wird mitgeliefert).
Absolut paßgenau; Lieferung mit TÜV-Gutachten und Montageanleitung.
Zusatzausstattung:
Heckflügel, Frontgrill, Heckblende, Sportfahrwerk.
KOENIG body styling kit (GFK) with front-spoiler, rear skirt, fender widenings front and rear, side skirts and door panels.
Optional: Fitting either by laminating or easy adhering with KOENIG special adhesive; (will be delivered with the parts).
Perfect fitting; Delivery with TÜV-certificate and assembly instruction.
Options: rear wing, front grille, rear panel, sports chassis.
Zugelassen auch für die Schweiz! < 2% Spurverbreiterung.
Licensing admitted for Switzerland; less than 2% track widening
Bereifung:
Wahlweise
VA 9" x 17 mit 235/40 ZR 17
HA 11" x 17 mit 275/40 ZR 17
oder
VA 8,5" x 17 mit 235/40 ZR 17
HA 10" x 17 mit 255/40 ZR 17 oder 265/40 ZR 17
oder
VA 9" x 16 mit 225/50/16
HA 10" x 16 mit 245/45/16
Types:
Optional
Front 9" x 17 with 235/40 ZR 17
Rear 11" x 17 with 275/40 ZR 17
or
front 8,5" x 17 with 235/40 ZR 17
rear 10" x 17 with 255/40 ZR 17 or 265/40 ZR 17
or
front 9" x 16 with 225/50/16
rear 10" x 16 with 245/45/16
KOENIG Hochleistungsauspuffanlagen; hochwertiges Material, schöner Klang, turbogeeignet. Auch für Katalysator.
KOENIG high performance exhaust system; long life high, quality material. Also with catalyst.
KOENIG-Sportfahrwerke - straffer und dennoch komfortabel.
KOENIG sport chassis - more rigid but still comfortable.
BMW 5
Koenig Specials – car tuning
Heidemannstr. 29 RG. 80939 Munich. Germany · Tel. 089-37066916. Fax: 089-7238813
www.koenig-specials.com. info@koenig-specials.com

The gain for the 520i-540i is claimed to be in the 3–5 bhp range. MK-Motorsport also offers a steel cat converter conversion for the M5. This upgrade is applicable to the e34 M5 3.6, which came with ceramic cats as standard. Breathing also gets better with a high-flow air filter available for all e34s.

Engine packages focus mainly on the baby six. A 200 bhp 2.7-liter conversion from earlier e30 days is present, but the later 225 bhp 2.8-liter conversion for the M50 2-liter is more desirable. The buyer gets new crank, pistons, connecting rods, and sports cams, larger capacity injectors, plus sports air filter and rear muffler. Similarly, the tuner offers an "engine A" package that converts the 525i to 240 bhp 3-liter I6 power, matching the ACS5 3.0 4v conversion to the letter.

A second retrospectively applied pack is "engine B," taking the 525i to 3.2 liters and 265 bhp via boring and stroking. The 2.8- and 3.2-liter displacements come from the e39 5 series era. All 2.8/3.0/3.2-liter packages MK-Motorsport offers apply to the BMW M50 I6 24-valver. To keep things neat, dress-up valve covers also abound. The two-valve 520i/525i have special cam covers available, as do the 6-cylinder 530i/535i.

MK-Motorsport hasn't overlooked the 535i with M30 I6. Under the engine kit code MK-52K a package of sports camshaft plus MK-Motorsport's replacement front and rear section mufflers boosts output by 37 bhp, with claimed torque of 330 Nm at 4,500 rpm. Compared to the 535i's standard factory figures of 0–62 mph in 7.7 seconds and top speed of 235 kph, MK-Motorsport's mods improve those readings to 7.1 seconds and 250 kph.

The German tuner also has an engine kit for the e34 M5 3.6. This involves re-chipping the ECU, a steel cat conversion and removal of the standard M5 speed limiter. Credit the megachip for an extra 27 bhp, produced at 400 rpm higher than normal, raising the M5's top speed by 20 kph. Combined with the steel cat, the total power hike is 45 bhp. MK-Motorsport also offers to chip the M5 3.8's ECU and jettison the speed limiter from that car. However, the tuner leaves the M5 3.8's suspension alone due to the car's EDC.

MK-Motorsport has suspension kits for all other e34 variants, from the six-pot 520i to the 540i V-8 and M5 3.6. Sedans and Tourings are catered for, as are cars with and without self-leveling rear suspension. With MK-Motorsport's lowering springs, the front is dropped 40 mm, and rear ride height by 15 mm. To improve the e34's torsional rigidity the company has one strut tower brace for 6-cylinder cars, and one for V-8 e34s.

After making special metric rims for Michelin TRX tires in the '80s, MK-Motorsport moved to a distinctive block spoke conventional rim. These are available in one- or two-piece design, with a choice of normal or staggered setup. In the MK-1 style one can have 17 × 8.5-inch rims with 235/45 ZR tires, or 17 × 10-inch rims at the rear with 255/40 or 265/40 ZR tires. Similarly the buyer can choose 18 × 8.5-inch rims with 235/40 ZR tires front and rear, or 18 × 10-inch rear rims with 265/35 ZR tires. The MK-2 two-piece design can be had with 18 × 8.5-inch rims and 235/40 ZR tires at all four corners, or with 18 × 10-inch rims and 265/35 ZR rubber at the rear.

MK-Motorsport also offers the obligatory tuner body kit. This is a four-piece affair of discreet nature consisting of front spoiler, side skirts and rear apron. This package isn't

Opposite: **Koenig offered patrons a choice of tuned M30 I6, blown specimen with 290 horses or the mega 500 bhp twin turbo M5 3.6 bolide. Founder Willy Koenig was a racer after all (courtesy Koenig-Specials, http://www.koenig-specials.com/).**

U.S. tuner Dinan initially achieved fame for its turbo conversions, but transitioned to supercharger kits as the '90s progressed (courtesy Dinan, http://www.dinancars.com/bmw/).

available on the e34 M5. The company also adds subtle "MK" grille badgework and decal insignia for visual effect. MK-Motorsport also has "MK-color-line," which is optional Shadowline treatment in chrome or black. Compared to Germany's other tuners the overall look of an MK-Motorsport car is low-key. The loudest statement is declared by the wheels, with care that other visual treats don't take attention away from the rims.

MK-Motorsport's products from 1994 were fitted to the e34 5 series, as well as the e36 3 series and e31 8 series. Note the distinctive block pattern alloys (courtesy MK-Motorsport, http://www.mk-motorsport.de).

Where can MK-Motorsport's wares be purchased? As with other tuners, their work is available through selected BMW dealerships in Germany. The company will sell to individuals in Germany, as well as on an international basis. Marking the modern state of German tuners, MK-Motorsport sells individual accessories, kit sets and complete cars. The last item should always be of interest to BMW, since they have their own special 5 series, the M5! BMW gets on well with the tuners, even though their work is a natural rival for the M5.

E34, as Dialed in by Dinan

Dinan was started by Steve Dinan, and it can trace its history back to 1979, but rose to prominence in the eighties as a purveyor of turbo conversions and other go-faster goodies. After turbo e28 M30 cars, Dinan moved on to the e34 535i, adding a Garrett TB04 with 10 psi of boost onto a stock CR 3,430 cc I6. The engine's Bosch Motronic ECU was modified to work with an added knock sensor and intake manifold pressure sensor, to calculate boost enrichment supplied by oversize injectors.

For chassis chores Dinan relied on Bilstein shocks and its own design springs and sway bars, and larger disk brakes with carbon fiber metallic pads that gripped and arrested forward

BMW's e34 M5 brought major refinements over the e28 M5, when it made its 1989 European market debut. A Canadian spec M5 3.6 is shown (courtesy Dean Novak, http://www.m5board.com).

momentum. The e34 turbo rolled on Dinan's 16 × 9-inch rims with 245/45 tires. The driver was informed of urgent developments thanks to console shifter surround-mounted oil temp/voltmeter/turbo boost ancillary gauges. The cost was $65,775 in 1991 money, and that purchased 330 bhp at 5,700 rpm and 340 lbs./ft. at 4,000 rpm, producing 0–60 mph times in the low 5-second bracket with a 165 mph top speed for a 5-speed base car.

To keep costs down Dinan switched from turbo to supercharger as the decade wore on. That spelled an e34 540i 6-speed with Powerdyne ceramic bearing puffer with bypass assembly, ECU rechip and Turbotronics-10 piggyback module which was fitted to the stock AFM to handle boost enrichment. A dual fuel pump and free-flow exhaust upped the ante to $7,995 at mid-nineties prices. Dinan's auxiliary gauge pack saw the voltmeter replaced by a rear differential oil temperature sender.

A semblance of balance was introduced by Dinan's full house "Stage IV" suspension kit, comprising Koni adjustable shocks, sports springs and camber adjustable hardware for the front and rear suspension. The 17 × 9-inch Dinan rims and BMW 850CSi-sourced 13.6-inch disks with 4-piston calipers kept it all safe, and with 402 bhp at 6,000 rpm and 363 lbs./ft. at 5,000 rpm it had to be safe. The supercharged 540i's 0–60 mph time of low 5 seconds and 180 mph top speed could be considered merely brisk next to Dinan's custom e34 540i turbo SCCA World Challenge racer. Dinan continued its racing connection as an engine builder for the Grand Am Cup racing series. As a U.S. tuner in the modern idiom, Dinan sells its products through selected BMW dealerships.

Koenig Gives the e34 a Kick!

Racer Willy Koenig founded the German tuner Koenig-Specials, a tuner associated with the creation of wild modified Ferraris. It all started with the first Ferrari 365 BB to land in West Germany. That was back in 1974 and bigger things lay in store, like the 1,000 bhp twin turbo Testarossa called "Koenig Competition." However, Koenig has tuned other great marques, including BMW; especially well known is the work they have done with the e31 8 series. Less well known is their e34 5 series related hardware.

Koenig-Specials' tuning kit for the 211 bhp 3,430 cc I6 involved a modified cylinder head, sports camshaft, altered valve timing, rechip and a sports exhaust system with "KOENIG" writ large on the rear muffler. This took the old 3.5's power to 250 bhp and 255 lbs./ft., cutting 0–100 kph to 7 seconds and increasing top speed to 245 kph. A supercharger kit improved power and torque to 290 bhp and 300 lbs./ft. respectively. The supercharger kit necessitated lowering the stock 9-to-one CR to 8:1 to avoid detonation. Performance was improved with 0–100 kph now dispatched in 6.2 seconds, accompanied by a top speed of 255 kph.

Koenig-Specials also looked after the e34 M5 3.6, their modified Motronic system removing the spoilsport 155 mph speed limiter. A hop-up kit took horsepower to a dizzying 380 bhp, while their twin turbo conversion made a stratospheric 500 bhp, 450 horses with catalytic converter! Koenig has a puffer for your Bimmer, especially if it's a 1990s era 540i/740i/840Ci. Koenig-Specials still offers the supercharger kit for the BMW V-8 which includes the supercharger, CR lowering pistons, ECU remap, intercooler, installation and test to the tune of a 2007 stated price of 25,000 euros! Quality doesn't come cheap; neither

BMW M Power
motorworks
YOKOHAMA

do 440 bhp and 600 Nm of torque, which is what the loot buys. Koenig also offers its firm, but comfy, sports suspension that comes with specially valved Koni shocks.

Having spent all those euros on hot hardware, one would also wish to look hot. No problem: Koenig-Specials made a multi-piece West German TÜV-approved e34 5 series GFK body kit. The marvelous makeover included a front spoiler, rear apron, wide fender extenders, side skirts and rear door cladding to smooth things out. Optional were front grille and rear lighting area decorative trim panels, plus a rear trunk wing. Koenig threw in its special adhesive to make sure boy racer didn't come unstuck. Quality of fit was guaranteed and with less than 2 percent track widening, it was all Swiss legal. Sixteen-inchers were available, but the icing on the cake tasted sweeter if one specified Koenig's 6-spoke 17s, 17 × 9 inches with 235/40 ZR tires front and 17 × 11 inches wearing 275/40 ZR rubber rearwards. Back in the early 1990s Koenig-Specials took no half measures with the e34.

E34 with Motorsport Flavor

It's hard to separate the finest tuner speedmobiles from the M5 in Germany, but the M5 has the advantage of a global dealer distribution sales and service network. Find a BMW dealer and they can look after your M5. With the e34, BMW designed an M5 for sale all over the world, not just Europe. The 1989 MY e34 M5 3.6 was a car that could match or better the outright performance figures of the Euro spec e28 M5, while adhering to the strictest pollution laws that might be out there. This point was lost on some reviewers who put the e34 M5 3.6 up against various exotic machinery that wasn't available worldwide.

BMW Motorsport had become a victim of its own success: make it look easy and soon people will believe that it is easy. Thus, though the Motorsport technicians went painstakingly through the M5 plan, filtering out areas of weakness and introducing refinements, critics were mostly underwhelmed. It was obviously competent, but was it exciting and likeable? Could a car that delivered all this performance, provided room for five, and was as readily available as a Big Mac be as good as an Aston Martin?

Finding opposition for the M5 was hard. The closest car was the special Vauxhall Carlton modified by Lotus, which was turbocharged and faster than the M5 3.6, but was available in fewer places and was more of a rough draft in comparison. BMW was on its own with the M5 concept, and had one ready for the e34 range almost from the start. The e34 M5 3.6 made a 1989 European model debut with a 315 bhp long-stroke version of Motorsport's 24-valve DOHC I6.

The motor in the new M5 was called S38B36, and would be the only e34 M5 power plant for all world markets. Dimensions of the 3.6-liter I6, actually 3,535 cc, were 93.5/86 mm, showing that the bore was almost the same as in the M1/M6, but that the stroke had been lengthened by 2 mm. The engine had a 10-to-one CR and high-lift 264-degree cams. Inlet valves were 37 mm, exhaust valves 32 mm, and stiffer valve springs were used to help

***Opposite, top:* Coded S38B36, the e34 M5's 3.6-liter I6 was the first Motorsport power plant specifically engineered for unleaded gas/catalytic converter operation. The DOHC 24-valver made 315 bhp (DIN) for all markets (courtesy Mel Abrahams). *Opposite, bottom:* Pre-1991 MY M5s had a standard rear bench seat console locker that turned the sedan into a 4-seater (courtesy Dean Novak).**

The e34 was the first Five to offer an air bag. A driver's side air bag was standard M5 3.6 equipment for cars exported to North America (courtesy Dean Novak).

achieve a new higher redline of 7,250 rpm. Some of these figures might not seem that spectacular, but comparisons should be made to the previous U.S. spec M5.

The clue was in the S38 engine designation, something used for the U.S. spec e28 M5s. So the Motorsport engineers were rising from a 256 bhp (SAE) base to the latest model's truly impressive 310 bhp (SAE) at 6,900 rpm. The racing six was spinning faster with a new lighter but stronger crankshaft. The greater weight of the e34 body combined with the marginal displacement rise made torque delivery a key issue with the latest M5. To help, an electronically controlled flapper valve varied intake manifold tract length. Torque for the 3.6-liter I6 was written down as 265 lbs./ft. at a mountain-high 4,750 rpm.

While the labcoats could say the engine could switch from short to long intake runners or vice versa, and make 75 percent of its torque across most of its rev range, 265 lbs./ft. wasn't an immense figure when one had 3,846 lbs. to haul around town. However, it was a clean engine, so the owner's conscience was clear and he could sleep at night. The M5 3.6 exhaled through two ceramic catalytic converters and mufflers sourced from the e32 750i/iL cars. Monitoring the motor was a Bosch Motronic M1.2 engine management system.

A black box to govern actions, and a black cam cover with the words "BMW M Power," alerted the curious that this was no normal e34 5 series. Onlookers might have noticed that

Zero to sixty in the low sixes and a derestricted top speed of 160+ mph made the M5 3.6 a unique entry among early '90s sports sedans (courtesy Dean Novak).

the M5 3.6 sat a little lower than a stock 535i, by 0.8 inch, to be precise. Firmer shock absorbers were used, sway bar diameter went up from 23 to 25 mm at the front and 15 to 18 mm at the rear compared to an e34 535i.

Making a distinctive statement were the M5 3.6's two-piece cast magnesium 17-inchers, the famous Turbine rims. The notable feature of this rim design was its inner turbine blade, possessing vent cooler centers. As the rim rotated, the vent coolers would blow air on the M5 3.6's brake rotors, fending off fade. It wasn't a gimmick: several owners who have swapped to the later Throwing Star design have noticed that their M5 3.6 brakes fade quicker when the car is tracked hard. The funny thing about the vent cooler centers is that they made the M5 look like it had whitewall tires. This must have been a first for BMW, because they don't usually give optional equipment without charging extra!

The M5 3.6's Turbines were 8 inches wide, with the front brakes upgraded to 12.4 inches, 0.2 inch thicker than stock e34 disks. Rear rotors were initially the same 11.8-inch type found on a 535i, but for the 1990 MY they became vented. Nivomat self-leveling rear suspension was standard equipment on the M5 3.6, as was a LSD with 25 percent locking action. Although BMW was still offering metric rims on its best Euro e34s, the M5 3.6 used normal Michelin 17-inch ZR rated 235/45 MXX2 tires.

Stirring the M5 3.6 into action was the familiar Getrag 280/5 overdrive 5-speed manual. Working with a shorty 3.91 final drive, the power team was in harmony, with even steps

For the '95 MY BMW Motorsport replaced the M5's Getrag 280/5 with a new 6-speed Type D box, a very '90s thing to do (courtesy Jonathan Baker).

being taken on the way to a speed-limited 155 mph. What if the limiter was removed? The 0.32 Cd M5 3.6 cleaved through the air more easily than the boxy e28 M5, but the e34's weight would have made 162/163 mph the brick wall. Comparing Euro to Euro, the M5 3.6's 6.3 second 0–60 mph dash was equal to that of the old e28 M5.

Do bear in mind the extra comfort and safety brought by those extra kilos, plus in most cases the M5 3.6 was optioned in one form: loaded! The fractional gains over the e28 would seem like small beer as one dialed up an amigo on the car phone, enjoyed the comfort of climate-controlled a/c, as well as the safety of a full-size driver's side air bag. The last item was standard equipment on the U.S. M5 3.6 when it was introduced as a 1991 MY entrant. The M5 was where Cadillac met Corvette. There were three ways to have leather in an M5: Standard, Extended and Complete Leather. Standard Leather covered just the seating. Extended Leather added cowhide to the center console, door pulls and glovebox door. Complete Leather went mad, adding the natural stuff to all previously mentioned locations, plus the upper dashboard surface, A pillars, upper door panels, sun visors and rear parcel shelf!

The M5 was about having something extra, like the standard illuminated gearshift pattern which used fiber optics, or the "Four Seasons" glass moonroof optional on pre–1991 MY M5s. There was also the rear bench console locker, standard equipment on pre–1991 MY M5s. This locker turned the M5 into a four-seater, which made sense, because who actually enjoys being stuck in the middle with the intrusive driveshaft tunnel of a rear-drive car?

Too little luxury, or too much padding? BMW Motorsport made the choice easy with two special edition M5 3.6-based cars. These 1991 MY models were known as the M5 Cecotto and the M5 Winkelhock. BMW got in two touring car stars associated with the BMW marque to specify the e34 M5 3.6 according to their respective tastes. Johnny Cecotto went for full luxury, and 22 examples of his loaded M5 were built. The Joachim Winkelhock version was a stripped-out racer in the mold of Porsche's Club Sport cars. The M5 Winkelhock had no power rear windows, no a/c and a 66-amp battery commensurate with the reduced number of gadgets.

The M5 Winkelhock had a smaller 80-liter gas tank and less sound-deadening material. However, it came with 17 × 9-inch rear Turbine rims wrapped up in 255/40 ZR tires. Overall the asset stripping resulted in an 88-lb. weight saving. One could select a/c, but that involved going back to a normal 85-amp battery, negating some of the savings. In total, 51 M5 Winkelhocks were constructed and all were Jet Black/Sterling Silver in color. The M5 3.6 was a car suited to a racer, and one was indeed featured in the high-speed chase in the movie *Ronin.*

To fix the M5 3.6's few flaws, BMW Motorsport came up with a 3.8-liter edition, first

Big torque was the S38B38's mission statement. It produced at least 300 Nm and as much as 400 Nm between 1,800 and 4,750 rpm (courtesy Jonathan Baker).

revealed at the 1991 Frankfurt show. The three-point-eight hit the market in the 1993 MY. The critics wanted the e34 M5 to pack more punch, and the three-point-eight delivered. BMW resisted hotting up their new V-8 and stayed faithful to the big six. The most powerful Five still carried an I6.

The size rise from 3.6 to 3.8 liters may have seemed a trivial adjustment, but there were many more changes to make this the ultimate example of the M30 family. To be exact, the new 3.8 liter was called S38B38, with new dimensions of 94.6/90 mm. Thus, the 3.6 I6 had been bored and stroked into a new, higher 10.5-to-one CR form, with a natty gray cam cover to top things off! A casual under-hood glance wouldn't reveal the hardware changes that the "M" men had worked into the sizzling six.

The 3.6's intake manifold tract-length-changing flapper valve now had its operation fully integrated with the motor's ECU. The ECU was itself upgraded to Bosch M3.3 with a hotwire air mass meter used as part of the fuel injection system. A hotwire produced very little breathing restriction for the motor. The 3.8 racing six had 6 throttle butterflies and, like the M50 baby sixes, 6 ignition coils. Taking efficiency and durability to the max, exhaust manifold diameter was up from 40 to 42 mm, with the latest M5 making the change to metal cats.

The important numbers were 347 bhp (DIN) at 6,900 rpm and 295 lbs./ft. at 4,750 rpm, or more of the good stuff at the same 3.6 engine speeds ... but there was more. Anxious to highlight improved torque delivery, the engineers had some impressive stats for the 3.8-liter. The 3.8 made 400 Nm at 4,750 rpm, but 300 Nm was produced at just 1,800 rpm. Even and seamless power delivery was the goal, and *CAR* magazine confirmed this when pitting the M5 3.8 against the Jag XJR and Audi A8 4.2 Quattro in January 1995: "There's no sudden kick, no point in the rev range when your head is dumped against the rest. Power simply wells like a tidal wave as the revs soar. What feels brisk and sonorous at 4,000 rpm borders on the violent at a yowling 7,000."[2]

It was claimed the M5 3.6 could touch 170 mph *sans* limiter, but this time there was no doubt that without the 155 mph governor the M5 3.8 could reach 170 mph. This Munich mile-muncher wasn't just quick, it was a Ferrari Testarossa's worst nightmare! As we have seen, German tuners were all too eager to lose the limiter for a few dollars more, creating the ultimate Maranello vs. Munich shoot-out.

The M5 3.8's extra verve was enough to drop the M5's factory 0–62 mph time from 6.4 to 5.9 seconds, and with the absence of the Lotus Carlton/Omega the M5 had the most horsepower in its class. Even a decade after the first M5, BMW was still having a hard time finding rivals to duke it out with. Audi didn't make one at all, Jaguar's supercharged XJ sedan came closest, and the Daimler-Benz E500 showed the differences that characterized BMWs and MBs for decades. The E500 was auto-only and it had a traction control device the driver couldn't turn off. The M5 was manual only and the traction control was the driver's right foot!

That's right, BMW offered ASC+T traction control on e34 525is and V-8s, but not on the M5. Smoke all the tread off the tires if that's your wish; Motorsport left the driving to the driver. To show its wide appeal, the M5 had always been available in LHD and RHD forms. The M5 3.6 had even been assembled in RHD form at BMW South Africa's Rosslyn plant between September 1990 and March 1993. The MB E500, on the other hand, was only available in LHD form. Daimler-Benz was still mainly building limos for third-world dictators, and automatic convertibles for society ladies to go shopping in.

The availability of a 6-speed on the 540i opened the door to the U.S. 540i M-Sport, an eventual replacement for this market's old M5 3.6 (courtesy Kevin To).

Chancellor Helmut Kohl wouldn't have liked the e34 M5: not enough room in the back seat. It had more appeal to tennis ace Boris Becker, who owned an M5 3.6 for a spell. However, Motorsport was more concerned with the state of the M5's chassis than its list of celebrity clients. Thus, they sent the M5 to the "Ring" for some fine tuning. The M5 3.8 used a special fully-automatic version of the e34's EDC called EDC III. This adaptive suspension used custom Boge shocks and there was a dash button that allowed the driver to stay in "full firm" mode.

EDC III had 5 electronic sensors that monitored road speed, body acceleration vertically for the front and rear axles, as well as longitudinal acceleration and braking, plus steering angle. In an emergency the system defaulted to full firm mode. The system's factory settings were learned during 6,000 test miles on the old Nürburgring. This impossibly long track taught a chassis all the slings and arrows that might be hurled at it by outrageous conditions! The whole exercise even resulted in an optional handling pack called, predictably, "Nürburgring."

Standard on the new M5 3.8 was the usual 17 × 8-inch rim with 235/45 ZR rubber, but the rim style had changed. In came a new 5-spoke "Throwing Star" design. On top of this the Nürburgring pack replaced the rear wheels with 17 × 9-inch rims with 255/40 tires, and a 19 mm rear sway bar was substituted for the regular 18 mm item. Servotronic steering was also part of the Nürburgring pack, and Motorsport retuned said steering so that it had more feel/heft than when specified in other e34s.

The more serious Canadian M540i matched the 4-liter V-8/6-speed power team to the '95 M5 3.8 chassis. Just 32 cars were built by BMW Motorsport (courtesy Rich Wedenig).

The e34 M5 had stayed true to the sleeper look, sporting a restrained body kit. The addendum consisted of a front spoiler, side skirts and rear apron; there was also an optional rear spoiler painted in matching body color. This last item was seldom seen, M5 owners being a breed that like to travel under the radar. Sometimes those pointing the radar gun were driving an M5. South Carolina police got the M5 3.6 for state trooper patrol with a special ECU chip, a goodwill gesture related to BMW's subsequent building of an assembly plant in Spartanburg in that state. The days of youngsters in stolen Mustang 5.0s were well and truly numbered. Wearing a baseball cap backwards was no defense against a power-chipped M5!

Apart from the Throwing Stars, visual differences between the M5 3.6 and 3.8 were few. The contrasting color of the lower aero body panels were changed from the 3.6's Diamond Black or Sebring Gray, to the 3.8's Diamond Black or Granite Silver. For the '94 MY a smaller Euro-sized air bag was available. With a less bulky boss, this was designed for use with a seat belt. Practicality as well as safety were on the M5 3.8's "to do" list, because for the '93 MY an M5 3.8 Touring was introduced. This variant was first displayed at the 1991 Frankfurt auto show, and was only ever available in LHD form.

For 1995 BMW Motorsport introduced a final set of e34 M5 improvements. These involved adopting the V-8-style winged kidney grille, standard 9-inch-wide rear rims and replacement of the Getrag 280/5 5-speeder with a 6-speed Type D manual box. Brakes were upgraded to floating alloy rotors, 13.6 inches front and 12.8 inches rear. The Nürburgring pack was now standard equipment, but no longer included Servotronic, which was now an option. With the alterations the M5 now rode on new-style 5-spoke "Parallel" rims. Wheels were now 18 × 8 inches front and 18 × 9 inches rear with 245/40 ZR Michelin MXX3 times four.

There were a number of special edition M5 3.8s. First off was the "20 Jahre Motorsport edn," built for the 20th anniversary of BMW Motorsport GmbH. All 20 were Mugello Red and had the Nürburgring pack plus black Throwing Stars. The cars also had a center console dash plaque stating the car's 1–20 number. To commemorate the cessation of RHD M5 3.8 production, 50 special UK M5s were offered.

The M5 "Limited Edition" cars were built from March to June in 1995. Fifteen had Rosso Red metallic with Champagne Extended Leather interior and poplar wood trim. The other 35 were Orinoco Green metallic, with duo Petrol and Mint Extended Leather interior and graphite bird's eye maple wood trim. Once more a center console plaque stated the car's 1–50 sequence number.

Rarer still was the M5 Touring "Elekta," a series of 20 special Tourings for the Italian market, unofficially organized in association with "BMW Individual" in June and July of 1995. The Elektas came in Sterling Silver metallic with Marine Blue Nappa Extended Leather, or in British Racing Green with Hazelnut Nappa Extended Leather. All cars had black leather-covered dash and door tops. Some had a decorative metal shifter insert with the "Elekta" name tag. Right from the start of 3.8 Touring production all M5 wagons had the 9-inch-wide rear rims with optional 255/40 tires. This predated the standardization of the Nürburgring pack and change to 18-inchers for the '95 MY.

Apart from the obvious load-lugger greenhouse, M5 sedans and Tourings differed around the license plate area. Sedans had black plastic inserts between taillights and license plate; the Tourings had textured black paint instead. The special touches that distinguished the M5 were legion, and the care taken to build one was tremendous. Skilled artisans were dedicated to making something as close to perfect as humanly possible. The emphasis is on the word human rather than robot, since the M5s had a large labor input in their construction. This was reflected in the kind of build quality flaws one finds at Rolls Royce, Aston Martin or any place where they still try to involve people in the production process. However, the sight of body-shop guru Leonhard Fuchs smoothing out imperceptible body flaws on an M5 3.8 sedan could only bring a smile to the face. The tiny hammer he was using was painted in Motorsport tri-color livery! Magic took place at Garching.[3]

Due to emissions laws or tiny market demand, some regions received special 4-liter V-8 e34s instead of the M5 3.8. The 1993 MY was the end for the M5 in the U.S., and that '93 U.S. M5 used Throwing Stars even though it was still a 3.6-liter car. For the 1996 MY, 200 540i M-Sports were earmarked for America. Each was a curious blend of Getrag Type D 6-speed, EDC III, and 17 × 8-inch Throwing Stars with 235/45 ZR tires. LSD was optional, as was ASC+T, something the M5 never had, and even a 5-speed auto was possible!

North of the border, Canada received a less cuddly vehicle. The 1995 Canadian M540i was a run of 32 4-liter V-8-powered Garching-built e34s arranged in association with BMW Individual. Although Motorsport built, this model used the U.S. 540i 6-speed as a base, so there was no special chassis number series. However, the cars did get a dash plaque with the 1–32 build sequence number. These cars were up to '95 M5 3.8 standards in almost every respect. They came with the latest Nürburgring pack, implying staggered Parallel spoke 18-inchers, as well as the '95 M5 floating alloy disk brakes. Unlike the '95 M5 3.8, Servotronic was standard, plus ASC+T was actually available.

A final special 540i, again using the 286 bhp 4-liter V-8 untouched, was the '95 RHD "Manual Limited Edition" created just for Australia. Australia and New Zealand did get the M5 3.8 when it first came out, but by this stage it made sense to default to a set of 70 6-speed 540is. Indeed, it was the only e34 540i variant sold down under with a manual gearbox. This sport configuration put it up against the hot HSVs (Holden Special Vehicles), sedans with tuned 5-liter V-8s that made more power and cost half the price, but lacked the BMW's refinement and handling polish. Like the U.S. 540i M-Sport, it had the Nürburgring pack with EDC III, but with 17 × 8 Throwing Stars. The Australian car came with ASC+T as standard equipment, and a silver plaque under the handbrake handle with the 1–70 sequence number.

All in all a total of 12,254 M5s were produced. That figure includes 891 Tourings and 265 produced in South Africa from CKD form.

Years before the Hydrogen 7, BMW created this experimental Wasserstoff LH2 car (courtesy Ulrich Thieme, http://www.e12.de).

Left: The specs of this 700 bhp turbo M30 I6 include Crower H-Beam billet rods, plus a dual 3-inch stainless steel Mandrel bend side exhaust system (courtesy Zane Coker and Performance BMW http://www.performancebmwmag.com/). ***Right:*** Hardy & Beck had a formal name change to H&B at the start of 1982. This made it easier to refer to the company, and place the tuner's logo on rim center caps, spoilers, etc. (courtesy H&B, http://www.hbspecialists.com/).

The South African e28 M535i wasn't sold with such add-ons as the M-Technic body kit. Some quarters considered the M-Technic body kit garish and "boy racer" orientated. On this car non-stock ROH "Milano" 3-piece 16 × 7.5-inch alloys are present (courtesy Peter Crow).

A 1988 UK RHD e28 M5 with M-Technic body kit and 16-inch rims. This car has had its engine retuned to 320 bhp and is fitted with racing harness/bucket seats. The original black leather interior is in storage (courtesy Jamie Myles).

Built in the U.S., for the U.S., the e53 X5 SAV called South Carolina home, but was exported worldwide (courtesy Al Burdulis).

Left: A 4-liter version of the S38 motor, specially created by Paul Burke Imagineering to produce over 700 horsepower (courtesy Ken Hawkins). ***Right:*** Utilize iDrive to change the race-inspired S85 V-10 from 400 to 500 horse mode, but go to Hamann to add a further 60 ponies thanks to their "HM/M+60 sport-kit." Note that to switch to 500 bhp mode one needed to visit the M Drive menu, accessed using the "M" button (courtesy Hamann, http://www.hamann-motorsport.de).

Present is a '97 540i Touring. The color is Biarritz Blue, with alloys denoted "style 32." '97 was the first MY for the e39 Touring in Europe, this car has been updated with clear turn signal lenses (courtesy Jonathan Beard).

Baby six, big six, Alusil V-8s and even a V-12, modified versions of BMW's full engine range were available in the Hartge H5 program (courtesy Hartge, http://www.hartge.de).

The e60 M5 made a 2005 MY European debut as a high-output, low-displacement counterpoint to AMG's sluggers. A 2005 M5 in Sweden is featured (courtesy Daniel Aslund).

Left: A UK spec RHD Daytona Violet metallic M5 3.8. The 3.8-liter M5 was available in fewer markets since BMW didn't wish to compromise the S38B38 power plant with emission regs (courtesy Jonathan Baker and http://www.m5board.com). ***Right: Autocar*** magazine refers to the e39 528i as probably the best midsize executive sedan ever made, and close to perfection (courtesy Adam Tier).

A tuner's work is never done. The e70 required attention and Hamann obliged with the e70-based "Flash," which has a wide-body aero kit among other fine touches (courtesy Hamann, http://www.hamann-motorsport.de).

The Alpina B5 was largely BMW-built. Alpina parts were brought to BMW's Dingolfing factory and added to e60/e61s, with the cars being finished off at Alpina's Buchloe facility (courtesy Alpina, http://www.alpina-automobiles.com/).

Two slight problems with the e39 diesels were their cast-iron blocks and recirculating ball steering. This made them less pleasant to punt around than their I6 gasoline counterparts (courtesy Paul Baylis).

For 2006 BMW replaced the 545i with the 540i and 550i. The latter is present here, resplendent in '08 spec with Space Gray exterior (courtesy Louis Laderman).

For regular Euro e12s, the 528i was the flagship model. By the time this 1979 car arrived the 528i had already been upgraded from 177 bhp to 184 horses (courtesy Ulrich Thieme, http://www.e12.de).

Left: In view of the 535d's greater firepower, BMW kept things in balance with larger brakes than possessed by the 530d. Front and rear disks now measured 13.7 inches and 13.6 inches respectively (courtesy Andre Mauvis). *Right:* BMW's 21st century 6 series has been well received. As in olden days it's technically related to the 5 series. A 2007 U.S. spec 650i convertible is displayed (courtesy Aaron Carter).

The BMW South Africa M530 racing/road car program was under the technical direction of Peter Stark. The M530 was like a 4-door e9 CSL Batmobile (courtesy Ulrich Thieme, http://www.e12.de).

One of the 64 RHD B9s Sytner BMW constructed in the '80s. The sole UK Alpina agent added imported Alpina hardware to new e28 528is. However, the very last 260 bhp Alpina B10 3.5-liter e28 (car #77) was a RHD car made by Alpina (courtesy Peter Thorpe).

Aus Freude am Fahren kamen wir zum Motorsport. Was lag näher, als die dabei gemachten Erfahrungen mit unseren Kundenwünschen zu kombinieren?
So haben wir in den letzten 10 Jahren einiges beobachtet, registriert, analysiert und aktiviert. Unser Betrieb im saarländischen Beckingen – im Schatten großer Stahlwerke – ist eine Edelschmiede für rollende Kraftwerke geworden.
Das Hartge BMW-Programm
323 i RS
Wir haben für Ihren 323i die richtige Potenz: 180 PS
Ein kleines bißchen mehr – das wollten die meisten unserer 323i-Kunden – das Gefühl von Überlegenheit, der Sicherheit beim Überholen, den Fahrspaß der dazugehört und die gewisse Exclusivität.
Wir fanden das realisierbar und haben deshalb einiges entwickelt und verbessert:
335 i
Wenn schon, denn schon. Hartge 335i.
Wir erfüllen einen langgehegten Wunsch: Wir bauen den 3,5 l-Motor des 635 Csi in den kompakten 323i – natürlich mit erheblichen Modifikationen: Großes 5-Gang-Getriebe des 635 Csi mit Spezialkardanwelle, verstärkte Hinterachse, Hinterachsgetriebe des 635 Csi mit spezieller Aufhängung und 40% Sperrwirkung.
535 i
Bereits lieferbar: Der neue Hartge 535i
Die erfolgreiche BMW 5er-Reihe hat ihren Nachfolger. Da es aber werkseitig keinen neuen 535i geben wird, haben wir uns dessen angenommen. Das Ergebnis ist eine Limousine mit den Fahrleistungen eines Sportwagens.
635 Csi
Das optimierte 6er Coupé
Wir haben uns vorgenommen, die ohnehin guten Fahrleistungen der 6er Coupes durch die Mobilisierung einiger vorhandener Reserven noch zu erhöhen. Für den 635 Csi mit Motronic gibt es den Hartge Bausatz mit 240 PS.
735 i
Der souveräne 7er
Souveränität und Vitalität sind Eigenschaften, die ein 735i seinem Eigner vermitteln soll.
Wir helfen hier ein bißchen nach und bieten für den 735i mit Motronic ein Top-Paket:
Die Leistung um 37 PS, das Fahrwerk mit 15'' Rädern und 50er Reifen und die Aerodynamik. Selbstverständlich alles TÜV-abgenommen.
Stärkere Abtriebswellen, Spezialbremsanlage mit Vierkolben-Bremssättel vorne und innenbelüftete Bremsscheiben, ⌀ 271 mm.
Motor: 3,5 l, 240 PS bei 5.500 U/min, Drehmoment 320 Nm/4.000 k/min, komplette Auspuffanlage mit verchromten Fächerkrümmer, 5-Gang-Schongetriebe. Fahrleistungen: 0–100 km/h 7,0 Sek. Spitze über 230 km/h.
Er besteht aus einem bearbeiteten Spezialzylinderkopf mit Ventilen, Ventilfedern, Spezialnockenwelle, Dichtsatz und verchromten Fächerauspuffkrümmer.
240 gesunde PS in Verbindung mit einem speziellen Fächerauspuffkrümmer sorgen für eine angenehme Leistungsentfaltung und einen besseren Drehmomentverlauf.
Das Ergebnis: 180 PS/6.200 U/min., Drehmoment 220 Nm/4.300 U/min., 0–100 km 7,5 sec. Spitze max. 215 km/h.
Das Fahrwerk: Verstärkte Bilstein-Federbeine und Federn, einstellbare Stabis, Federbeinbrücke aus Aluminium (auch für alle anderen Modelle lieferbar), 15'' Räder und 50er Reifen.
Fahrwerk: Hartge-Bilstein-Sportfahrwerk mit 25 mm tieferen Sportfedern. 16'' BBS/Pirelli-Radsatz mit 55/50er Reifen.
Auch 628 Csi/632 Csi-Modelle werden bei uns auf Wunsch modifiziert.
Dazu kommt ein verbessertes Fahrwerk mit Hartge-Bilstein-Abstimmung, 25 mm tieferen Federn, 15 oder 16'' BBS/Pirelli-Radsatz.
Auf Wunsch: Hartge Front- und Heckspoiler.
Gesunde 180 PS, alltagstauglich verpackt und vieles „gewußt wie" vermitteln einen bemerkenswerten Fahrspaß.
Leistungen: 240 PS/5.500 U/min., Drehmoment 320 Nm bei 4.000 U/min. 0–100 km: 6,4 sec. Spitze max. 240 km/h, Verbrauch ⌀ 15,6 l/100 km.
Frontspoiler: handgearbeitet in GFK, lackierbar, optimal paßgenau und harmonisch. Erhöht den Abtrieb und damit die Fahrsicherheit, verbessert das Fahrverhalten.
Das Fahrwerk besteht aus Hartge/Bilstein-Stoßdämpfern mit 25 mm kürzeren Sportfedern und einem 16'' BBS/Pirelli-Radsatz mit 205/225er Reifen.
HARTGE GmbH
An der B 51
6645 Beckingen
Tel. 0 68 35/21 53
Telex 443 747 hartg d
HARTGE
BBS
BOSCH
Castrol
GETRAG
MAHLE
PIRELLI
WEBER

The $43,600 US e34 535i made an '89 MY debut. This '92 US 535i is one of only 56 5 speeds imported that model year (courtesy Mike Cekalovich).

Left: Whether it was 208 bhp (SAE) or 211 bhp (DIN) it was the same 3,430 cc M30 for all markets, and it could drink 87 octane unleaded even with a 9-to-one CR. *Right:* The lavish leather interior of a U.S. spec 535i. BMW was still offering a stick shift at the top end of town, but most U.S. e34 535is had the ZF 4HP22 EH autobox with triple electronic mood program (courtesy Mike Cekalovich).

Opposite: An Alpina rival, Hartge's association with the Kohl Automobile BMW franchise saw it become a household name in 1980s West Germany. Hartge adopted the "H" model designation prefix later in the '80s (courtesy Hartge, http://www.hartge.de).

The 520/520i used BMW's M10 4-cylinder and disk/drum brake combo; thus, the e12's character approximated that of a big 2002 (courtesy Peter Kilner and Peter Hackney, http://team-orange.blogspot.com/).

Left: A 1985 M535i complete with standard equipment metric rims and M-Technic body kit. 1985 was the first model year for the e28 M535i (courtesy Duke Samouce). ***Right:*** To keep the Five competitive, BMW dropped the 3.5-liter I6 into the e28's engine bay to create the 1985 U.S. 535i. The 3.2-liter motor was discontinued in North America at the end of the 1984 MY (courtesy Shawn Doughtie and http://www.mye28.com).

8

The e39 5 Series

The Conservative One

Steady Progress

The e39 5 series is BMW's quiet achiever. Slipping under the radar, lying between the classic e34 and new-wave styling BMWs like the e60 and e65, the e39 is in danger of being overlooked. The e39 hails from the functional '90s when Bimmers packed high tech with a conservative face. That face was attributable to designer Joji Nagashima, the man responsible for the BMW Z3, e36 and e90 3 series. Back in 1991 when the e36 replaced the much-loved e30 3 series, the newcomer was considered a radical change, but not an unwelcome one. The nineties saw a succession of pleasant, offend-no-one shapes from BMW.

Nagashima's e39 exterior styling didn't make waves. It took some cues from its little brother the e36, like the rear ¾ look, but was more '90s organic mainstream. The e34's sharp creases and flat planes were replaced with arcs. Bland but good, the e39's rounded form had balanced proportions; it was not unlike a modern BMW 501. The only qualm was the slight awkwardness with which the ever-widening BMW hood power band crease met up with the A pillar. Naturally, the expected "C pillar" was there, just as much a part of BMW as the blue and white roundel.

So there it was, the vanilla milkshake of cars: everyone likes vanilla. Above the e39 was the even more sedate e38 7 series, recognizably the e32's replacement, minus the old Seven's radical edge. Don't let the styling take attention from the driving; this was a BMW and the public needed to know that the e39 was a safe bet after 1.4 million e34 sales. In addition the luxo sedan segment in Europe was shrinking. Unless a sedan wore the three-pointed star, 4 rings or a BMW propeller, buyers weren't interested. Big Ford or Opel? Forget about it!

It was a great incentive for the remaining players to raise their game. Daimler-Benz certainly did with its already released W210 E class. A very capable car, it would have been even more endearing had the bean counters decided not to decontent quality. Cheap fixings wouldn't halt diesel taxi fleet sales, but the three-pointed star had become tarnished.

Developments were also transpiring over in Ingolstadt. Audi was always the purveyors of solid-build quality and stylish interiors, but now that style had leaked through to the outside too. For 1998 Audi released the hounds with a new stylemeister A6 complete with 30-valve V-6, and the options of Quattro and Tiptronic. The only fly in the ointment was

Comparing 520i to 520i, the e39 tipped the scales 77 lbs. lighter than the e34. The latest Five made great use of aluminum to kill kilos (courtesy Darren Kelly).

lower driving satisfaction. Woolly steering and jiggly ride aside, this was a classy contender for sedan honors. The new Five would need some world firsts to be a worldbeater.

The e39 5 series was the world's first volume-produced sedan to have aluminum suspension. Front and rear subframes, wheel location members, brake calipers and the optional alloys were made of aluminum. The e39 15 × 6.5-inch starter alloys, wearing 205/65 VR tires, used aluminum tape in their construction. This added up to a 15 percent drop in unsprung weight, a 143-lb. weight saving that meant better handling, and the e39 did handle better. Right from the base 520i, all e39s possessed multi-link rather than semi-trailing arm rear suspension.

BMW had moved on from the twitchy times of semi-trailing arms, introducing "Z arm" rear suspension on the 1986 Z1 sportster, as well as the 1991 e36 3 series. For the new Five multi-link meant 4 control arms in an aluminum frame. The control arms were rubber mounted to the frame, and the frame was attached to the unibody using rubber mounts too. This created an elastokinematic road shock absorption system that permitted firmer springs and shocks without adversely affecting ride comfort.

The e39 Five was a car with 50/50 weight distribution, and things got even better for I6 gasoline-powered variants because they were the first Fives to feature rack and pinion steering. Overall the e39 was a very safe-handling automobile, with a class-leading ride/handling combo naturally biased towards sport, even if said handling wasn't quite as involving as it was on the elder e34. It should be noted that although it was lighter, 77 lbs. lighter comparing e34 520i with e39 520i, the new e39 was a physically bigger beastie.

Critics felt that the e39's rear ¾ styling was too close to the e36 3 series. A 1998 318iS coupe with 16-inch Borbet rims and body kit is shown (courtesy Dale Mah).

In spite of not looking that imposing, the e39 was 2.2 inches longer, 1.9 inches wider and 0.9 inches taller than an e34. Even though the new car felt more cosseting and less exciting, the extra size made for improved rear leg room, which has been a long-standing 5 series stumbling block. The e39 was also a more fuel-efficient car, using its weight savings and low drag factor to achieve better fuel efficiency. An early 4-speed auto U.S. spec 528i was good for a 14/34 mpg city/highway combination using premium gas in real-world driving conditions. The drag coefficients ranged from the slim-tired 520i's 0.27 to the 540i's wide-footprint 0.31. Very effective, even though public interest in low drag factors had passed by this stage. Still, it did make for low wind noise at speed, and the e39 variants were capable of higher top ends than their e34 equivalents.

Electronic Aids, Courtesy of the e38

It had become expected that BMW would introduce its latest thinking on the low-volume 7 series, letting the features filter down through the range once they had proven themselves. This was the case with the e39 5 series, which inherited much of the good stuff, after a little pause, from its big brother the e38 7 series. BMW made ASC+T standard across the board on the new e39. As before, it maintained traction by braking individual

The e39 528i made its North American debut as an early '97 MY entrant that retailed for $38,900. This particular 1997 U.S. 528i has been modified with 2001 MY–style grille/clear indicator lenses, H&R lowering springs/Bilstein shocks and Jim Conforti Shark Injector ECU chip (courtesy Alex Selamat).

rear wheels up to 25 mph, and from that point used the throttle. In cutting engine power, computer manipulation of the ignition advance angle, plus the duration the fuel injector solenoids stayed open, were harnessed.

The e39 was still a driver's car, so BMW gave the pilot the choice of turning the traction control off via a console button. Coming from the e38, BMW introduced DSC (Dynamic Stability Control) to the e39. This system did what ASC+T did, as well as cover individual braking of the front wheels for even more control. All this was in the late nineties, all the more impressive when one considers that some new cars don't come with electronic stability control even in the final moments of the 21st century's first decade. DSC also involved DBC (Dynamic Brake Control), which when sensing an emergency braking situation via the force applied to the brake pedal, automatically invoked max braking effect up to the point of lockup.

These electronic driver aids did what a very skilled driver was supposed to do in a crisis, much like ABS had shown to motorists 15 to 20 years earlier. DSC was standard equipment on the pricey U.S. spec 1998 540i automatic, and the following model year it was made standard on all 540is. BMW wanted to make sure brokers were safe on their way to the New York Stock Exchange! In an egalitarian move, DSC was made optional on the 1999 MY I6 cars.

Another life-saving option derived from the e38 was RDC or Reifen Druck Control. RDC was BMW's tire pressure monitoring system, activated by a black rectangular dash button with the picture of a tire and an exclamation mark. From the 2000 MY onwards, 5 series owners could press the button and know how their e39 stood. This was BMW's first tire pressure monitoring system and had pressure and temperature sensors in each rim as part of the valve stem, plus an antenna in each wheel well. BMW subsequently moved on to their RPA Tire Defect Indicator system, as seen on the M5.

RPA uses speed pulses from the car's ABS system sensors. As a tire pressure monitor RPA is much less accurate than RDC, which could be a problem given BMW's later reliance on runflats where tire pressure is crucial. However, RPA is simpler and has fewer parts making it cheaper and an easy retrofit. RDC was more complex and its hardware added to unsprung weight with negative implications for handling. RDC caused a headache for tuners where aftermarket rims were to be installed.

A more acceptable e39 inclusion was the e38 sourced multifunction steering wheel. Take vital control buttons, the ones used frequently by the driver, and place them around the steering wheel boss, so that hands never need leave the rim. The handy pushbuttons included were for stereo, cruise control and climate control's air recirculation.

In a further move to make the living easy, BMW made available PDC, or Park Distance Control. Long gone were the days of 2002-style panoramic visibility. Steeply raked windshields, low seating and small glass had made safe and accurate curbside parking a lottery. To get out of parking by ear, PDC involved sensors placed in the back bumper, with an audible warning going from paused sounds to a continuous beep depending on object proximity. For 2001 BMW put sensors in the front bumper too. It was possible to adjust system sensitivity so PDC wasn't too alarmist.

The e39 was also the first Five to get the option of double-glazed windows for a hushed ambiance, plus rain-sensing wipers. Infrared sensors worked out how much rain was on that windshield, turning on the wipers and adjusting the wiper interval accordingly.

With the e39 BMW offered a greater range of fruit, with more of it included at no extra cost. It was such a shock that in 1997 the *Daily Express* was moved to say, "Standard equipment much improved on the new model, including, at last, a stereo."[1] At one time folks spent a fortune on optional Becker or Blaupunkt radios. BMW said they didn't want to interfere with the exec's audio choice, but competition heat prompted change.

To match Lexus showroom appeal the e39's interior wasn't as stark as previous Fives. The cassette deck was now hidden behind a soft-touch dash flap, and the cassette player head unit was now part of the dash. Things were sounding positive since, depending on the export market, the e39 started with a 10-speaker hi-fi set. At additional expense this could be upgraded to a full 14-channel 400+ watt orchestra with BMW digital sound processor.

Other visual changes were abounding, too. BMW ditched the e34's forward-opening hood in favor of a conventional unit, and the BMW angled dash was less angled than in past years. However, BMW's S.I. indicator system with its colored light show, informing owners a wallet-pounding inspection one or two was just around the corner, was still in evidence. The deadly serious econometer still resided at the tach's base, too.

Check Control and OBC were also back ... in a fresh form. The basic onboard computer readout now resided in the instrument binnacle, and included Check Control as a pictogram. However, the deluxe 9-function OBC was entirely part of the center console, and used MID (Multi Information Display). This informed interested parties of OBC, Check Control and stereo musings with an alphanumeric LCD display. Moving in hi-tech circles, the e39 was also the first Five with an in-dash monitor, filtering from the big daddy e38.

Upgraded to 3.5- and 4.4-liter displacements, the e39's M62 V-8 was much altered from the M60. Even though the noise-absorbing engine cover is removed, one still can't see the key difference: the change from Nikasil to Alusil block (courtesy Jim Levandoski).

Depending on the market, one could select the e39 "Communication Package," a.k.a. the "Rupert Murdoch Special." Feelings of self-importance would run high because the pack consisted of an integrated GSM phone (fitted to the e39 sliding front armrest eject box), with hands-free operation and a windshield antenna. Completing the collection were the e39's optional multifunction tiller and deluxe OBC. The funny thing about electronics, especially when auto-applied, is that development takes place at a cracking pace and what was once state of the art could resemble a museum display in as little as 10 years.

As the BMW 507 and 2002 have shown, an enduring classic goes easy on the gadgets. Also, a word of warning to purchasers of post-e34 Bimmers: the electronic dash info displays can suffer from dead characters over time, not unlike parts of illuminated signs that have stopped working ... with comic results. The only solution is a new replacement unit.

BMW's designers were also working on something more elaborate for the e39's HVAC center. On basic e39s with a/c, one was welcomed by 3 rotary dials. Deluxe variants had the fully automatic pushbutton climate control a/c with 2 digital temp readouts, one for each side of the car. The deluxe climate control could feature AAR (Automatic Air Recirculation). Saving the driver from having to manually hit the recirc button during an olfactory assault, a sensor for pollutant concentration did the job automatically.

Impressive, but there was one e39 odor that wasn't coming from the great outdoors.

Maintaining the old 282 bhp (SAE) rating, but the new 4.4's 310 lbs./ft. made the e39 540i more adept at covering vast Texan distances (courtesy M. Ernst).

Blame the a/c evaporator core. Even after a short period, a/c e39s (and most e39s have a/c) can produce a gym locker or smelly sock-like odor with the a/c working. The underlying cause of the problem is unknown, but it seems especially to affect cars in a humid climate. The design of the evap core housing could be the culprit. The particular core placement, where it gets little exposure to fresh air, even in non-recirc mode, could be the cause. For solutions, try running in vent mode for as long as possible. There are also odor-quelling sprays. Ultimately the core has to be taken out and cleaned, but there is still no long-term fix. It's a trait that seems unique to the e39, sadly.

Fortunately, there is one important thing the e39 doesn't stink at: auto safety. Yes, the e39 has driver-curbing electronic safety aids, but when it comes to the crunch the e39 is king of passive safety too! Little surprise here, because according to the wise heads at BMW, the e39 unibody was 82 percent more rigid in torsional stiffness than the e34. Indeed 40 percent of the e39's unibody used high-strength steels, compared to 12 percent on the e34. Independent tests proved the e39's fortitude. The Insurance Institute for Highway Safety bestowed upon the e39 "A Best Pick" rating for the 40 mph offset crash test. This is a stern test, given the impact energy is concentrated on just part of the structure.

The mid to late '90s was a time when there was an explosion of interest in the supplementary restraint system known as the air bag. Once restricted to the top end of town, it was now reaching a wider audience. The air bag count rose sharply once the feature

High gasoline prices and the efficiency of the I4 520d turbodiesel's 136 bhp/206 lbs./ft. made this version the thrifty choice in Europe (courtesy Ulrich Thieme, http://www.e12.de).

became a safety selling point. Rivals Daimler-Benz and BMW started upping the number fitted in a game of auto one-upmanship. As a European 1996 MY entrant the e39 was available with just 2 front air bag units, for driver and passenger. A few months later the new Five hit the U.S. with 4 air bags, the additional ones being front side air bags.

With the rise of the SUV, and situations where vehicles of varying height share road space, came the arrival of ITS during 1997 for the '98 MY in the U.S. The new Inflatable Tubular Structure was a head-level front air bag system designed to save front occupants in side collisions with tall vehicles. ITS was joined at the same hour by the availability of rear side air bags, taking the possible air-bag count to 8. This tally was increased to 10 for the 2001 MY when rear head air bags, which deployed from the C pillar, were introduced.

Right from the '96 MY the e39 had a front passenger seat detector that wouldn't permit the front passenger air bag to deploy unless a front passenger was actually there. Improving the thinking air bag, for the 2001 MY the e39 received a two-stage severity release for the front air bags. The deployment force depended on crash severity. It's curious how the air-bag total went from 2 to 10 on the e39 in just 5 years. It makes one wonder what car makers were up to in the preceding 10 to 15 years. Sadly, safety didn't sell back then.

Making 184 bhp, then 193 bhp for the 2001 MY, the 530d shared direct injection common rail turbodiesel technology with the 520d/525d (courtesy Paul Baylis, http://www.greenkeepers.fr/).

From 520i to 540i, Not Too Little, Not Too Much...

Aside from new features, there were also new variants in the e39 show, with a notable absentee. After 21 years the 518i econoplate was retired; there would be no gasoline I4 in the e39 family. The 518i's role would be taken by the upcoming upsized e46 318i. Six cylinders befitted the e39's position in Europe as a larger exec sedan, and for Europe revisions were afoot for the I6 cars.

The volume-selling I6s got a new M52 I6. The new six in Europe featured an aluminum block and Nikasil cylinder bore coating, which had been seen earlier on BMW's M60 3–4 liter V-8s. The new M52 tipped the scales 44 lbs. lighter than the outgoing e34's M50TU I6. However, the new M52s sold in the U.S. 528i had a cast-iron block. Nevertheless, there were incremental performance gains for all players.

The only familiar name in the e39 game was the range commencing 520i. This iteration still had 150 horses, but now achieved 136 mph thanks to better aero, with 0–62 mph down to 10.2 seconds. As a first-rung big Euro exec car, the latest 520i was more capable and convincing than its e34 predecessor. In spite of the engine improvements BMW introduced on the e34 520i, the 2-liter I6 never seemed at ease aboard the e34 big bus. The e39 520i manual had a balance that had been missing since the e28 520i.

Interest was also abounding for the oddly titled 523i—odd because it wasn't a 2.3-liter car as the name suggested. The new 523i was powered by a specially tuned, high-torque 2.5-liter version of BMW's I6. The junior e36 of the same vintage also shared the motor. Previous 325i/525is had 192 bhp, but the new 523i's motor made 170 bhp at 5,500 rpm, with 181 lbs./ft. at 3,950 rpm. Low notes for a Bimmer: the Munich men had sacrificed top-end power for improved drivability, and placed the 323i/523i into a thriftier German fiscal motoring category due to the 170 bhp output.

Performance didn't suffer: with a terminal velocity of 141 mph and 0–62 mph in 8.5 seconds, the 523i nearly had the measure of the old e34 535i! A sound e39 variant, certainly, but all eyes were on the new 528i, a name not present since e28 days. The latest e39 528i had little technically in common with the old 528i, but much in the sense that this could be the best-value-for-money quality sedan on the market. This edition of the new M52 had bore and stroke dimensions of 84/84 mm. The figures for the 2.8-liter DOHC 24 valve six weren't exceptional at 193 bhp at 5,300 rpm and 206 lbs/ft at 3,950 rpm; CR was 10.2 to one. Daimler-Benz and Audi had 2.8-liter sixes that equaled such figures, the 193 bhp plateau being merely a German fiscal cutoff point, but the rivals couldn't quite match the free-spinning nature of BMW's six, and more than that, it was a question of being surprised.

The surprise was that this was as far up the range one needed to go to attain bliss point. It was only right that the BMW should take over the old Jag "grace, pace and space" line. Browns Lane wasn't building anything at the time that fitted the cliché, but BMW was. It seemed astonishing that a 3,333-lb. sedan with room for 5 could match, and easily better, its claimed manual gearbox figures of 146 mph and 0–62 mph in 7.5 seconds on just 2.8 liters and for such modest outlay.

Did one really need a V-8, or the extra presence and price of an e38 7 series? These questions were posed by the e39 528i. The 520i/523i/528i all had Vanos working merrily away on the intake side. The standard 5-speed direct fifth manual box was also a boon, easy to shift and a key aid to the flattering figures. Final drive ratios for the early Euro e39s ranged from the 520i's 3.46 to 3.15 for the 523i and 2.93 for the punchier 528i. ABS was standard and worked with 11.8-inch front vented disks, with 11.9-inch rear rotors. The rear disks on the 520i/523i were solid, while those on the 528i/535i were vented.

Things continued apace for a few more years until it was time for a technical upgrade for the 1999 MY, changes that coincided with the intro of the new e46 3 series. Single Vanos (Variable Nocken wellen Steuerung) now became Double Vanos on BMW's gasoline I6s, and the M52 became the M52TU. BMW's six now had variable valve timing on the intake and exhaust sides. This upgrade also marked the introduction of a dual resonance intake system, plus extra turbulence intake passages.

The biggest news concerning M52TU was that it marked the arrival of a world-market all-alloy BMW I6 with cast-iron liners. Up to that point Europe got e39s with Nikasil aluminum block I6s, whereas U.S. e39 528is had a cast-iron block; from the '99 MY they shared the same design. The big reason for the change was trouble with the Nikasil coating. German manufacturer Mahle, maker of pistons, had developed the Nikasil process, with great results in motor racing.

Although Nikasil had proven itself in well known racing engines, like the ones used in Porsche 917–935 sports cars, there were problems experienced with road cars. Nikasil

The M62 V-8 was like an M60 V-8, but with all the bugs ironed out. Examples from the 1999 MY featured Vanos, although max power output remained 286 bhp (courtesy Jonathan Beard).

bore-coated engines had trouble dealing with the high sulfur content of U.S. gasoline, causing a bore-wear issue as the protective Nikasil coating was eaten away. This was especially true for the top of the cylinder bore, causing a CR drop from combustion chamber sealing failure.

For examples of the problem look to the Nikasil M60 3–4 liter V-8s sold in North America in e34s and e32s. A noticeable number of these engines experienced bore-wear problems, leading to poor running and in some cases even complete engine failure. This was the reason why BMW didn't let the U.S. e39 528i receive the Euro spec Nikasil M52 I6. To head off the M60 V-8 public relations fiasco at the pass, BMW extended the warranty for U.S. e34 and e32 V-8 owners to 6 years or 100,000 miles, whichever came first.

To knock the problem on the head, BMW replaced the M60 V-8 with the updated M62 V-8, and only the latter was fitted to the e39 5 series and e38 7 series. The Nikasil 3- and 4-liter V-8s were replaced by Alusil block 3.5/4.4-liter V-8s. The Alusil motor also dealt with other M60 V-8 woes, and those of the early M40 I4s upon which it was based. These foibles concerned front crank oil seal leaks and prematurely worn valve gear, due to a lubrication deficiency. The ghost of BMW's '50s V-8, which had a borderline in-block oil cooler, had come back to haunt the company.

The emphasis with the new M62 was on improved reliability and torque. The new

The e39 Touring first reached North America in 1999 MY. The 2.5 liter e39s, like this Touring, arrived in this market for the 2001 MY (courtesy Frank Gilbert).

535i sported 10-to-one CR, and its 3,498 cc V-8 made 235 bhp at 5,700 rpm with 236 lbs./ft. at 3,300 rpm. Its big brother was still called 540i, even though it had a 4.4-liter V-8 making 286 bhp at 5,700 rpm and 310 lbs./ft. at 3,900 rpm. The 535i and 540i both had the same CR. For 1999 the 535i/540i got revised V-8s with Single Vanos.

The outputs of the Single Vanos V-8s were the same, but were delivered at different rpm. Maximum power and torque for the 535i now took place at 5,800 and 3,800 rpm respectively; for the 540i the figures were 5,400 and 3,600 rpm. Power outputs for the 520i/523i/528i stayed at 150/170/193 bhp in spite of Double Vanos. BMW was trying to improve the civility of its engines; there was also the issue of tightening emissions.

In Europe and the U.S., manufacturers couldn't ignore the increasing need to be "green." More Vanos helped BMW meet U.S. LEV (Low Emissions Vehicle) standards. Thanks to high tech one could own a powerful V-8 and avoid the gross polluter class. V-8 e39s also had recirculating ball steering, by necessity rather than desire. Space constraints ruled out the use of the gasoline I6 e39's rack and pinion system. However, both I6 and V-8 cars were available with a 5-speed auto with the slight difference that the sixes had a 0.74 fifth, whereas the V-8s possessed a shorter 0.80.

535i/540is had a shorter auto fifth to go with their taller final drives. BMW's Steptronic

The e39 became the first Five since the e12 to have its master power window control panel relocated back to the door. Note also the buttons for the 3-position memory powered seats (courtesy Frank Gilbert).

brought greater driver involvement for auto 5 series fans. This sport shift was BMW's version of the Porsche/Audi Tiptronic device, allowing clutchless sequential shifts with a normal torque converter autobox. Be sporty when the mood arises and enjoy the smooth changes only a real auto can deliver the rest of the time. The setup was getting quite useful now that auto exec cars had 5 ratios to play with.

Starting with the shifter in "D," the e39 auto owner knocked the wand towards himself, to position "S." Then the shifter was pushed forward to go up a ratio, or back to go down through the box. There were + and — shifter console markings to aid the driver. With Steptronic one could be like a racing driver, the old gated manual shift pattern being long gone from most motorsport. It was also a more modern way of holding a particular gear through a corner compared to BMW's old Switchable autos.

The joys of Steptronic weren't for everyone, though. In Europe its availability was initially restricted to the 528i and higher, even though e39s southwards could have the normal electro-hydraulic 5-speed auto *sans* Steptronic. In America neither the 5-speed auto nor Steptronic were available on the 528i when the e39 reached North America. The U.S. e39 528i made a spring 1996 debut as an early '97 MY entrant. The model retailed for $38,900 and included ASC+T, sunroof and 4 air bags. Gearbox choices lay with a 5-speed manual or 4-speed auto, the latter being optional.

The e39 was the first Five to feature a factory-fitted GPS system with in-dash monitor, moving from a CD-ROM to DVD-ROM–based system for the 2003 MY (courtesy Frank Gilbert).

The U.S. 528i was partnered by the $49,900 540i, with more equipment and 5-speed Steptronic standard. A 6-speed stick was optional. For the U.S. a 4-speed auto continued to be available on the 528i until the end of the '99 MY. Slightly earlier BMW fans with enemies could take comfort, and cover, thanks to the special e39 light armor 540i Protection. This variant was announced in 1998 and was the first factory-built 5 series with armored protection. The 540i Protection used Aramide fiber, not steel, for its cladding. Thus, the weight penalty was restricted to just 320 lbs.

The 540i Protection came standard with self-leveling rear suspension and BMW Servotronic steering, plus DSC and EDC. Also thrown in was a "Siege Pack," which contained sat nav GPS, cell phone and runflat tires with overinflation monitoring. However, perhaps it wasn't quite time for the Godfather to trade in his Caddy, since the 540i Protection came with bullet-resistant rather than bulletproof glass. The 540i Protection could save lives, but the e39 was also into saving fuel, and with that in mind featured new versions of the 525td and 525tds.

Better Diesels and a New Touring

The e39 525td and tds had revised versions of the M51 diesels seen in the e34, designed to deliver cleaner emissions, improved refinement and greater torque. The cars had a new

A 2000 MY U.S. spec 528i, containing the Double Vanos M52TU I6 with aluminum block (courtesy Fabrizio Plaza).

catalytic converter, plus an ECU rechipped to meet stricter EU (European Union) stage 2 emissions. The e39 diesels also had intelligent engine mounts. These electro-hydraulic mounts were told to go soft at idle by the ECU, to cut NVH.

The gains are shown by stating the stats on the e34 and e39 525tds. Both diesels made 143 bhp, but the e39 525tds produced the output at 4,600 rpm, not 4,800 rpm. Torque was up from 192 to 206 lbs./ft. at 2,200 rpm. The e39 525td and 525tds ran from 1997 and 1996, respectively, to the close of the '99 MY. The intercooled 525tds boasted commendable factory figures of 131 mph and 0–62 mph in 10.4 seconds, and yet its thunder would soon be stolen by a newcomer that was the real future of BMW diesel motoring: the 530d!

The 530d joined the 525td and 525tds as a range-topping 3-liter I6 during 1998, and rewrote the rulebook on diesel motoring expectations. As a sedan the 530d had claimed performance figures of 140 mph and 0–62 mph in 8 seconds. The extra sparkle was partly due to the extra half liter, but mostly related to new diesel high tech. The 530d featured a direct injection common rail turbodiesel motor, involving technology developed by Fiat and Bosch. The 530d used four valves per cylinder, the older 525td/tds merely two.

BMW diesels still used a cast-iron block; the 530d had a strengthened crankcase/block and a variable geometry turbo. The turbo changed its size depending on the revs: small turbo at low rpm for quick spool-up; big turbo at higher revs to make power. The 3-liter diesel made 184 bhp at 4,000 rpm and more importantly 288 lbs./ft. at 1,750 rpm. This new diesel design quickly became known for monster torque. For the 2001 MY things got

BMW's new e39 530i was on display at various car shows. In this case it was the Paris Auto Salon (courtesy Paul Baylis).

even sexier when the 530d was recalibrated to 193 bhp, proving it was OK for high flyers to drink derv!

BMW took the direct-injection common-rail turbodiesel to the 2/2.5-liter class with the 520d I4 and 525d I6 for the 2000 MY. These new models replaced the 525td/tds. The 520d's 1,951 cc 16-valver made 136 bhp and a tremendous 206 lbs./ft. at 1,750 rpm, eclipsing the 525td. The 6-pot 2,497 cc 525d rated out at 164 bhp. It all spelled diesel dominance in Europe. Fuel prices have always been historically high in the old country, making diesel the automatic choice.

With the second wave e39 diesels the 520d/525d/530d started to make up a big percentage of the product mix, a trend which would continue with the e60. Stumble across a BMW in Continental Europe and more often than not it will be a diesel. However, a wagon would be less common. The wagon, the postwar staple of the typical nuclear family, was fast going the way of the dodo. America discovered the SUV, and Europe latched onto tallboy people movers like the Renault Scenic.

Wagons were now well-heeled, with Audi, BMW and Daimler-Benz making models that cost a lot, didn't carry a lot, but were nice to be seen in. The e34 Touring was easy on the eye and so was its e39 successor. The e39 Touring arrived in Europe for the 1997 MY; in the 1999 MY, it came to North America. In Europe the e34 Touring lingered on until the e39 version was ready to roll. As with the e39 sedan it was a larger animal than its predecessor. The e39 Touring was 1.2 inches longer than its sedan counterpart, and 242 lbs.

heftier. It was 6.3 inches longer and 1.8 inches wider than the lunchbox-like e34 Touring, and boasted 53.5 cu. ft. of cargo space.

For a vehicle that set great store by style, the e39 Touring had a commendably flat load space, thanks to the unintrusive design of the rear suspension. Lifestyle accessories were on hand to make picnics and weekend trekking a pleasant experience. There was a lockable under-floor storage area, and a 75-kg-rated pullout platform that might have saved someone a bad back. The e39 Touring also packed the convenient separate-opening tailgate glass hatch, as seen on the e34 Touring.

In spite of the e39 T's bigger dimensions, it was lighter than a comparable e34 Touring. The e39 528i Touring was 90 lbs. lighter than the e34 530i Touring. The older car had a V-8, but both had all-alloy engines. The e39 Touring had a slight rear weight bias of 45/55, but this only had a tiny effect on the Touring's handling feel compared to the sedan. In Europe, just the 525td was unavailable in Touring form out of the regular e39s. As with the e34 there was some overlap as the e39 Touring continued into the 2004 MY alongside the new e60 sedan.

Changes for 2001 and Beyond

For 2001 the e39 received some major rejigging for its final 3 years. Cosmetically it was hard to miss the new "Angel Eyes" headlights: the dipped-beam lamps had an illuminated outer ring and a blue center, while the rear lights were changed to jewel-effect units. Formally the new lamps were called "CELIS" by their manufacturer Hella. Round revealed front indicator lights also figured in the restyle. BMW was keeping an angel eye on the opposition, even though rivals had made little impression on the e39's lead in 5 years.

A change that wouldn't be seen, unless one was doing a tire rotation, was a brake change to e39s below the 540i. Lesser e39s now adopted the 540i's 12.8-inch front vented disks, and switched to solid disks at the rear, if those rear disks had been previously ventilated. The e39 was also the recipient of larger kidney grille trims, a popular retrofit on pre–2001 e39s. The e39 now had a sharper, more menacing visage. To complement the visual aggression, Munchen's engineers put more fire in the e39 belly with upgraded I6s.

For 2001 there were three new gasoline I6 variants, direct replacements for the 520i/523i/528i. The 520i was now a 170 bhp 2.2-liter machine, fixing the 2-liter's torque shortfall. There was a change from 80/66 mm bore and stroke to 80/72 mm and 2,171 cc for BMW's wee six. Engine CR was up to 10.7 with torque, formerly 140 lbs./ft. at 4,200 rpm, rising to 155 lbs./ft. at a more relaxed 3,500 rpm, implying less need to stir the stick.

BMW had also finally decided to unleash their middle child's true spirit. The sober 523i was transformed into the hi-po 525i. It had the same 10.5 CR and 2,494 cc as the 523i, plus the same max torque, but at a lower 3,500 rpm. However, output was a loftier 192 bhp at a screaming 6,000 rpm. The retuned 525i now lived at a different German fiscal threshold, with an engine coded M54B25. The 525i's big brother was the new 530i, using the M54B30. It was the end of the 528i, with the 3-liter possessing measurements of 89.6/84 mm. The 530i also had an attractive 231 bhp at 5,900 rpm and 221 lbs./ft. at 3,500 rpm.

The revised e39s cemented BMW's position in the I6 sports sedan segment, with the 530i's power plant in particular making rivals seem a trifle dull. The North American lineup

A UK RHD 2002 530i Sport, the look of an M5 combined with the revised M54B30 3-liter I6 (courtesy Peter Thorpe).

was also expanded to embrace the new 2001 525i (the 523i was not previously available), working with the new 530i and existing 4.4-liter 540i powerhouse. Lexus had good reason to be scared!

To underscore the e39's inherent sportiness was the presence of "Sport" variants for Euro 525i–540i models. These Sport editions were value packs for those who couldn't cope with the cost or severity of the e39 M5. For the money one received an M5-style body kit, larger sports seats, multifunction steering wheel, aluminum interior trim inserts and sports suspension. Such Sport cars sat lower and wore 17-inch Parallel spoke rims, 8 inches wide at the front with 235/40 tires, 9 inches wide at the rear with 265/35 tires, once again ZR rated.

Amongst the Sport variants only the 535i Sport was unavailable with the pack's shorter final drive; it made do with the normal 535i 2.93 ratio. More extravagant still was the U.S. 2003 MY 540i M-Sport edition. This 6-speed manual, or 5-speed auto, car came with an extended sport kit that encompassed a full M-Tech ground effects body kit, M-Tech II sports suspension and 18-inch rims. Rather than lose sales to Daimler-Benz, BMW made the M5's handling abilities available to American patrons unwilling to give up an autobox.

Final amendments to complete the e39's successful run was the 2003 MY change from

A 2003 U.S. 530i manual on display, representing the final model year for the e39 sedan (courtesy John Carrier).

a CD-ROM–based sat nav GPS system, to a DVD-ROM–based set-up. This move cut the number of discs needed to cover North America from 8 to just 1. However, in judging which might be the best e39 to buy today the choice won't be ruled by which had the most equipment. The I6 gasoline cars had the nicest steering, benefiting from a rack and pinion system. Indeed, the six-pot cars had the best balance in the e39 family, and even in this group one would lean towards the Euro versions.

The early U.S. 528i had a cast-iron block, meaning more weight in the nose than the Euro Nikasil 528i. All-alloy their engines may have been, but the e39 V-8s carried even more weight up front, making for duller turn-in when cornering. The 535i/540i also carried the penalty of vaguer recirculating ball steering. However, if one likes automatics, then the pendulum swings to the V-8s, since the auto takes the edge off the sixes. Even with modern 5-speed Steptronic the autos are 1.5 seconds tardier when sprinting to sixty, although the 530i copes somewhat better.

In spite of V-8 torque, Steptronic and microchips could do little to banish that slight shift pause one would never get in a manual 528i. Team the V-8s with a manual, a 5- and 6-speed for the 535i/540i respectively, but it would be a He-Man experience next to the 6-cylinder cars. One could always try a diesel, and with fuel prices being what they are,

Top: Outside the M5, if one wanted a 6-speed e39 the path led to the 540i. The coolest 540i was the 2003 U.S. 540i M-Sport. *Bottom:* The 540i M-Sport had an M-Tech ground effects kit, 18-inch rims and sports suspension. A total of 1,265 540i M-Sports were made for the U.S.; this is car number 496, which happens to be a 6-speeder (courtesy Bill Johnson).

there could be little option. However, e39 diesels have cast-iron blocks and recirculating ball steering, making them less pleasant for the enthusiast.

An enthusiast wishing to tote a load could do far worse than try the e39 Touring; Alpina liked them. Transport pets without hurting your credibility, but the purist would always lean towards the sedan. This probably leaves the 2000 MY 5-speed 528i optioned with M-Tech suspension as the one to go for. No Nikasil, no worries: the benefit of an all-alloy block combined with early e39 styling. The 2.8-liter I6 seems the best performance/economy compromise. The original e39 variant and still the best!

9

BMW in Flux

The 1990s

The 1990s saw BMW in a state of flux. After 3 decades of planned progress it seemed to have lost its direct focus. Munich had launched its extravagant V-12 8 series GT mobile, the ideal competitor for Stuttgart's new MB SL. The stage was set for a clash of the titans, but the powers that be didn't foresee the recession of 1990, so why not make an electric car? Yes, BMW would spread the joy of motoring to an electric buggy. The BMW E1 electric car was unveiled at the 1991 Frankfurt Motor Show, too big to fit in the trunk of an e32 750iL, but socially restrained nonetheless.

BMW E1— Plug and Playtime

The E1 was 136.2 inches long, and came with a 45 bhp electric motor and no ashtray ... since it was a zero emissions vehicle. However, the E1 was practical: it had 2 air bags, a 200 km range and 120 kph top speed. At 900 kg with a 900-liter storage capacity, this was no 4-wheeled gimmick; it was a real small car that didn't need fossil fuel.[1] Like the 21st-century Toyota Prius, the BMW E1 stored the energy generated during braking. This no-waste conveyance could be filled up, or charged up rather, by removing one of the BMW kidney grilles and inserting the provided plug into the mains for juice.

BMW—The Green One

While there were no official electric e39s, BMW was getting serious about the business of recycling. Recycling operations at the Landshut factory in Southern Bavaria commenced in July 1990.[2] The process of taking a car apart and salvaging parts is as orderly a procedure as building said car in the first place. Liquids are drained, gas is recovered and the car is then dismantled. Work is easier and more can be saved if the car is designed with recycling in mind. The e39 was the first 5 series where this was the case.

In Germany a BMW or MB owner can go to a center where the car is checked out with a quote for the work needed to make the car pass the TÜV vehicle roadworthy inspection. If the owner decides the repair work is uneconomic and it has reached the end of its working life, then the automobile is recycled, not scrapped. During dismantling, hardware like final drives, turbos, and long blocks can be saved, reconditioned and sold with a warranty to benefit owners of previous model generations. Junking is no longer part of the job.

As part of spreading this formal green-minded practice, joint recycling programs between manufacturers have developed, with reciprocal arrangements to recycle each other's cars.[3] BMW and Renault entered into this relationship in 1993, with BMW recycling Renaults in Germany, Renault returning the favor concerning Bimmers floating around France. However, concerns for the planet's survival take a back seat to a company's survival. BMW always wants to produce more cars, not fewer.

BMW and Rover

The cost of car development is always rising; BMW spent more designing the dash on the e36 3 series than Rolls-Royce did on the entire new 1981 Silver Spirit. To design a new car requires a big budget, with costs that can only be amortized by large-scale production runs and economies of scale. In the '90s there was a fear that one had to get large, or disappear into economic oblivion. A quick method to get bigger is via merger. Merger sounds kindly, but buyout is more accurate and common. BMW had done this in the '60s with Glas, and now its attention turned to England's Rover Group.

With a view to safeguarding its future BMW purchased the Rover Group from British Aerospace in 1994. Initially it looked like a good move. Back in the mid–'70s, British Leyland, as it was then known, was on the verge of self-destruction, but then things started to get better. A period of stability ensued through nationalization, followed by a successful 1980s era when the English auto consortium ran as a privatized concern. It had been the policy of the UK Conservative government under Prime Minister Margaret Thatcher to pursue privatization where possible. It was a good revenue raiser and promised more profitable and efficient industry.

The good economic times and reliance on the free market system brought sound results. BL (British Leyland) had morphed into the Austin Rover Group, introducing well-received, locally designed 1980s volume sellers, as well as one derived from a particularly good joint association with Japanese manufacturer Honda. However, the tide was about to turn once more. By the late '90s BMW hadn't achieved the hoped-for headway from having turned Rover around, and losses were mounting. To be a sales winner one must have products people want, and Rover had a problem. Their 1980s home-grown cars were aging; so too were their Honda-based models. The Rover 800/Sterling luxury car had been reskinned and re-engined, but was still based on the original Honda/Acura Legend.

There was also a limit on the amount of funds BMW was prepared to pump into Rover. The Munich management had been wary of red ink since 1961, and apart from the sales slowdown caused by the 1973 fuel crisis, had managed to stay in the black during the interim. This was of little comfort to Rover; Britain's last volume automaker, representing fabled brands like Austin, Morris, Triumph and Land Rover, needed cash for new models. BMW boss Bernd Pischetsrieder, coincidentally a nephew of Mini designer Alec Issigonis, had been instrumental in getting, keeping and spending over $3 billion on Rover. Pischet-

Pictured in Portugal, the X5 3.0d had the torque of the 4.4i and even greater thrift than the e53 3.0i variant (courtesy Nuno Forneas).

srieder resigned in 1999 amid big Rover losses, with Rover being sold in 2000 for a nominal sum, and BMW bearing the burden of Rover worker pension liabilities.

During the ensuing carve-up, Land Rover, the money maker, went to Ford, BMW kept the new Mini, and the rest went to the Phoenix Consortium. In fact the Rover 75 was based on a mooted front-drive 3 series platform that was eventually rejected by BMW. Daimler-Benz had a similar "growing pains" experience when it merged with/bought Chrysler. Billed by Benz as the coming together of equals, the relationship speedily went south.

With Rover, BMW quickly installed its own management. Former BMW GB boss Dr. Walter Hasselkus was appointed Rover Group CEO in 1996, joining BMW notable Dr. Wolfgang Reitzle, who happened to be chairman of the Rover Group.[4] Daimler-Benz also experienced a management culture clash and put their people in high positions at Daimler-Chrysler. Unable to turn around Chrysler losses, Daimler-Benz sold Chrysler to private equity in 2007. The experience of both German companies proved that to get things done one can't rely on others.

BMW Z3 and X5—Roadsters and SUVs

A second way to get bigger is to expand the product portfolio. This side of things proved more successful for Bernd Pischetsrieder as BMW went about expanding its range,

When the e53 reached North American dealers, it was in gasoline-only 3.0i/4.4i form. The I6 variant arrived later than the V-8, sharing its engine with the e46 330i and e39 530i (courtesy Kathy Shaller).

and guarded against adverse U.S. currency fluctuations. The solution was to start making cars in America ... but where? The answer was supplied by Pischetsrieder and his friend Dr. Helmut Panke as they drove around the American South during 1992 in a rented minivan (rumored to have been of Chrysler Corp. origins), looking for a U.S. factory site.

Their conclusion: Don't locate in Detroit, move far from the U.A.W., take advantage of state government incentives and set up shop on the greenfield (union-free) area of Spartanburg, South Carolina. The Spartanburg facility became operational in November 1994 and quickly became associated with turning out college preppy Z3s and the e53 X5. The Z3 was a Miata-chasing 2-seater, a modern-day MGB, if you will. The e53 was an early upscale crossover vehicle.

If you wanted a truck that drove like a car, then you needed a Sports Activity Vehicle (SAV). Market research showed that when buyers traded up from a Ford Explorer/Grand Cherokee they either went for a giant (Ford Excursion/Chevy Suburban) or they went the mini luxo route.[5] The latter involved vehicles like the BMW X5 and MB M class. Working with the same reasoning of designing what people want and building it where they live, Daimler-Benz made their SUV at a factory in Tuscaloosa, Alabama.

As ever, the experiences and products of DB and BMW were similar, but different. These were two SUVs that handled, but the M class had a separate chassis and was much better off-road, whereas the X5 had unibody construction and was tuned for on-road action. The e53 had all independent suspension and used e39 5 series parts to cut costs. BMW's SUV was first and foremost a BMW, and secondly an SUV. Thus, the big Bimmer had a rear bias torque split of 38/62 percent, and no low range because it was never intended to be a mud plugger.

The e53's good-handling on-road nature approximated that of the 1970 Range Rover,

When combined with manual transmission the I6-powered X5 had good pep. This 2002 X5 3.0i 5-speed has towed 4,500 lbs. (courtesy Robert Bell).

although the latter possessed sound off-road skills too. However, the early Range Rover wasn't as widely available as the X5. The X5 was as ever-present as two all-beef patties on a sesame seed bun in the country where it mattered, and used a Range Rover trick to overcome the absence of a low range. A benefit of BMW's association with Rover was that it was able to purloin Range Rover's Hill-Descent Control device. HDC made going down steep inclines an automatic foolproof feat.

The X5 made its world debut in January 1999 at the North American International Auto Show in Detroit. Initial power plants comprised 3 choices: 3.0-liter I6, 3.0-liter I6 turbodiesel, and 4.4-liter V-8. These were familiar e39 5 series engines, with all three e53 variants exported to Europe. The X5 4.4i made a fall 1999 U.S. debut, and was later joined by the X5 3.0i gasoline model with standard 5-speed manual power team, once the M54B30 motor arrived.

The Z3 and X5 were all about BMW fitting into U.S. environs. BMW had a Californian design studio and American Chris Bangle as styling boss. Who could have foreseen such BMW developments back in the '60s? BMW acknowledged the increasing popularity of lifestyle SUVs over sedans by pricing X5 versions lower than like-engined e39 equivalents. It also gave buyers an incentive to choose the SUV. For example, in June 2000 the X5 3.0i

BMW kept the e53 in synch with the 5 series. The 2003 MY was the end of the road for the e39, so the 2004 MY brought several changes for the e53 X5 (courtesy Jack Tulling).

was priced at $38,900 with the 4.4i V-8 edition coming in at $49,400. These prices were slightly less than the e39 528i/540i were retailing for back in the spring of 1996!

The X5s also tended to have a higher spec level than their sedan counterparts. Such traits were repeated in all world markets. In adding cars like the Z3, X5, and BMW Compact, as well as the subsequent X3 and 1 series, BMW grew by going outside the comfort zone. Daimler-Benz has done the same with their A and B class, attracting converts through new models with pricing never previously associated with the marque.

In trying to have something for everyone — small, thrifty turbodiesels in Europe; gasoline V-8 SUVs for North America — BMW did have its American gremlins. There were quality concerns at Spartanburg; early Z3s had very poor body panel fit. The first X5s were felt to have the sort of cheap interior alien to Munich's finest. Plus there were X5 reliability woes, but not nearly as many as experienced by the MB M class. On debut the M class chalked up one of the worst new car reliability records of any vehicle sold in the U.S.

Reliability of the X5 and M class did get better, with higher quality materials fitted to the X5 in the interim as well. However, quality control at the BMW and MB U.S. factories is still not up to the level of the U.S. greenfield sites established by Japanese and Korean firms. Fortunately the X5's driver appeal allowed quality shortfalls to be overlooked. It has always been the ultimate SUV driving machine and the German tuners agree.

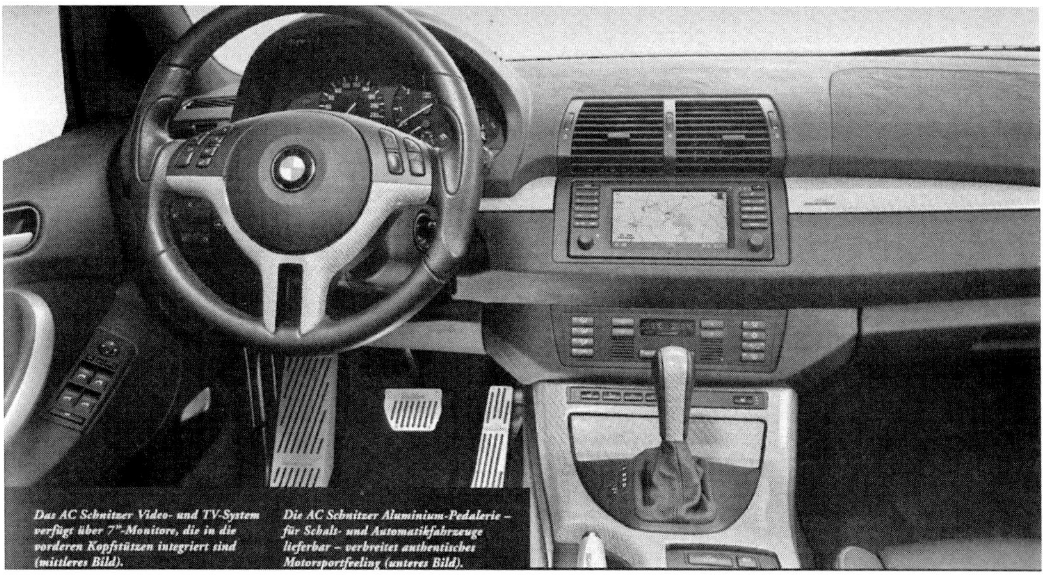

Top: **Pictured on grass, but with lowered (30 mm) sports suspension and 19-to-22-inch rims, an ACS5 e53 is best on-road.** ***Bottom:*** **Feel free to personalize your e53 X5 with carbon fiber interior panels, aluminum pedal set and multimedia LCD screens. Only your budget is the limit (courtesy AC Schnitzer, http://www.ac-schnitzer.de/en/).**

The X5's on-road raison d'etre was shown by the aftermarket tuners, especially Hartge. Hartge did an M5-based conversion that blew any e53 off-road pretensions out of the water. Take one e53 X5 and swap in the e39 M5's 400-pony V-8, as well as any e39 M5 driveline that could be squeezed aboard. Throw in sports suspension and remember not to trek too far from the beaten track, because Hartge's M5-engined X5 was 2-wheel-drive only! For those determined to explore the Yukon, Hartge also offered an all-wheel-drive 380 bhp conversion with their bored and stroked 5-liter version of the BMW M62 V-8.

Breyton Design first came to public attention through its aftermarket rims; thus, experience the spirit of Breyton with its X5 wearing 23-inch "Spirit" wheels (courtesy Breyton Design, http://www.breyton.com/).

AC Schnitzer also shares the view that the X5 is for road burning, rather than bush burning. The German company calls the e53 X5 an "Off-Road saloon"! Chipping the popular X5 3.0d variant pushed up power from 193 to 255 bhp, with torque reaching a monumental 407 lbs./ft. For gasoline X5 3.0is, a supercharger kit used a max of 0.35 metric bar boost pressure. The 3.0 I6 figures boosted to 295 bhp and 281 lbs./ft., with the kit called ACS5 "COMPRESSOR."

For total performance, AC Schnitzer's e53 sports suspension set lowers ride height 30 mm, with rim choices running in the 19- to 22-inch range. With an emphasis on AC Schnitzer's "5 spoke" program, their Type IV rim can be worn by the e53. For cosmetics, AC Schnitzer integrates the tailpipe's exit with the rear body kit apron for a neat finish. On the inside, video and TV in-car systems are available among customization choices.

Breyton Design said their X5 was at home anywhere, but would anyone want to get those Magic Sport rims covered in mud? (courtesy Breyton Design, http://www.breyton.com/).

That such expensive upgrades seemed at odds with mud plugging was hardly an issue. In AC Schnitzer's words, "The effect on the off-road capacity — in reality only rarely utilized — is minimal...." The tuning firm Breyton Design is of similar mind when describing their special e53 as "optimised by Breyton Design. Regardless of the terrain, this car is at home everywhere." The company is right in referring to the e53 as a car, especially after Breyton Design has worked their magic.

Breyton Design offers an e53 body kit and 20- to 23-inch rim choices. Try the Magic Sport or Type Seven styles in 22-inch form, or the Spirit at 23 × 11 inches wrapped with 315/25 ZR tires. For the e53's interior an 8-piece carbon fiber trim panel set makes things stylish. Under the hood the "Breyton D-Box" 3.0d tuning kit involves a reprogrammed ECU that takes power onto 262 bhp and 600 Nm of torque or 444 lbs./ft. This enhancement is ideally complemented by Breyton's dual stainless steel muffler set.

10

Tuning the e39

Motorsport and Tuner Choices

Alpina Tries Diesel

As the first well-known BMW tuner, Alpina occupies a special place in the BMW improvement universe. By the turn of the century this car manufacturer — a better description of its operations than tuner — was providing 700 cars per annum for motorists with very particular needs. Those needs only partly involved greater speed; for a price, Alpina guaranteed performance with harmony. The Buchloe concern was interested in efficiency, plus the importance of being green.

Alpina only uses metal cat converters, like on its winning 1987 M3 Group A racer. Indeed, the entire Alpina exhaust could be described as being green and efficient. The firm used a twin scroll system with stainless steel elbow joints and heated lambda probes. The Emitec metal cats used an Engelhard coating. A bold example of high performance working with conservation was the mighty, and thrifty, 1999 e39-based Alpina D10 Bi Turbo.

The Alpina D10 Bi Turbo, a joint Alpina and BMW project, was first shown at the Geneva Motor Show. A triumph of ecological speed, it was the world's most powerful and fastest diesel production sedan, with a terminal velocity of 159 mph, with the e39 Touring edition capable of 157 mph. An impressive achievement, but little surprise given the great abilities of the base e39 530d and Alpina know-how. Moving into the e39 era, Alpina extended its sphere of influence to cover right hand drive cars.

Previously (before 1993), if one lived in a right-hand-drive locality, the importing agent brought in engine, suspension, body kits, etc. and fitted them to a new right-hand-drive car, creating a RHD Alpina. However, Alpina had concerns over the integrity of the completed car. Did it have all the right stuff to make it a genuine Alpina B9 or B10? To make sure it really was an Alpina, when the badge said so, it was possible to get RHD Alpinas from Alpina themselves now, and one would certainly want all the pieces put together properly with the Alpina B10 4.6 V8.

As the name signified, the B10 4.6 V8 was Alpina's take on the e39 540i. The Buchloe gnomes had created a newly cast 4.6 liter version of the Alusil M62 4.4 liter V8. The Alpina V8 had larger dimensions of 93/85 mm, 1 mm and 2.3 mm bore and stroke increases over the stock 4.4 respectively, sportier cams, and hand-polished intake ports, and Alpina carefully checked the combustion chambers to make sure they all displaced the same ccs. The Alpina

Alpina's B10 4.6 V-8 predated BMW's e39 M5, and put forth performance with great civility using an automatic transmission (courtesy http://www.thealpinaregister.com/ and alpina46).

V8 had oil-sprayed Mahle pistons, steel mesh cats and a remapped M5.2 ECU that was Bosch blessed.

It all added up to a 10.5 CR engine making 340 bhp at 5,700 rpm and 346 lbs./ft. at 3,800 rpm, which helped spirit the B10 4.6 V8 0–62 mph in 5.7 seconds and towards a top end of 167 mph ... as an automatic. That's correct, the B10 4.6 V8 was an auto-only car and featured Alpina's own clever auto system called "Switch-Tronic." Switch-Tronic involved a modified ZF 5HP24 autobox. There were plus and minus buttons on the expensive-looking Alpinaized BMW multifunction tiller.

The Alpina experts reprogrammed BMW's somewhat recalcitrant Steptronic to permit the Switch-Tronic system to change up at 7,000 rpm. It was all about getting rid of the dreaded auto shift pause, as well as letting the driver pretend he was a Formula 1 gladiator. Alpina also made other alterations to make their 5 series just right. The B10 4.6 rode on Bilstein twin tube shocks, with braking courtesy of cross-drilled rotors. Wheels were Alpina's usual turbine blade design, 18 × 8 inches with 235/40 tires front, 18 × 9 inches with 265/35 tires rear. ZR rated Michelin MXX3s were the B10 4.6's tire of choice.

Alpina lowered the car's final drive from the stock 540i 2.81, to a more acceleration-friendly 3.15. B10 4.6 occupants only heard pleasant V8 purrs in the opulently appointed interior, where custom seats with thicker-than-standard leather awaited, if the Alpina buyer eschewed the idea of squeezing into sports buckets. Alpina could still work in side bolsters that were more aggressive than 540i equivalents. There was also leather trim for the center console shifter surround, and a headliner plaque stating the B10 4.6's build number.

Top: Alpina's Switch-Tronic auto system worked with the usual ZF 5HP24 autobox, to bring real driver involvement to shiftless living (courtesy Alpina, http://www.alpina-automobiles.com/). *Bottom:* Alpina's 6-cylinder B10 3.2 was manual only, and through rack and pinion steering was even closer to the enthusiast's ideal than the B10 4.6.

This 1998 Estoril Blue B10 3.2 is car number 133 out of a sequence of 194. The Alpina rear spoiler has been replaced by an M5 item, with the sports sedan riding on Eibach coil over suspension (courtesy Mark Blackburn).

Alpina still found room for improvement. For 1999 and 2000 they introduced a tweaked 4.6 V8 with Bosch Motronic ME M7.3. Power was now 347 bhp at 5,700 rpm and 354 lbs./ft. at 3,700 rpm, with newly associated performance claims of 0–62 mph in 5.5 seconds with a top speed of 173 mph. Finally, for the 2001 MY Alpina released the B10 4.8 V8S, replacing the 4,619 cc unit with a bigger 4,837 cc V8 making 375 bhp at 5,800 rpm and 376 lbs./ft. at 3,800 rpm. The still auto-only B10 V8 was now good for 177 mph; Alpina didn't believe in speed limiters.

Whereas the B10 4.6 and 4.8 were automatics, the B10 3.2 I6 was manual only. The e39 528i was such a popular and able car, it made sense to use this model as a base for the B10 3.2, which used a ZF S5–31 manual 5-speeder. In the style of the e36 M3 Evo 3.2, Alpina turned the 2.8 I6 into a version making 260 bhp at 5,900 rpm and 243 lbs./ft. at 4,300 rpm with dimensions of 86.4/89.6 mm. The outcome was a claimed 0–62 mph in 6.5 seconds with 162 mph top speed, plus the handling and steering advantages of using an I6 e39.

As was typical of Alpina they offered their B10 3.2 in sedan and Touring forms. For the 1999 MY Alpina replaced the B10 3.2 with a 3.3-liter edition. The 3.3-liter version of the BMW baby six had bore and stroke of 86.4/93.8 mm; CR was lowered to 10.2 from 10.5 on the B10 3.2. The 3.3-liter had a new crank and torsional vibration damper, plus redesigned Alpina intake and exhaust manifolds. Engine figures were now 280 bhp at 6,200 rpm and 248 lbs./ft. at 4,500 rpm. Claimed top speed remained 162 mph, but 0–62 mph was down to 6.3 seconds.

In the 3.2 to 3.3 liter transition there was a mind change from Siemens DME MS 41 to MS 43 concerning the ECU. Alpina chose iron blocks for its I6s; they were more rigid.

In the spirit of the BMW e36 M3 Evo, Alpina converted the BMW 2.8-liter I6 into a 3.2-liter with 86.4/89.6 mm dimensions (courtesy Mark Blackburn).

For the 2001 MY, Switch-Tronic became available on the B10 3.3, increasing 0–62 mph to 6.6 seconds and decreasing top speed to 161 mph. As with the B10 V8s there were the usual Switch-Tronic benefits of torque converter lock-up in Switch-Tronic mode, with auto upshifts at the raised redline.

Switch-Tronic was a joint development venture between Alpina, Bosch and ZF. The smart auto ignored incorrect downshift requests, and would start off in 2nd automatically after coming to a halt if the driver forgot to change out of high gear. The B10 3.3's Switch-Tronic differed from the unit used on the V8s, by using the e39 I6's ZF 5HP19 auto. Among the various tailor-made options one could select sports seats with Alpina's asymmetric blue/green stripe upholstery, or BMW's e39 Comfort seats.

Between a Rock and a Hartge Place

Rival Hartge had similar bore/stroke engine conversions for BMW's I6s and V8s. As with other tuners, apart from Alpina, there was a reverence for the e39 M5, with special items available for this model, without any more extensive mods. Starting off was Hartge's H5–2.8, based on the 528i. Customers got a ported/polished head, valve size increased 1

This 1999 Alpina B10 3.3 was ordered with powered sunroof, power rear window sunblind, automatic dimming mirrors, 6 CD changer audio unit, trunk lid spoiler, white indicator lenses, Shadowline and tinted windshield for 49,020 pounds sterling (courtesy Kevin Troubridge).

mm, CR rose from 10.2 to 10.5, plus an e34 M50 525i intake manifold. Sports cams and power chip took output to 221 bhp, with Hartge sports exhaust making that 231 bhp at 6,000 rpm and 221 lbs./ft. at 4,900 rpm. The 0–62 mph time dropped to 6.7 seconds, and top speed rose to 154 mph, which was why the "2.8" script on the intake manifold was in red!

Higher up was the Hartge H5–3.2 with 3,172 cc I6. With bore and stroke dimensions of 86/91 mm and 10.5 CR, this package made 265 bhp at 6,200 rpm and 239 lbs./ft. at 4,000 rpm. On top of this, Hartge did a mild 3.5 I6 for the H5–3.5 with a 3,478 cc (86/100 mm) 280 bhp output at 6,000 rpm, and 280 lbs./ft. at 4,200 rpm on a 10.5 CR. A special hotter 3.5 with larger 86.4 mm pistons, and displacement of 3,485 cc, was available for the e36 M3 3.2. This version used standard M3 Evo conrods, a glued spacer to lower the CR from 10.8 to 10.5, special intake manifold and rechip, plus a red "3.5" on the cylinder head. The output was a huge 350 bhp at 6,800 rpm with 295 lbs./ft. at 4,350 rpm.

More restrained upgrades came in the form of rechips for the 530d's ECU, taking outputs to 220 and 231 bhp for pre– and post–2001 MY cars, respectively. If one liked the M62 540i, then Hartge's H5–5.0 350 bhp conversion made things more appealing still. Birds, the UK Hartge agent, started to offer Dinan supercharger kits from late 1996. These kits used a Powerdyne blower limited to 9.6 psi boost, and poly-vee belt drive from a custom crank pulley with auto tensioner, making the arrangement maintenance free. Bigger capacity injectors and remapped ECU took care of boost enrichment. The Spirit S28 pack for the 528i made 276 bhp, and the S42 kit for the 540i was rated at 422 bhp.

Hartge also had a carbon fiber Ram Air induction kit for the 540i and M5, plus sports cam M5 set. A sports cat for the e39 M5 was good for an extra 30 bhp. To keep the extra hp in check, cars without EDC could have a sports suspension kit that lowered ride height, by 35 mm on I6 e39s and 25 mm on V8s. Hartge rims were 18 × 8.5 inches with 245/40 tires, or with larger 19 × 9.5-inch rims out back with 245/35 or 275/30 ZR covers. Hartge claimed their sports suspension and 19-inch combo produced good ride comfort on the e39.

For appearance, a Hartge H5 e39 car could have a special front spoiler, rear apron, and aerofoil rear wing, plus a pair of Hartge roundel badges. Like Alpina there was also a Hartge large design stripe insignia body decal kit, blue in color and measuring 150 × 50 mm. On the inside your e39 could be sportified with an 11-piece carbon fiber interior trim kit.

The Increasingly Popular AC Schnitzer

In 1986 the Kohl group switched its association from Hartge, at the Hartge brothers' choice, to Schnitzer. In short order AC Schnitzer became a German tuning household name, and by the e39's release, product development had moved in-house. However, Team Schnitzer still did the motors. The early AC Schnitzer e39 528i-based S5 2.8 had a special intake manifold, rechip and sports exhaust for 218 bhp and 0–62 mph in 7.1 seconds for the manual, 8.4 seconds for the auto. The S5 2.8 came with special front spoiler, teardrop mirrors, side skirts, roof spoiler and a choice of 2 rear spoilers.

In September 1996 BMW (GB) Ltd. became the distributor for AC Schnitzer in the UK. For the previous 6 years the concession had been handled by a specialist. Upwards from the S5 2.8, was the 3.2 liter S5 3.2. AC Schnitzer deals with engines on an exchange basis, doing headwork, including a special block, forged crank, special pistons and sports rear muffler made of V2A steel, plus the ubiquitous rechip. Early S5 3.2s had 260 bhp, and 244 lbs./ft. at 4,200 rpm and could do 160 mph with 0–62 mph in 6.9 seconds. Later 3.2s were re-rated to 235 bhp and 252 lbs./ft. at 3,000 rpm.

For the 540i, AC Schnitzer continued to offer their 315 bhp hop-up kit for the 4.4 V8. This involved sports cams, heavy-duty valve springs, sports rear muffler and a rechip; torque increased to 326 lbs/ft. There was also the e39 M5-based ACS5 Sport, which involved adding a different intake manifold kit, rechip and sports rear muffler. A DFC (Damper Force Control) sports suspension set with electronically controlled shocks was specially developed for the e39 M5 and tested on the north loop of the Nürburgring, and in town for civility.

The ACS5 Sport got an "S5 Sport" trunk lid decal, and was the only ACS5 variant to receive a rear wing with a carbon fiber strip and integrated brake light. Regular e39s, with or without self-leveling, can have sports suspension that lowers ride height by 30 mm. For a more rigid body and better handling there is the 520i–540i sway bar kit, adjustable with 2 settings, and an aluminum strut tower brace. AC Schnitzer Type II (16 × 8 inch) and Type III (19 × 9.5 inch) rims are around, the latter being 30 percent lighter.

BMW didn't release an official e39 M5 Touring, so one simply visited Hartge, chose the H5-5.0 V-8 option/assorted hardware and voila (courtesy Hartge, http://www.hartge.de).

Body kit parts are made of PU-Rim material, and powered/heated sports mirrors with AC Schnitzer script inset can be complemented by AC Schnitzer body decals and pinstriping. Indeed, a short shift kit has an aluminum shift knob with the words "Short Shift," plus a picture of a race helmet with open visor. Interior trim can be in silver or anthracite as part of a nine-piece set. On request there can be a carbon fiber cover for the e39's dash monitor.

Steering wheels can be a 3-spoker with root wood and Nappa calf leather or carbon fiber trim with perforated leather grips. The normal BMW multifunction wheel, with leather/carbon fiber trim added, can also be selected. TV monitors are available for the front headrests, with a 310 kph speedo listed for special request. After all, according to their slogan, the ACS5 e39 is "Made by winners, made for fun."

Motorsport Tuning the MK Way

MK-Motorsport knows how to hot up an e39 too; their "Engine kits A" and "B" are good for 30 bhp gains (520d–540i). They include a sports air filter, MK-muffler, rechip and speed limiter removal on the faster e39s. The "B" kit for the 523i/528i also includes sports cams, allowing the cars to hit 148 and 158 mph respectively. Then there is the "MK-streamline system I" and "II" for the 530i, where "I" has a header, steel cat, exhaust with

76 mm pipes, rechip/speed delimit and sports air filter. It meets Euro 3/D4 emissions law and adds 38 bhp/44 lbs./ft. "II" brings sports cams and special power chip for 65 extra ponies.

"MK-supercharger-system" kits boost an early 520i to 240 bhp, with the stage II 530i version reaching 376 bhp. The company's bore/stroke kits prove the adage that there's no replacement for displacement. These kits consist of a new crank, rods, pistons, cams, sports air filter and end muffler. For example, "MK engine C" takes a 520i to 2.8 liters and 225 bhp, "MK engine K" makes the 540i a 5-liter car with 400 lbs./ft. and a 177-mph-plus top speed. Kit "K" also includes the "MK header" and steel cat, with MK's special intake manifold (referred to as "big suction pipe") worth over 15 bhp. MK also does their own design carbon fiber valve covers for the I6s.

AC Schnitzer's 3.2-liter version of BMW's I6 is as good as that of any other respected tuner, plus the firm's five-spoke rim design is a key point of distinction (courtesy AC Schnitzer, http://www.ac-schnitzer.de/en/).

To arrest forward progress, count on the "MK brake system BS355/6 kit." Front grooved 355 mm disks, 6 piston calipers, stainless steel brake lines, aluminum parts, special pads and racing brake fluid are provided. It needs a fitting set with two 6 mm spacers and 10 special wheel screws. MK also sells cross-drilled disks.

For suspension, MK's 520i–530i/d spring set lowers the front 50 mm, and rear by 30 mm; ditto for the 535i/540i. All e39 Tourings without self–leveling can have a 50 mm front and 15 mm rear lowering job. There are MK shocks, and a strut tower brace for I6 e39s in aluminum or blue carbon fiber, plus sway bar sets for I6 and V8 e39s. On the exhaust end, MK's header is good for an extra 3–5 bhp, and the stainless steel header for the V8 is claimed to bring up to 23 horses.

With wheels MK has a one-piece MK-1, 18 × 8.5 inches front with 235/40 ZR18s, 18 × 10 inches with 255/35 or 265/35 ZR18s at the back. Rims are available in a wide range of colors at extra cost. The two-piece MK-2 uses titanium nuts, with one wheel screw of this sturdy design serving as the valve. Front and rear can be 18 × 8.5 inches with 235/40 or 245/40 ZR18s. Larger 18 × 10-inch rear rims with 255/35, 265/35 or even 275/35 ZR18s can be substituted. MK's one-piece MK-3 comes in a 19 × 9-inch size, with 245/35 front and 275/30 ZR19s rear. The MK-3 can be presented in a "chrome line" finish. Cosmetically one's MK e39 can have a front spoiler, rear wing and MK-color-line Shadowline in chrome or black.

For the e39 M5 a rechip alone adds 20 bhp, with "MK Engine kit A" including a header, end muffler and ECU delimit for 48 bhp and 189 mph. Kit "B" uses a "streamline header" and equals 50 bhp, kit "C" adds an air filter, MK steel cat, MK cams, modified head/combustion chambers for 100 bhp! Just for the M5 is a stainless steel "MK-performance end muffler set," with a hand-made muffler (wider cross section) and 76 mm pipe exit, worth 10 bhp alone. Also, 30 mm lowering springs, MK-2 or MK-3 rims and the MK BS355/6 brake set can be added to the M5.

This time there is a choice of cross-drilled front disks, plus the usual brake hardware made of aircraft-quality aluminum that make up the set. MK throw in their ceramic competition sport brake pads and for the rear, as per regular e39s, the M5 can have cross-drilled disks for the standard rear calipers. For the body only the M5 can have MK's rear wing, and this item comes with MK special glue!

In the multimedia age automatics are welcome at tuning houses. AC Schnitzer is happy to deal with BMW's Steptronic, but only the M5-based ACS5 Sport gets their rear wing (courtesy AC Schnitzer, http://www.ac-schnitzer.de/en/).

MK-Motorsport offers a range of supercharger kits for the e39 5 series, hence the "Kompressor" tag on this 540i (courtesy MK-Motorsport, http://www.mk-motorsport.de).

Breyton Design — Setting the Wheels in Motion

In keeping with the future of tuning, Breyton Design, established 1982, was started by a computer tech engineer rather than a racer. Edmund Breyton helped design the early AMG body kits and rims of the '80s, with Breyton Design making its name exporting alloy wheel sets to North America and Asia, unusual for a Euro tuner. The firm has set great store by CAD/CAM design technology, and gained fame for its "Softline" (1994) and "Competition" (1995) rim designs.

Since late 1996 Breyton, like others, produced a 3.2-liter version of the e39 528i. The reworking of Breyton's engines was carried out under the watchful eye of Martin Eppinger, a former Formula 3 engine builder. Breyton's 3.2 had dimensions of 86.4/92 mm, gas flowed head, emissions-friendly sports cams, 7,500 rpm redline valve springs and a new steel billet crank, lighter con rods, 10.2 CR, sports air filter and a fuel pressure regulator permitting 4 metric bar of pressure, instead of the usual 3. The rechipped I6 motor used the large capacity injectors of the old M30 3.5 liter I6 to make 264 bhp and 254 lbs./ft.

The early Breyton e39 body kit had a subtle front spoiler that integrated with the stock lower valence, and a rear apron with cutout for Breyton's oval exhaust and slimline reversing side mirrors. A later style body kit for facelifted 2001 e39s is available with side skirts and revised side mirrors. Breyton's sports suspension was based on a 528i with M-Tech. Front springs were reduced by 40 mm and the rears by 10 mm.

Initial choices were 17–18 inch Softline or Competition styles, 225/45 ZR17s at each corner or four 235/40 ZR18s, or with larger rear footwear, 245/40 ZR17s and 265/35 ZR18s respectively. Later and larger rims were introduced as the 20 × 9.5-inch "Magic Sport" and the "Type Seven." All of Breyton Design's work naturally carries German TÜV approval.

Top: Flying the flag for MK-Motorsport, the BMW e39 can accept their one-piece 19-inch MK-3 rim style (courtesy MK-Motorsport, http://www.mk-motorsport.de). ***Bottom:*** Observe a post-2001 e39 5 series wearing Breyton Design's Magic Sport rims, available in a huge 20 × 9.5-inch size (courtesy Breyton Design, http://www.breyton.com/).

For Bimmer to Bentley — Visit Hamann

Hamann Motorsport started in 1987. Its founder Richard Hamann raced in various categories: motorcycles, open wheelers, touring cars, sports cars and even with the BMW M1. He once held the lap record at the Nürburgring Nordschleife. As a tuning house Hamann liked to fit large, normally aspirated engines and effect custom requests. Their 420 bhp 5.8 liter 850i conversion gained notoriety. Over time the business became more formal and today their tuning line covers BMW, plus Mini, Porsche, Ferrari, Lamborghini, Land Rover and even Bentley!

In late 1996 Hamann was producing the Hamann 532i, an e39 curtain raiser with a 350 bhp version of the e36 M3 Evo's 3.2 I6. A "350" trunk lid decal was a little clue, and the car's body kit was an even bigger one. The front spoiler/rear apron, side skirts, roof spoiler and trunk wing were set off by 5-spoke rims made for Hamann by OZ Racing. The rims used 1-inch spacers and the fender lips were slightly flared for tire clearance. Hamann's sports suspension still retained decent ride comfort. The prototype car was lowered 40/25 mm front/rear, changing to 40 mm and 20 mm on later Hamann e39s. Tourings are just lowered at the front by 40 mm, with an adjustable aluminum strut tower brace available for I6 e39s in general.

The simplest thing one can get from Hamann is a rechip, necessitating Super Plus 98 octane gas if the best is going to be derived from a gasoline e39. Expect a 15 bhp gain on I6 cars, 25 bhp on the V8 535i/540i. On the 520d power becomes 163 bhp with 249 lbs./ft. at 1,750 rpm and 0–62 mph down to 9.8 seconds. More involved are Hamann's bore and stroke conversions for I6 and V8 e39s. There is the HM 2.6 pack (2,532 cc) with 194 bhp, 220 bhp HM 2.8 (2,791 cc), 240 bhp HM 3.0 (2,977 cc), two HM 3.2s (3,143 cc and 3,151 cc) with 261/265 bhp for Single and Double Vanos 528is respectively, plus a 286 bhp HM 3.3 (3,268 cc) motor topping the I6 range.

Owners of the 540i can enlist the HM 4.8 (4,784 cc) kit for 350 bhp, or the HM 5.0 (4,941 cc) pack with 360 bhp. Hamann's sports mufflers improve looks and efficiency. Made of V2A stainless steel, the 2-pipe (76 mm) version is complemented by a raised-pipe "Racing Look" edition, plus a 4-pipe export-only version! The Hamann header/cat 540i/M5 pack is export-only too. Hamann's brake kit includes two 355 × 32 mm slotted/vented front disks and two 4-pot front calipers, which are painted red with other colors involving a surcharge. Special pads and Stahlflex brake lines are also in the mix.

Hamann has an e39 hood with natty vent slots, and did a special e39 aero study special edition called "Daytona Beach." Chrome-plated air vents were let into the front fenders and rear steel fender extensions were welded in. Hamann's "Competition" front spoiler and special side skirts completed the picture. Wheels are always important in a tuner's portfolio, and Hamann has a split-rim 5-spoke "PG3," which is painted silver with polished flange treatment available as a 19 × 9-inch set, or with bigger 19 × 10, and 19 × 11-inch rear rims.

Hamann's "Anniversary" model is a one-piece, split-rim, multi–spoke affair painted silver with a polished INOX stainless steel protection lip, sized 19 × 8.5 inches, or with 19 × 10-inch rear rims. When putting Hamann rims on an e39 with RDC one needs Hamann's "Tire Pressure Check Sensor System." More commonly purchased is Hamann's e39 short shift kit. Gasoline cars may have a 300 kph speedo which requires Hamann's recalibrated speedo module. Pre–2001 MY e39s can be fitted with Hamann kidney grille trims. There's also an aluminum handbrake lever, plus an aluminum oil filler cap.

The "Hamann Threaded Sports Suspension" kit involves coil over, height-adjustable shocks, allowing the front and rear to be lowered by as much as 60 mm and 30 mm respectively. It helps the e39 M5 deal with the ol' Ring, and Hamann's standard or "Racing Look" 4-pipe (80 mm) sports mufflers make it sound better while doing so. Natural choice for the

At first BMW didn't think about doing an e39 M5, but the presence of hot sedans from Daimler-Benz, Audi and Jaguar made it change course (courtesy Taylor E. Spalt).

M5 would be the PG3 rim, 19 × 10 inches with 275/30 ZR tires front, 19 × 12 inches with 335/25 rubber rearwards.

Enhance the M5's look with a rear diffuser fitted to the stock rear apron, or for substance attach the "Hamann Sport kit HM/M450," another export-only item. HM/M450 includes Hamann's header, steel cats, sports mufflers with 4 (76 mm) pipes, sports air filter and ECU remap with speed delimit for a claimed 187–190 mph. The "450" tag stands for the engine's new output. Torque is also 26 lbs./ft. up on stock.

Motorsport Discovers the V8—e39 M5

There wasn't going to be an e39 M5 originally; BMW thought a 540i with sports suspension/6 speed would be enough. Management was using the M tag liberally on the company's smaller cars, which saw M3s with automatic transmission and quasi–M power plants, i.e., 240 bhp S52 U.S. 3.2 I6. BMW's rivals also poured on the pressure with cars like the MB E50 and E55, Jaguar XJR I6 and V8s, Audi S8 and even BMW's semi-in-house buddy, the Alpina B10 4.6. It was like BMW forgot to turn up at its own birthday party!

BMW's 4.9-liter V-8 made 400 bhp in ECE terms. The S62 V-8 carried the same rating worldwide, but U.S. versions had the catalytic converters placed closer to the motor due to stricter pollution laws (courtesy Brian Beckman).

BMW got busy and the e39 M5 made its debut at the Geneva Motor Show, with production starting in October 1998 and the model arriving in the U.S. during fall 1999. The new M5 had a freshly cast 4,941 cc V8 version of the Alusil M62, denoted S62. With bore and stroke of 94/89 mm it was the first M engine with hydraulic lifters, and featured Double Vanos with increased water jacket area and coolant passages around the intake ports, plus a sky-high 11-to-one CR. The S62's oil-cooled pistons were unique to each V8 bank.

Among the fine touches were hollow cams, 3-layer steel head gaskets, and 2 suction pumps to help return oil from the cam covers, cylinder head and block back to the sump using electromagnetic valves controlled by the lateral force sensors of the M5's DSC. This safeguard worked even when DSC was off. Cautionary yellow lights circled the rev counter from 4,500 rpm to the 7-grand redline. Extinguishing one by one as the motor warmed up, they let the driver know how soon and how hard the V8 could be worked. Such a "keep off the grass" signpost is necessary because in the cockpit they can't hear the V8 scream!

Sitting atop the V8's aluminum plenum chamber was a "BMW M Power" script on a carbon fiber plaque and that familiar M logo with tri-color livery. The V8's ECU was represented by Siemens MSS 5.2, with power rated as 400 bhp at 6,600 rpm and 368 lbs./ft. at 3,800 rpm. BMW claimed 0–62 mph in 5.3 seconds, but top speed was limited to 155 mph. With weight at 3,863 lbs., good brakes were needed and supplied by vented floating (front) disks, 13.6 inches front, 12.9 inches rear. U.S. e39 M5s missed out on the 2-piece

A Dinan-enhanced e39 M5. The U.S. tuner had its own line of wheels and suspension to take the Motorsport sedan in a different direction (courtesy Mark Odom).

floating disks. The other difference between Euro and U.S. M5s was closer cat placement to the engine on the U.S. edition, due to stricter emissions law.

The M5's gearbox was once again the Getrag Type D 6-speed, but stronger than the e39 540i's version. The M5 also capitalized on the e39's aluminum suspension, with appropriate reinforcement. There were firmer shocks, bigger sway bars, polyurethane rather than rubber bushings, and steel ball joints. The M5 sat 15 mm lower at the front and 10 mm lower at the back compared to regular e39s and quicker Servotronic V8 steering, with ratio changed from 17.9 to 14.7:1. A dash "Sport" button sharpened the M5's fly-by-wire electronic throttle response and altered the power steering pump valving to give the recirculating ball helm more weight.

The M5 had a subtle body kit of front spoiler, side skirts and rear apron, which was applied to the facelifted 2001 e39 Sport variants. The M5's trunk spoiler was a delete option. The M5 side mirrors could fold up electrically. The e39 M5 had a reasonably slippery drag coefficient of 0.31, in spite of wide Parallel Spoke II alloys with Satin chrome finish, 18 × 8 inches with 245/40 tires front, 18 × 9.5 inches with 275/35 ZR tires rear. The M5's instrument binnacle gauges had aluminum bezels, and an oil temp gauge replaced the e39's econometer. There were 2 designs of steering wheel, the later style for the 2001 MY being the same as for the e46 M3. Gray gauge faces arrived for '01, along with other e39 fresheners.

E39 M5 interiors consisted of the "Sport" with aluminum trim panels (not available in North America), the U.S. M5's Sport trim had Bruyere Club wood, and the "Exclusive"

This 2001 (January build date) RHD UK spec e39 M5 was featured on the cover of the September 2004 issue of *Used Car Buyer* magazine (courtesy Gary W. Gillespie).

had walnut burl panels. The "Exclusive" tag was later changed to "Luxury" in the North American market. There was a choice of Extended Leather or Complete Leather. The power rear sunblind was not available with Complete Leather, due to Alcantara trim on the rear parcel shelf. Complete Leather also featured Alcantara for the headliner, A pillar, upper B pillar and C pillar. The 2000 MY was the end for Complete Leather in North America, so for the '01 MY the Alcantara headliner was included with Extended Leather. U.S. M5s had power moonroofs standard, and all M5s had an illuminated shift pattern.

BMW made at least one prototype e39 M5 Touring, with Titanium Silver paint and black Exclusive Leather interior, but BMW thought there wouldn't be enough demand. The irony was that the e39 M5 turned out to be the best-selling M5 to that point in time: 20,482 e39 M5 sedans rolled off the normal 5 series Dingolfing assembly line. Motorsport itself couldn't cope with such volume, and the opposition couldn't match the e39 M5; in that respect it was a real M car!

11

The e60 5 Series

The Mold Breaker

Styling—Bangle in Search of Truth and Beauty

The new e60 5 series enjoyed a glittering unveiling at the 56th International Film Festival in Cannes on May 22, 2003. Glittering and fitting because the e60 has been the most outlandish 5 series to date, its slogan in television and print advertisements declaring "100% Drive, 0% Compromise." It has also marked a transition from BMW's brash old line of "The Ultimate Driving Machine," to the softer "Sheer Driving Pleasure." One constant has been the need to make the 5 series hold true to BMW's tradition of fun and quality motoring, which implied retention of rear drive.

BMW manager Guenther Seemann summed up the situation succinctly in June 2007: "It's also an issue of sportiness. You do not find a Formula One car with front-wheel drive." The 5 series continued to be manufactured at BMW's biggest factory, the Dingolfing works. At the commencement of e60 assembly, Dingolfing had 23,000 workers making 1,250 cars as a mix of 3, 5 and 7 series per day. Even bigger was the change in styling direction that accompanied engineering additions, which made the e60 one of the most controversial new cars.

This was the first Five to receive stylistic guidance from Chris Bangle and Adrian van Hooydonk; specifically, the e60/e61 exterior was penned by David Arcangeli. The end result was efficient: the slim e60 520i had a Cd value of just 0.26 and top speed of 143 mph, but with a sting in the tail. BMW felt that in ever more competitive times it was necessary to distinguish its cars from the pursuing pack. In the words of BMW's head of product and technology communications Thomas Gubitz, "We have to make sure our cars don't become boring. Our designs may prompt some negative comments, but we don't want to be mediocre."

So it was that the new e60 sported the e65 7 series' controversial blend of convex and concave shapes known as "flame surfacing." A bold profile swage line, highlight headlight eyebrows and tea tray rear deck, it was a courageous break from evolutionary Bimmer styling. Chris Bangle had something to say on the matter: "Humans need time to get used to newness." As discussion on BMW's new look got slightly toxic, Bangle offered this July 2004 retort to the critics: "Hey, we're talking about cars here, back off. We're not dropping bombs on people." It's just as well no one mentioned the Edsel!

Top: The U.S. e39 M5 came with a power moonroof standard, and its V-8 had enough thrust to reach the moon (courtesy Gary T. Kerr). ***Bottom:*** An Orient Blue e60 520i in Hong Kong. This 520i has PIAA 4700 KXtreme Force halogens, K&N high-flow air filter and non-runflat Dunlop Sport Maxx tires (courtesy Bunbun).

Chris Bangle stated the need to combine truth and beauty; he felt Marilyn Monroe had managed this and sincerely believed the e60 5 series had too. It's left to individuals to assess the veracity of this claim, and it seemed that the e60's spec sheet could create contention too. The latest Five brought several devices, some from the e65 7 series and some new to BMW as well as the 5 series itself. For a car known for its good handling, steering is a logical place to start.

Those Wacky e60 Gadgets

The e60 featured Active Steering (AS), a system combining quick and slow steering response on the one car. AS was a world first and standard e60 equipment in a few markets like Australia. Figure in a planetary gearset with 2 input shafts, and one output shaft integrated in the split steering column. The first input shaft was connected to the steering wheel; the second was driven by electric motor via a self-inhibiting helical gearwheel that reduced the gearing ratio.

AS had a separate ECU and cut the number of turns lock-to-lock to just 1.7, initially, making parking and low-speed maneuvers a piece of cake. At freeway speeds AS became more indirect, that is, slower. One wouldn't wish a car's steering to be videogame quick, like Pole Position, while executing a high speed lane change. As a system AS worked with DSC III, Dynamic Stability Control being a standard e60 feature monitoring yaw rate and steering angle changes. AS made DSC work less.

The e60 also had a talent for seeing around corners, if Adaptive Headlights (AH) were fitted. As with the old Citroen DS, AH implied bi-xenon front lamps that could swivel up to 15 degrees. AH moved the lights according to steering angle, yaw rate and road speed, and it also knew when to shut off. AH knew when you were stopped at traffic lights with wheels turned, or reversing, and in those situations it slept. Another e60 lighting trick, from the e65, was Brake Force Display (BFD). BFD enlarged brake lamp area during emergency braking.

Another e65 derived lesson was the inclusion of thinking sway bars; BMW called it Dynamic Drive (DD). DD cut e60 body roll when cornering, with the system made up of two active sway bars, valve block with sensors, dual oil pumps, accelerometer and ECU. DD took no action when the car went straight; it had a swivel servo motor working on half the sway bar to curb body roll and give the driver a greater sense of security and control. This was yet another area of interest for motorists attending the BMW display at the 60th International Frankfurt Motor Show in September 2003.

There were many attractions on show with the e60, including its Tire Defect Indicator (TDI). TDI observed wheel speed/revolutions using ABS system signals, providing the driver with a warning light and acoustic signal. In order for TDI to work, the car had to be moving at or greater than 15 kph, with a loss in tire pressure over 30 percent, whereupon

Opposite, top: **The e60 545i was the successor to the e39 540i, retailing for $54,300 on its 2004 MY North American debut. Note that for the Chinese region the e60 was available in long-wheelbase "Li" form to compete with that market's successful stretched Audi A6.** ***Opposite, bottom:*** **The label may have read 545i, but the e60's N62B44 Valvetronic V-8 actually displaced 4.4 liters. However, it made 333 bhp so complaints were few (courtesy David Flanigan).**

DF 30

"Tire Defect" appeared in the instrument display. This system lacks the sensitivity of BMW's older tire pressure monitoring system, and there have been cases of blowouts where the driver has received no dash warning.

Having TDI assumed greater importance with the e60 5 series, since a large percentage have been fitted with special runflat tires. The original entry-level e60 520i was fitted with Trapeze pattern 16 × 7-inch rims wearing 225/55 tires and a space saver. In the U.S. the 530i was issued with all-season 225/50 17-inchers as stock equipment. However, go one level higher and it was all runflats, with the exception of the M5. Runflats weren't new—recall the Dunlop Denovos fitted to Mini 1275 GTs in the '70s—but the construction properties offered on the Bimmer runflats were different.

In Europe new Fives with 17-inch tires, or larger, got runflats. These super tires had reinforced sidewalls, support strips and temperature-resistant rubber compound. Thus, one could do 80 kph for 150 km on flat tires, even with a full load. Independent tests have shown that a BMW with 4 completely deflated runflats can still be driven safely, without too much of a negative impact on handling. Even in a deflated state all 5 series safety equipment like ABS and DSC III continue to operate. The setup used specially contoured double rim humps (EH2) to prevent the punctured tire from jumping off the rim.

Five series owners still had the option of fitting a normal tire, since the rim would accept such fare. But that returned one to that old standby, the space saver, with the inconvenience of having to change a flat. The DeLorean DMC 12 had its full-size spare mounted on an optional rear window luggage rack, but such solutions are considered too avant-garde in the 21st century. The debate on the best way to prepare for a flat continues. At least the e60 was making light work of slippery conditions, with Dynamic Traction Control (DTC) as part of DSC III.

Unlike most rivals DSC III could still be turned off on the 5 series, although DSC III did come on automatically when the car was started, and in wintry conditions it was wise to leave it on. DTC was thinking traction control, permitting some rear-wheel slippage where beneficial. In deep snow, slush or mud the driver would want the rear wheels to turn a little, so the drive wheels could get some bite. DTC obliged in such scenarios. To activate DTC one depressed the DSC button for a continuous period. While DTC was operational, DSC III intruded later than usual.

Next on the list of labor savers was Active Cruise Control (ACC). ACC used a 77 GHz radar sensor to check on the distance between cars, and was capable of detecting a vehicle nearly 400 ft. ahead. The system cut engine power with application of the brakes and engine braking where necessary to maintain a programmed vehicle distance. ACC could get an e60 back up to speed once a safe distance was restored, but it couldn't actually stop the car. In cases where strong braking was required, the driver got an optical and acoustic signal.

The e60 put the 5 series well and truly into the modern drive-by-wire era. Get rid of mechanical linkages, or combine hydraulic devices with ECU brains to produce smart brakes and considerate suspension, with a view to helping the driver. Many such automated aids and warning devices used to be found only on something like a Boeing 767. In the late sixties BMW was proud of its multi-colored warning light grid introduced on the dashpod of the e3 sedan. The engineers looked forward to the day when audible warnings would become possible on cars, and that day had arrived!

Even the humble S.I. indicator system could now inform the driver how far until the

Unveilings at the Cannes Film Festival and Frankfurt Motor Show were all well and good, but it was the e60's showroom response that really counted. Fortunately the German public warmed to the Five that Bangle built (courtesy Ulrich Thieme, http://www.e12.de).

next oil change, plus the month and year of the next service. However, BMW's modern info star has been "iDrive," a system first seen on the e65 7 series. Think of it as Windows for motorists, replacing hordes of dash buttons with a graphic menu presentation where the PC's mouse is replaced by a "Controller" dial selector. iDrive was revised for inclusion on the e60, to make it more user-friendly.

On the 5 series the Controller was sited with the shifter and handbrake in the center console. With basic versions of the e60 a 5.8-inch b/w monitor was originally utilized, but choosing GPS sat nav or the deluxe climate control option upgraded matters to a 6.5-inch color screen with 8-bit color resolution. iDrive menu zones involved communication, navigation, entertainment, climate control and a fifth area, accessed by pressing the Controller in the main menu, covering presets.

iDrive improvements for e60 usage involved a better color-coded display, the ability to program presets for favorite functions, and a default "Menu" button allowing the driver to return to the main iDrive screen. The last was useful since iDrive is somewhat reminiscent of that old videogame Gauntlet. After wandering through a labyrinth it's easy to lose track of position. Other e60 driver aids included a standard multifunction steering wheel and the option of Head-Up Display (HUD).

Exactly the same price was demanded by the 530i and 530d. However, the 530d shown exacted a lower fuel usage penalty and unlike the 520i/530i didn't use carry-over e39 motors (courtesy Mick Jones).

HUD allowed a number of dashboard info items to be displayed on the windshield, directly in the driver's line of vision so he didn't have to take his eyes off the road. Such updates covered navigation instructions as guidance arrows, information and instructions for ACC, speed and various Check Control system warnings. HUD worked via a projector built into the instrument panel, with a rain and light sensor that adjusted display brightness. HUD was new to the 5 series, but it wasn't a new idea.

BMW's Park Distance Control (PDC) ultrasonic distance measurement device had been seen on the e39, but now the acoustic beep was backed up by an optional top-down-view graphic display. Obstructive objects that could dent the e60's sheet metal during a parking maneuver were shown as colored sections. The e60 could also be equipped with a dual band telephone with cordless handpiece, or the more popular "Bluetooth" option. Bluetooth represents a universal mobile phone preparation kit, interfacing with mobile phones without cables or wiring. The mobile phone must be Bluetooth compatible, and many are these days. When the e60 was first rolled out, choices were limited to the Nokia 6310, Ericsson T39 or Siemens S55. A Bluetooth-compatible phone started working within 33 feet of the car, and the 5 series owner could operate a phone via the multifunction wheel and dash display. Hands-free operation, a center console snap-in phone adapter/battery charger, and the ability to work up to 4 different phones are necessities, not luxuries, in modern times. The user's contact diary and phone functions could be stored and executed via the iDrive interface. The e60's audio/multimedia facilities could also be enjoyed using iDrive.

The e60's 530d engine brought several technical upgrades compared to the outgoing e39. Output was now 218 bhp, with micro-hole injectors used in the Euro 4 emissions-compliant 3-liter (courtesy Mick Jones).

On the audio front, the e60 was the first Five to be unavailable with a cassette deck; on its debut, the first musical rung was the "BMW Business Radio" with single-disc CD player and 6 speakers. Next up was the "BMW Professional Radio" with 10 speakers, followed by having a 6-disc CD changer located in the glovebox and a 6-disc DVD changer for CD/audio/video multimedia experiences. The last piece of hardware found a home in the e60's trunk, behind a flap in the left-hand wheel arch. The 5 series navigation system imparted directions using a voice facility/graphic arrows, drawing upon road traffic information from the BMW Professional Radio. With dynamic route guidance it worked out the quickest trip.

Top of the audio tree was the Harman Kardon 13-speaker LOGIC7 Professional hi-fi system with digital audio signal processing mode for 2-channel stereo signals and multimedia multi-channel signals. A matrix circuit split up every signal of an analogue or digital stereo recording into 7 individual signals. The signals were then specially processed in keeping with the car's interior. Acoustically a car isn't a great place to hear music, so technology tries to bridge the physical shortcomings of the environment.

LOGIC7 also added rear audio controls using a wireless remote control that worked through the iDrive control display menu. "Headset mode" allowed choices to be affected for rear seat occupants who took advantage of the two headphone console sockets. Basically

Open the pod bay doors HAL ... please? The e60's iDrive wasn't as scary as *2001: A Space Odyssey*'s HAL 9000, but it wasn't exactly intuitive either (courtesy Mick Jones).

the kids in the back could listen to Britney Spears without annoying the 5 series' other occupants. In other ways the Five's interior wasn't so divided. The e60 was the first Five since the e12 not to have BMW's once-famous angled dashboard, an ergonomic delight for the driver that left the front passenger out in the cold.

The latest Five had the dual binnacle dash look found on the e65 7 series and Z4 roadster, complemented by four choices of interior trim: Titanium II Dark, Aluminum Wave, Maplewood and Poplarwood. The e60 also received a new interior color scheme option on release, "Truffle Brown" combined with natural black, and three kinds of leather. The base cowhide was Dakota, followed by the microperforated climate control leather known as Nasca. Top of the line was the soft, extra-sumptuous Nappa leather choice denoted Exclusive.

Standard fitment for a normal Euro e60 was a flat weave cloth used on the "Basic" e60 seat, but as with the e39 there was more. Slim, sporty types went for the e60 Sport seat, while those wanting it all selected the Multifunction seat, which was the Comfort seat option. The Multifunction seat featured side bolsters that altered shape to give more support during hard cornering, and anti-whiplash pyrotechnically activated headrests to protect occupants during collisions.

Seat heating elements were optional, and if one selected Nasca leather it was possible to have variable speed blowers in both the seat squab and backrest. These blowers pumped

Unlike the e39 5 series, the e60/e61 enjoyed Double Vanos efficiency on the gasoline sixes and eights. Previously the only V-8 e39 to have DV was the M5 (courtesy BMW).

air through the seats, a handy device for warm climates where the 5 series may be parked *sans* shade cover for long periods. To cope with all possible climatic extremes there was a heating element for the rear seating too. Indeed, the rear backrest of the e60 sedan was an interesting technical item.

Normally split-fold seats would imply loss of the unibody's rear steel bulkhead panel located behind the back seats. To get around the loss of torsional rigidity the e60's rear seat backrest was itself reinforced and load-bearing. The backrest was a tubular steel frame hybrid structure embedded in a plastic coating, with the steel frame connected to the e60 unibody at four points. This made for load versatility while maintaining passive safety. Thus the e60 could have retrofittable through-loading and 60/40 split backrest with a choice of integrated ski bag, cooling box, storage compartment or sports bag in the "60" part of the backrest.

Storage versatility was matched by a very versatile HVAC system. Both standard and deluxe climate control systems fitted could be adjusted by the Controller, with choices viewable in the iDrive's Control Display screen. The deluxe setup had the added functionality of being able to control the right/left side interior temps, auto air volume and ventilation through the central dash vent with infinite adjustability, plus individual control of upper body air temperature.

The deluxe a/c's bi-directional solar sensors sensed the sun's effect on each side of the

Top: A BMW 330d in France. The e90 3 series was BMW's next attempt with runflats, and is considered the first runflat-tired Bimmer with acceptable ride comfort (courtesy Paul Baylis). *Bottom:* The e39 Touring lived on into the 2004 MY before giving way to the new e61 Touring, shown. This was the first time a 5 series sedan and Touring possessed different model codes (courtesy Nuno Forneas).

The e61's "Panorama Roof" had historical precedent in the e34 Touring's Double-Lever Sliding Sunroof option (courtesy BMW).

car, allowing precise adjustment of interior air temperature. Provisions for the rear seat's HVAC outlet were detailed too, with stratified rear air possible from this vent. To combat interior misting the e60's deluxe a/c had a window sensor that made the system go off recirculation mode/raise blower speed to get rid of interior moisture prior to final cooldown.

Then there were allowances for those times when your 5 series was left outside unoccupied in all climes. The e60's fresh air blower would run when the car was parked with the engine off, so the vent system could keep the interior a little cooler. Thus, the a/c didn't have quite so much to do when the car was restarted. However, if a high level of pollutants was sensed, the system automatically went to recirc mode as part of Automatic Air Recirculation (AAR). For those times when things got chilly, warm engine coolant was pumped through the HVAC heat exchanger when the e60 was left stationary.

Both standard and deluxe a/c systems had a new feature for the Five, in that they cooled only as much as was necessary. An external sensor monitored air temp and informed the a/c to cut the interior temp without making the air too dry. Finance permitting, one could also spring for the optional Comfort Glass, which involved infrared reflecting glass all round. Comfort Glass was claimed by BMW to reduce interior temperature by 5° C. If security helped you keep your cool, theft-inhibiting glass was also optional, composed of two layers of glass and a middle layer of polycarbonate in TPU film.

Building the e60

All of these gizmos and geegaws were wrapped up in a body that the stats told us was larger, but lighter. Length compared to the old e39 was 2.6 inches longer; the e60 was also 1.89 inches wider and 1.57 inches taller. The 5 series wheelbase had been extended to 113.8 inches, an increase of 2.4 inches and greatly responsible for improved rear leg room over the defunct e39. Tight rear leg room is a problem with the e34 and older Fives; the e60 was more like yesteryear's 7 series, with the added security of wide track handling.

Front track on the e60 was up 1.8 inches, with rear track 2.2 inches greater than the e39. With all the upsizing there was one notable area of reduction: weight. Figure an e60 to be 165 lbs. lighter than a like-engined e39 predecessor. Aluminum was key to the e60's construction. On the e60's release, BMW was the only car maker using an aluminum propeller shaft, with hollow drive shafts and a world-first hybrid aluminum/steel unibody. The e60 shell weighed under 772 lbs. with all attachments included.

From the A pillars rearwards the e60 was steel; forward of the A pillars the unibody was aluminum. The first part encountered in the e60's front after the bumper was foam,

The M Sport pack was also available on the e61, as indicated by this 2006 MY 530d M Sport Touring (courtesy Paul Twiss).

then an aluminum crossbar and two bolt-on deformation boxes. A bridge structure took the radiator and headlights, and was bolted to the engine and support arms. The goal with the e60 was to reduce repair costs associated with low-speed collisions.

The e60's hybrid nature also created expected engineering challenges. Metallurgical problems exist when two dissimilar metals, aluminum and steel, combine. To overcome the different thermal expansion coefficients of the metals, and the electrolytic corrosion caused when they meet, unorthodox techniques were employed. The punch rivets joining panels were 50 mm apart and new insulating glue was used to fill flanges. Flange surfaces had been specially designed and contoured to accept the use of adhesives. Glue application was carried out by an automated and camera-monitored production process. Modern industrial-strength adhesives make for strong bonds and good weight savings; examples of their extensive use include the 1991–92 GM F body coupes and the 2003 Jaguar XJ sedan.

The e60 ingredients list makes for interesting reading. It included glue, 48 aluminum bolts, and 599 punch rivets, combined with aluminum MIG welding and aluminum laser welding at Dingolfing, where 1,350 robots helped in a body-joining process that was 98 percent automated. The high tech continued with a Rotation Dipping paint application called RoDip. RoDip has been used by BMW since 2002 and involved preparing the unibody by applying a phosphate layer, and using water-based hydrofiller material which cut paint-shop solvent use by 40 tons per year.

Had the baby been thrown out with the bath water by using such unusual construction and manufacturing techniques? It would seem not, and the world needs "outside the box" thinking to create the next auto fleet of lighter, more fuel-efficient cars with a smaller carbon footprint. The e60 driver sat behind an e65 7 series style collapsible steering column, made of corrugated tube and slide pieces. To cope with side impacts the e60 had two crossbars located under the front seats.

The 5 series instrument panel also had a crossbar, and there were two crossbars around the rear axle, plus up to 8 air bags! Recognizing the importance of seat-belt usage, Euro e60s came out with an optical/acoustic warning for the driver and front passenger to wear their seat belts, to complement the 6 standard air bags. Optional in a "rear seat safety package" were thorax side air bags with an inertia reel belt system including force limiters/belt latch tensioners for the two outer rear seats.

The 5 series ITS curtain air bag now extended from the A to C pillars, which explained why the maximum number of air bags had fallen from the e39's 10. The e60 knew what to do with its safety hardware, with selective air bag/belt latch tensioner/active headrest deployment. Using sensors the car knew whether to deploy at full strength, half strength, or even not at all if the seat was unoccupied, and the decision was made quickly thanks to microchips.

Information was processed quickly using a fast databus system, jointly developed with BMW's suppliers. Signal transmission took place using plastic byte flight lightwave conductors. The byte flight databus was integrated with the car's onboard network concerning CAN buses and diagnostic system, thanks to using a central gateway module. On a more basic level, things on the e60 that went pop, like air bags and active headrests, used replaceable gas generators. Added together it was all good enough to earn the e60 a 5 star Euro NCAP safety rating.

Under that radical body, suspension changes were more modest. BMW continued with its front double pivot strut suspension, whereas the rear "Integral IV" was a revised version

LR55 WDF

L8 8EEF

BMW's gifts to you for 2004 were two turbos. With 272 bhp and an impressive 413 lbs./ft. the twin turbo 3-liter I6 was some present (courtesy BMW).

of the multi-link aluminum component setup seen on the e39. As ever, BMW offered sports suspension for the Five, which included firmer shocks/stiffer springs, plus the visual treat of a 15 mm lowering job.

Early e60 braking involved single piston calipers front and rear working on inner vented disk brakes. For the original 520i the disks were sized 12.2 inches on the front and 12.6 inches at the back. With the more powerful 530d/i the front disks were larger 12.8-inch items. An important change for better steering feel on diesel and V-8 Fives was a move to rack and pinion steering. Previously the e39 had used recirculating ball-type steering for such iterations, creating a somewhat numb-feeling helm. The e60 also had standard Servotronic power-assisted steering.

Indeed, the e60 brought a number of small, welcome trinkets to 5 series life. L.E.D. cabin lights were located in handy places like door storage bins. Radiator ribs closed up when the motor was cold to cut external noise pollution, and as with the e65 a brake lining wear sensor that worked with DSC III to calculate present pad wear as a function of driving

Opposite, top: **Still no room for a swimming pool, a Jacuzzi or a pony, but the e61-style wagon could lug 57.9 cu. ft. The BMW Touring's traditional separate-opening glass hatch was also handy when one wanted to give a snack to a trunk pet (courtesy Paul Twiss).** ***Opposite, bottom:*** **The 530d could outaccelerate the 530i to 100 mph, allowing this 530d M Sport to have the go to match the show (courtesy Andrew Hudson).**

Twin turbos and a weight of 3,652 lbs. seemed at odds with diesel economy, but the 535d was claimed to be capable of 35.3 mpg (Imperial) overall (courtesy Andre Mauvis).

behavior. The driver was informed of how many more miles could be traveled before the pads had to be changed.

If seat belts weren't worn, or the windshield washer reservoir was allowed to get low, one was treated to the dulcet tone of a pleasant gong chime. Luggage capacity was raised from the e39's 16.1 cu. ft. to 18.2 cu. ft. with a space saver, and even 19.5 cu. ft. if one was prepared to risk a runflat! In keeping with modern machinery, 6 L.E.D.s resided on the bottom of the side reversing mirrors for improved vehicle visibility. An optional sliding center armrest had an upper compartment for storage, as well as a lower portion that was climate controlled, the latter taking air from the rear HVAC outlet.

Meet the e60 Range, Gasoline and Diesel

Not many of the weird and wonderful options were included in the Euro e60's base sticker price on debut. This was the first Five to be priced in euros from the get-go. E60 life commenced with the 2.2-liter I6 520i at 35,100 euros, with 40,600 euros required for either of the 3-liter I6 powered 530d or 530i. Whereas the 520i/530i had carry-over e39 gasoline engines, the 530d was equipped with the new generation super diesel seen in the e65 730d.

More fiery and thriftier than the old 530d, the new 530d was easily the pick of the early e60 range. The amazing 3-liter diesel produced 218 bhp, about the same as a late '80s

Ford Mustang 5.0 HO, and more importantly exactly 500 Nm of torque, or 369 lbs./ft. The engine's fuel injection system operated at 1,600 bar, with a high-pressure pump that compressed only as much fuel as necessary. Micro-hole injector jets with optimized jet openings were better at atomizing fuel.

The new super diesel was able to inject fuel up to four times per stroke to boost refinement and reduce pollutants. With 6,000 fuel control maps and Bosch DDE5 Digital Diesel Electronics for an ECU, efficiency was expected and delivered with 32-bit technology and a 1.5 MB memory. Electronically controlled 6-volt spark plugs had only their tip raised to maximum temperature, and made for cold weather starting that was a snap *sans* preheating.

BMW's main priority was getting a good power plant range capable of passing Euro 4 and ULEV II emissions law dictates. Thus, the gasoline fleet used Siemen's MS 45 unit for the ECU and the e65 745i's N62B44 333 bhp Valvetronic V-8, with Double Vanos and variable length intake manifold made a home in the new e60 545i. Valvetronic could be attributed to BMW's Harald Unger and a project that started around Christmas 1991. It involved smart inlet valves that opened according to throttle position and a fuel saving that ran to 10 percent.

As a device Valvetronic comprised a sequence of action going from throttle movement

Transform a 520d SE into an M5 clone, with the M Sport pack. This 2007 520d M Sport has Comfort seats and non-runflat tires for its 19-inch rims. For the 2008 MY BMW introduced a new I4 gasoline 520i with a 170 bhp N46B20-coded 1,995 cc motor (courtesy Adam Kent).

Most tuners have an ECU chip upgrade for BMW's 2-liter turbodiesel, the ideal accessory for an e60 520d M Sport. Thrifty government officials could select an "edition fleet" version of the 520d/525d with an ECU detuned 150/163 bhp. The lower power ratings represented more frugal German market fiscal cutoff points (courtesy Adam Kent).

to an electric motor, then to an eccentric shaft and finally to an intermediate lever. The achieved objective was to deep-six the conventional, and restrictive, throttle butterfly. Less restriction meant better breathing and more power. The Valvetronic system made its debut on the revised MK II 316ti Compact 4-cylinder. Since BMW's I4s and V-8s were related, it was only natural that the innovation should reach the V-8s too.

Double Vanos did variable intake and exhaust cam timing, Valvetronic controlled valve lift, and together they helped the e60 545i achieve 0–62 mph in 5.9 seconds as well as a limited top end of 155 mph. Progress was also made with gearboxes. The e65 745i was the world's first mass-produced car with a 6-speed autobox, and this had been passed onto the e60. The ZF 6HP19 and 6HP26 weighed 18 and 31 lbs. less, respectively, than their e39 5-speed predecessors. The 6-speed auto was a modular design configured for the power at hand, the 6HP19 for the 520i/530i, and the 6HP26 for monster torque models like the 530d.

The new auto employed a Lepelletier gearset and, using the early e60 530d/i for comparison, resulted in a mere 0.2 second deficit concerning 0–62 mph sprinting compared to their 6-speed manual counterparts. Yes, even plebian versions like the 520i BMW offered the choice of 6-speed Steptronic, or conventional 6-speed manual with 0.85 ratio overdrive

6th. A special Sequential Manual Gearbox (SMG) with 6 forward ratios was available too, and responsible for a $1,300 gas-guzzler tax on the 2004 MY U.S. e60 545i. However, SMG on regular Fives proved less than popular, with the device being discontinued on non–Motorsport 5 series cars at the close of the 2007 MY.

Naturally BMW's excellent new diesels made a perfect pairing with the 6-speed Steptronic. The European public have taken to the modern diesel's good performance, refinement and high gas mileage like ducks to water: 54 percent of UK-registered 5 series sedans and 74 percent of e61 Tourings were derv drinkers in 2004. The "Technical Upgrade" 530d with M57TUD30 was soon joined by the 177 bhp 525d (M57TUD25), and for the 2006 MY the 520d with revised 2 liter I4 M47TUD20 was released.

The 520d boasted 163 bhp from 1,995 cc and, like BMW's other diesels, met Euro 4 emissions dictates. The diesel side of life was still handled by Austrian specialist Steyr, who built the diesel motors. Steyr's operations continue to be the research center for the BMW Group's diesel program, a program that included the twin turbo 535d. Introduced during 2004, the 535d represented the world's fastest-accelerating diesel car with the highest diesel output per liter (90 bhp per liter). The model was still a 3-liter car, using the 530d motor as a base before adding two turbos.

The 535d's small turbo operated from idle to 1,500 rpm; being small, it had a talent for spooling up quickly for instant boost. From 1,500 rpm to 2,500 rpm, the small and large turbochargers both worked. From 2,500 rpm to 5,000 rpm, only the big turbo was blowing. Small turbos spool up fast, while big turbos blow a lot but have lag; by using two units BMW cured most of the lag associated with turbo installations, with two factors working in the 535d's favor. First, it was a diesel, so it naturally had good low-end torque; second, it was auto-only, and thus received the torque-amplifying effect of a torque converter.

So the 535d felt more even in power delivery than a twin turbo gasoline car. The figures were tremendous, with 272 bhp at 4,400 rpm and 413 lbs./ft. at 2,000 rpm, with a redline situated at 5,000 rpm or 500 rpm higher than a 530d. That was only 5 horses shy of the 3.5 liter 1978 BMW M1 sportster, and with 0–62 mph in 6.5 seconds plus a top speed limited to 155 mph, a 535d wasn't far behind the M1 in outright terms either. Being much heavier than the M1 and given its accelerative potential, the 535d received uprated brakes measuring 13.7 inches front and 13.6 inches back.

With the e60 generation it wasn't just fast for a diesel; it was fast, period! An automatic 218 bhp 530d did 0–100 mph in 19 seconds, making the 231 bhp 530i's 20.1 seconds seem tardy. With all the diesel advancements the gasoline I6s were shined up to stop them from becoming the poor relations. For the 2006 MY fans said hello to the N52B25 525i with 218 bhp and N52B30 530i with 258 bhp. The sixes already had Double Vanos, but now they got Valvetronic plus magnesium in their construction to cut weight by 22 lbs.

Other model range changes for 2006 saw the 520i replaced by the 523i, which featured a detuned 177 bhp version of the N52B25 2.5 liter gasoline I6. The 545i was replaced by two V-8 variants, the new 4-liter 306 bhp N62B40-powered 540i and the 4.8-liter 367 bhp N62B48TU-engined 550i. BMW's model designations rarely correspond to metric engine size anymore; it's a tradition more honored in the breach than the observance.

An exciting 2006 development was the commencement of the M Sport pack, available on everything from the humble 520d to the mighty 550i. In a nutshell the pack's aim was

Opposite, top: Controversial on release, but BMW's post–2002/3 interior and exterior styling cues have been adopted by mainstream car makers across the globe (courtesy Nayan Williams). ***Opposite, bottom:*** After skipping the e39, all-wheel drive was back in a Five with BMW's I6 "Xi" variants using "xDrive," which possesses an infinitely adjustable torque split (courtesy Bob Schulte).

to give non–Motorsport Fives the e60/e61 M5's look. It started with a cloned body kit of front spoiler, side skirts and rear bumper/apron complex. On the inside, anthracite headliner, aluminum dash trim panels, plus the use of Alcantara material, were expected. The M Sport steering wheel, rocker panel kickplates and sports seats provided further visual distinction.

The M pack was an easy way to get the kind of stuff one usually visited a tuner for, with the convenience of having your friendly BMW dealer in the neighborhood. Other included items were dechromed windows, the e60 15 mm lowered sports suspension, and bigger wheels, 18 × 8-inch rims with 245/40 tires. The M pack is good for your e60, it boosts resale value and is as close as many would practically want to get to a M5, seriously.

Speaking of seriously practical, BMW continued to offer a wagon option on the 5 series. The wagon got its own model code, a first for a Five wagon, called e61. The e61 body was available with most power teams, including the M5's 5 liter V-10/SMG III combo, so there was no need to compromise. The e61 sports wagon body style has been critically judged to be more aesthetically pleasing than its sedan counterpart, and weighed 110 lbs. less than a comparably engined e39 Touring. The latest 5 series Touring had a useful 57.9 cu ft worth of load space, plus a lockable trunk floor cubbyhole and a luggage cover that opened with the tailgate.

The e61 also retained the convenient separate-opening glass hatch found on all 5 series Tourings since the e34. Suspension alterations have created a flat luggage area, with the same e60 level of suspension and wheel travel meaning that the handling gap between sedan and Touring was smaller than ever. There is some irony in that it's the high-end brands that continue to offer wagons, as well as SUVs. The choices didn't stop there; the 5 series had other relatives.

12

Living in a Niche

X5, M5 and Tuner Fives

The Phase 2 e53 and e70

Harking back to the '70s, the 5 series once again had a 6 series sibling. In the e12/e28 era the 5 and 6 series shared chassis hardware; in modern times they share a platform and access to the same BMW power plants that make them class leaders. Unlike in the old days the 6 series has to share the spotlight with a 5 series relative that gets bigger attention: the X5. When the 5 series improves so does the X5, and the 2004 MY e60 introduced a raft of upgrades for the successful e53 X5.

The X5 has always had a strong U.S. connection, being a Designworks studio creation originally styled by Chris Chapman. For 2004 it got a makeover. The 2004 X5 was the recipient of a restyled hood, bolder character lines and, predictably, larger kidney grilles. There was a new front bumper and spoiler with mesh complex and rear end changes that included clear indicator lenses. A soft close facility for the upper part of the tailgate also helped modernize the e53, as did an e65-style steering wheel and the availability of the e60's then-new Truffle Brown interior color scheme.

Let's not forget about safety. In 2001 the American Insurance Institute for Highway Safety (IIHS) ran an e53 X5 through its 40 mph offset crash test, with results that showed it to be the safest car ever tested by the body to that point in time. The revised 2004 e53 X5 achieved a 5-star Euro NCAP crash test rating. The e53 achieved those 5 stars after being subjected to a 64 kph front offset, plus side-on and pole-impact tests.

Great interest also surrounded the e53's mechanical changes. For 2004 the e53 took on the 218 bhp 3-liter turbodiesel, allowing the weighty one to sprint from 0–62 mph in 8.8 seconds, and achieve super fuel consumption of just 8.6 liters per 100 km. The e53 4.4i variant now received the latest Valvetronic V-8, which cut 0–62 mph to 7 seconds with a top speed of 210 kph, if one could afford the gas! The 4.4 V-8 was retuned for greater pulling power in its e53 application, making 320 bhp at 5,400 rpm and 324 lbs./ft. at 3,600 rpm.

Diesel or gasoline, it was now easier to put the power to the ground thanks to the new all-wheel-drive system on the e53. As with the X3, the X5 now used what BMW called xDrive. Available with e60-derived manual and auto gearboxes, it brought an infinitely adjustable torque split. All the drive could go to the front or rear wheel sets if necessary,

On the surface the e53 was slightly restyled for the '04 MY, but the major change lay with the adoption of BMW's xDrive all-wheel-drive system (courtesy Nick Zarnetske).

with multi-plate clutch and computer control managing the power split. One could find the xDrive wheel sensor and DSC (observing lateral acceleration, yaw rate, vehicle speed and steering angle) working together in the chosen torque split.

If xDrive couldn't stop an understeer or oversteer scenario, then DSC III stepped in. All this extra active safety was also made available on 2.5- and 3-liter e60/e61s in certain world markets, especially North America. The all-season security of xDrive has been available on I6-powered "Xi" e60/e61s since the 2006 MY. However, the biggest all-wheel-drive show on earth has come courtesy of BMW's high-performance V-8 X5 variants. These special X5s really deserved "M" badges, given their single-minded devotion to on-road speed and control.

Matters kicked off innocently enough with the 4.6iS, but during 2004 this variant was superseded by the 4.8iS. Both hot X5s were the only e53s to come out of the box with chrome-tipped real duals, but the 4.8iS upped the ante to the tune of 380 bhp at 6,200 rpm, the 4.6iS had a mere 340 horses. The 4.8iS' 5,005 lbs. were tamed by 369 lbs./ft. produced at 3,600 rpm, which was how Bavaria's Bigfoot got from 0–62 mph in 6.1 seconds and onto a top speed of 153 mph.

Large and loud acoustically, the X5 4.8iS also registered several decibels visually. Look-

For 2004 the e53 was available with the e60 Truffle Brown interior. In 2004 the revised e53 achieved a 5-star Euro NCAP safety rating (courtesy Nick Zarnetske).

ing somewhat like a refugee from Bling Central, this "phat" ride rode on 20-inch rims with 315 section tires and other accoutrements. The body kit came with a rear diffuser and the iS front valence was now part color-coded, complemented by the iS only e53 variant colors of Imola Red and Le Mans Blue. The Motorsport e39 M5-style warning-light-extinguishing rev counter looked purposeful, and valuably warned against a brake-torqued launch into warp speed too early in the going.

The X5 4.8iS had an oil temperature gauge instead of the usual econometer, probably because the sight of the needle registering 10 mpg or less most of the time would have been depressing. The sporty exhaust burble was sure to put a smile on the dial, as were the interior metal trim, aluminum running boards and swivel headlamps. The last two items were optional, but who wouldn't have got them after coming so far? The e53 iS versions were less about reason and practicality, and more about having a good time. Sometimes one just has to believe.

With 580,000 e53s built, the original was an unqualified success, and the 4.8iS a fitting swan song for the first incarnation. BMW created a followup with the e70 X5, a larger kind of X5 to distance the model from the X3 and possible X1. Don't rock the boat, don't make waves; the e53 had done so well BMW took care not to alienate the X5 faithful. Changes made were evolutionary and carefully considered. Dimensionally the new X5, making its debut as a 2007 MY vehicle, was 7.4 inches longer and 2.4 inches wider, with a wheelbase crucially longer by 4.4 inches.

Not content with the first SAV, BMW brought out the even sportier X5 4.6iS (courtesy Greg Smith).

The longer wheelbase was essential in allowing BMW to offer third-row seating and challenge 7-seat rivals like the MB GL and Audi Q7. For an additional $1,200 (2007 MY prices) two "jump seats" could be added to the trunk, and kids were part of BMW's customer clinic. Children spent a day in the e70 during its development in Germany and suggested 3 key changes, according to BMW: add armrests, add handgrips, and improve outward side vision.

Top: The X5 4.6iS featured a special hi-po 340 bhp V-8, with BMW raising this to 380 horses when they introduced the 4.8iS during 2004. ***Bottom:*** The e53 iS variants possessed the special exterior colors Imola Red and Le Mans Blue. These SUVs were "M" versions in substance (courtesy Greg Smith).

There was a candid admission concerning the reason for the e70's electronic handbrake, activated by a button on the transmission tunnel. A BMW designer revealed the truth: "It was the only way we could make the space to fit two holders big enough for American takeaway coffee cups." The e70 is the first X5 to have been designed under the stylistic influence of Chris Bangle. To be precise, the e70's exterior was penned by Pierre Leclercq, with Oliver Heilmer responsible for the interior.

In keeping with the revisions introduced for the early 2008 MY 5 series, the e70 X5 was the recipient of 8 iDrive preset "fave" buttons. Indeed, the e70 marked the first time that iDrive appeared on the X5. To make room for iDrive, the e70 required BMW's space-saving auto shifter, another item shared with the '08 MY 5 series. This short-gate shifter went back to center once a gear was selected.

Another first for an X5 concerned the unavailability of manual transmission on the e70. For the e70, BMW's 6-speed auto was revised with secondary damper unit and low-slip torque converter, with improved efficiency and up to 50 percent quicker cog shifting claimed. The e70 raised the X5 bar for interior trim and build quality, and was designed for even better on-road driving. New hardware involved rack and pinion steering, plus double wishbone front suspension. The latter was a first for a BMW since the modern era commenced with the 1961 1500. The only other recent Bimmer not to use MacPherson struts up front is the M1.

Handling was highlighted in bold by the e70's wider track compared to the e53, by 2.7 inches front and 2.9 inches rear. On release the new SUV could also be optioned with Dynamic Drive and Active Steering, plus it's the first BMW to boast good ride comfort on runflats. The original e70 Sport pack ran to EDC, DD and 19-inch rims. It should be noted that without BMW's Dynamic Package all e70 X5 variants were limited to 210 kph. Then there were the M5 inspired ingredients. DSC+ encompassed brake tensioning: the caliper pistons got poised for action when the system detected the driver lifting off the gas pedal abruptly.

The brake-drying trick on the e70s, like the M5, saw light braking at intervals in the wet to get rid of disk water buildup. With brake fade compensation, more braking effect was invoked when sensors detected fade, without the driver's having to apply more pedal pressure. Starting on inclines was also a breeze thanks to the hillstart assistant that automatically braked as the driver moved his foot from brake to gas pedal on a slope. The brakes one found on a 2007 MY X5 involved 13.7-inch front and 12.6-inch rear rotors.

In spite of the new e70's larger size and extra features, the dreaded carbon footprint wasn't much worse than with the e53. Weight gain was limited to no more than 33 lbs., even though the e70 was 15 percent torsionally stiffer than the e53. An aluminum hood, instrument panel and suspension arms, plus thermoplastic front fenders, and a revised brace of power plants that included a 272 bhp gasoline 3-liter I6 and 3-liter turbodiesel with aluminum crankcase that put out 231 bhp at 4,000 rpm and 383 lbs./ft. at 2,000 rpm all helped.

The gallon-stretching efficiency of the e70 X5 3.0d meant that one could reach far-off places even with the e70's tiny 85-liter tank. Those wishing to burn rubber rather than diesel could choose the X5 4.8i, now rated at a more tractable 350 bhp at 6,300 rpm with 350 lbs./ft. at 3,400 rpm. Whichever engine option taken, be left in no doubt that BMW designed your e70 for on-road action, with a default torque split of 40/60 percent front to rear and no low range, but the e70 did have HDC (Hill Descent Control).

Top: For 2007 BMW replaced the e53 with the larger e70 X5. The e70 brought rack and pinion steering, plus double wishbone front suspension (courtesy Aaron Carter). ***Bottom:*** The e70 was launched with automatic only, involving the space-saving shard shifter and transmission tunnel handbrake button (courtesy Hamann, http://www.hamann-motorsport.de).

For the 2008 MY, BMW restyled the e60 so slightly that changes defied detection. Functionally the front lower valence was altered to permit ACC (Adaptive Cruise Control) (courtesy Peter).

The e70 exhaust system was cavity hidden, but could a real off-road rig really get by on runflats? Runflats could take an e70 with puncture 145 km at a limited 80 kph. Note that by specifying the 7-seater option, one got a tire repair kit, no spare included, and there were other losses when 7 seats were gained. The third-row seating was at the expense of the e70's 3.2 cu. ft. trunk cavity storage hold. Max e70 cargo capacity was 61.4 cu. ft., and it should be considered that the SUV's side curtain air bags terminated at the second-row seating.

Then there were the refinements one couldn't get on an e53. Try optional Xenon lights with parking light rings 100 times brighter than conventional parking lights. High-Beam Assist (HBA) automatically went back to low beam when a car approached, or the distance to the vehicle ahead dropped below a set level. E70 gadgets also extended to road bend following adaptive fog lamps and 5 series-derived HUD. For towing travails, towing stability control stopped the pendulum sway between X5 and trailer through judicious use of throttle and brakes.

Visibility problems concerning low unseen objects made the standard parking camera with front and rear sensors welcome. To make sure all 7 occupants were comfortably seated the optional 4-zone climate control system was pleasant. This option came with rear seat a/c controls. The e70 had its limitations, not quite being a full-action, heavy-duty 7-seater like its rivals. However, for those wanting a sometimes seven-seater, without driving a bus, it achieved a niche, and BMW has always been about niches.

In 2008, 5 series cars had innovative options like lane drift warning and night vision display, the latter using a thermal imaging camera (courtesy of the owner).

Tuners know about niches too, and they know the e70 X5. Various companies have incorporated the e70 into their program. Hartge's sports suspension kit includes springs, shocks and sway bars to lower the e70 by 50 mm. There are power chips for the 3.0d, 3.0i and 4.8i, although only an optimist could think that Hartge's 200 mph or 300 kph speedos would be necessary. More useful is the Hartge load floormat in black, or other colors on request, made of velour with extendable flap to cover the rear bumper. Hartge e70 carbon-cased reversing side mirrors will help one look good while having a good look. So will the company's sports stainless steel dual round or oval tailpipes, and runflats can be matched with Hartge rims. The Classic 2 design can be chosen with 22 × 10.5-inch rims and 285/30 ZR tires at the front, and 22 × 12-inch hoops with 335/25 ZR tires rearwards.

AC Schnitzer has the measure of the e70, using BMW's quote concerning the SUV: "Perfect for extreme sight seeing." AC Schnitzer refers to their modified 5 series and X5s by the ACS5 moniker. They take the X5 3.0d to 265 bhp using a power chip, add two rear sports mufflers with chrome round outlets and sports suspension that lowers the whole deal by 25 to 30 mm as the X5's price rises! At least one will be riding on style with AC Schnitzer's Type IV 20-to-22-inch or Type VI 20-to-22-inch rim sets, accompanied by proprietary front spoiler and rear apron.

Hamann calls its special e70 the "Flash," which denotes a wide-body aero body kit

Top: Part of the '08 changes were clear front and rear lamp lenses, visible on this 2008 535d M Sport (courtesy of the owner). *Bottom:* An interestingly optioned 2008 e61 is present in the form of this all-wheel-drive twin turbo 535Xi Touring (courtesy Arnold Pravinata).

This 2008 550i has black Dakota leather, Sports pack, sports auto transmission, Harman Kardon LOGIC7 audio system, iPod USB adapter and Style 167 alloy wheels (courtesy Louis Laderman).

including front spoiler, side skirts, roof spoiler and rear apron. The Flash also draws upon Hamann's other catalogue pieces. An ECU remap boosts the 3.0i by 14 bhp, takes the 3.0d to 265 bhp and 600 Nm, and the 4.8i gains 18 horses. Rim sets are Hamann's PG3, Anniversary I, Anniversary II, and Edition Race, ranging in size from a 20-inch PG3 to the Edition Race's 23 × 10.5-inch size shod with 315/25 rubber.

Hamann's progressive lowering springs reduce an e70's ride height by 40 mm front and 30 mm rear, or just 40 mm front if self-leveling suspension is involved. The desirable brake upgrade pack brings slotted/vented 405 × 34 mm front disks, special pads, steel flex brake pipes and aluminum 6-piston fixed calipers. For the rear Hamann has slotted/vented 345 × 28 mm disks and 4-piston calipers. The Flash sports exhaust system includes gasoline motor sports headers, sports cats and mufflers with a 2-pipe oval 145 mm exit, or 4-pipe round 76 mm outlet, both in stainless steel. Fit Hamann's DVD, TV and PS3 multimedia pack to your Flash and you might not need your house anymore!

In all the extravagance of modern motoring, BMW is still an eco-warrior. Eco-think has run to a BMW prototype petrol/electric hybrid e53 with 1,000 Nm at 1,000 rpm. There has also been a followup to the 2000 hydrogen-powered e38 750hL, in the form of the 2007 MY production "Hydrogen 7," a 191 kw V-12 dual fuel petrol/hydrogen e65 760Li with 200 km range on hydrogen, 500 km on gas. Cars will be environmentally friendly and capable of chatting with each other, according to BMW.

The Alpina B5 sedan was a supercharged version of the BMW 545i automatic that had 493 bhp (courtesy Martin Kulin).

In a wireless LAN or Local Area Network, vehicles pass information to each other concerning weather, traffic, etc., based on car sensor values, e.g., use of windshield wipers, airbag deployment and average speed using, for example, DSC activation. It's networking for cars, adhering to "swarm theory," whereby animals and insects pass along info to each other, resulting in the whole group's acting more intelligently. For cars the process is fully automatic, with no driver intervention required. An early glimpse of this futurescape is afforded by the "Flex-Ray" system on the e70, which covers just EDC so far.

Many e70 qualities were shared with the updated early '08 MY e60/e61 unveiled on January 8, 2007. The latest Fives adhered to the original e60 basics, but with new front and rear bumpers, and restyled headlights and taillights using LEDs. The front and rear lamps were clear and those at the front had chrome accents. The car's lower front valence had been revised to accept the new Adaptive Cruise Control (ACC) with Stop & Go. ACC Stop & Go, in development back in mid–2003, was designed to bring the car to a halt using an additional "close-proximity radar." Now a production reality, it will stop the car if traffic is heavy enough, but if the car in front stops too suddenly the driver is urged to brake via visual/acoustic signals. In cases where the halt function has transpired, if the car in front starts to move, so too will your car!

Another smart driver aid introduced was the lane drift warning system. Available on the revised Fives for '08, it used a camera sited near the interior rear view mirror. The driver was warned when he had veered off course by a vibration through the steering wheel rim.

The Alpina B5 was an even more comfortable, and colorful, place to be than a normal 5 series because Alpina, like BMW Motorsport, avoided runflats and chose conventional tires (courtesy Martin Kulin).

Yet another innovation was the optional night vision, using a thermal imaging camera to detect items on and next to the road up to almost 1,000 feet away. One received a high-contrast image on the sat nav screen. Many of the e60's features for '08 seemed like promises from *The Jetsons* cartoon come true. The e60 was the first true drive-by-wire Five.

The gateless automatic shard shifter took some getting used to, and a new 6-speed sports auto arrangement with F1 style paddles replaced the outgoing SMG option. iDrive got reworked with 8 presets, programmable for two drivers to make life easier. One surprising thing about the '08 Five was its marginal side impact protection rating in a luxo car safety test conducted by the U.S. Insurance Institute for Highway Safety. The side impact test simulated getting T-boned by an SUV or truck, a likely scenario in modern times.

The e60's poor showing relative to rivals Cadillac, Honda and even Kia was less a reflection of declining passive safety at BMW than it was an indication of the improvement offered by competitors. Fortunately BMW still had peerless power plants. In the U.S., as of March 2007 production, the 525i was replaced by the detuned 230 bhp N53B30-powered 3-liter 528i. The 530i was fired and the twin turbo gasoline 535i (N54B30), based on BMW's 3-liter I6 with 306 bhp and direct fuel injection/aluminum crankcase, was hired.

To paraphrase Enzo Ferrari, the best stats are the ones we give ourselves. According to

Opposite: **Alpina's unique interior accoutrements helped distance the B5 from BMW's Five, making Buchloe's car rather special (courtesy Martin Kulin).**

Reaching onto the BMW parts shelf, Alpina purloined the 745d's non-LSD differential. It was the toughest unit BMW made (courtesy Martin Kulin).

BMW the 535i made 400 Nm from 1,300 to 5,000 rpm, with a 154-lb. weight saving over BMW's 4-liter V-8. The twin turbo I6 was unveiled at the February 2006 Geneva Motor Show. The first model to use it was the 335i coupe. The 550i continued on into '08 apace.

Alpina B5—Like an AMG ... Only Better

Moving into e60 times, Alpina not only tested alongside BMW, but its cars were assembled at BMW's Dingolfing factory too. Alpina mechanicals were brought to Dingolfing and fitted to e60s and e61s, with the cars taking a final trip to Alpina's Buchloe operation for completion. Each engine was built by one Alpina engineer, and for the e60/e61 that meant a supercharged V-8 for the Alpina B5 sedan and Touring. This was the only 5 series-based Alpina variant offered by this stage; the I6 cars ended with the e39s. All manual transmission cars were defunct too: the B5 was auto only.

The heart of the matter was a special version of the e60 545i's 4.4 called H1 by Alpina. The block and crank were made by Austria's Steyr works to Alpina's recipe and the supercharger was set to a max of 0.8 bar boost pressure. Alpina added an additional throttle body of its own design, plus an intercooler placed between the car's radiator and a/c condenser. The emphasis with the H1 was on economy/refinement as well as power. The radial compressor's blower had a planetary gearset with 15:1 offset and spun to 105,000 rpm when the tach read 6,000 rpm, and yet supercharger whine was virtually absent.

Irksome noise was missing, but power was present: 493 bhp worth at 5,500 rpm, with

The B5S Touring zoomed to 62 mph in 4.7 seconds, with 195 mph top speed. The B5S cars rolled on 20-inch rims (courtesy Alpina, http://www.alpina-automobiles.com/).

516 lbs./ft. at 4,250 rpm from the 4,398 cc motor. The B5 sedan blasted to 62 mph from rest in 4.7 seconds, and onto an initially electronically limited top speed of 186 mph, subsequently 195 mph. The B5's stats were all the more wondrous because they were achieved in hot weather testing in Dubai, no less. Handling the torque was an improved version of ZF's 6HP26 auto, with stronger first and second gear cogs, plus a new torque converter.

Alpina brought its own automatic gear selection software and familiar Switch Tronic system, with pushbuttons on the steering wheel. Unless one floored the gas pedal the autobox started off in second, just like a traditional Mercedes! The Alpina approach to suspension involved using BMW Motorsport springs, but overall the ride comfort was softer than an e60 M5. Continuing with the MB analogy, one could describe the Alpina B5 as the gentleman's M5, or an AMG with better handling!

Alpina used the best of BMW where possible to cut costs, allowing the B5 to price out on a par with the M5. The B5's brakes came from the BMW 760Li in Mideast spec. A heavy sedan, especially when loaded with the options of that market, supplied the B5's 14.7-inch front and 14.6-inch rear rotors. For decoration there was "B5" script on the B5's brake calipers. When it came to runflats, Alpina just said no, preferring Michelin Pilot Sport 2s specially developed for the B5.

Initially the B5 started rolling on 19 × 8.5-inch rims with 245/40 tires front and 19 × 9.5-inch rims with 275/35 tires rear. Alpina retained its famous turbine alloys pattern and art deco body decals; there were also embossed Alpina metal badging on the floormats and

Hartge tweaks the e60 M5 electronically so that it can belt out 544 bhp and 409 lbs./ft., all part of their "H5.0 Complete Conversion" (courtesy Hartge, http://www.hartge.de).

Alpina blue-faced instrument gauges. With the B5 one was never allowed to forget an Alpina was at hand! For exterior visuals Alpina borrowed the e60 M5's side skirts, but used its own rear spoiler design.

Alpina also placed some special input in the DSC III's electronic mapping, allowing the pilot to drift the B5 with DSC III still on. In spite of this level of control there was no limited slip differential on the B5 for its 2005 MY debut, which was quite odd. However, Alpina never rested on its laurels, incorporating the revised '08 e60/e61 into its program in the form of the Alpina B5S released during 2007. The new version offered greater punch, 523 bhp at 5,500 rpm and 535 lbs/ft at 4,750 rpm, allowing the sedan to do 0–62 mph in 4.6 seconds with a top end of 197 mph. The Touring edition was hardly tardier with 4.7 seconds and terminal velocity of 195 mph. The B5S employed 20 × 8.5-inch front rims, 20 × 9.5-inch rear rims, with 245/35 and 285/30 20-inch tires used front and rear, respectively.

Giving the M5 a Hartge Day's Night

Hartge, like other tuners, has chosen to concentrate tuning the popular diesel models. The goal is to widen the diesel power band, characteristically known for being somewhat narrow. In normal driving a Hartge-modified car uses BMW factory fueling maps, but a

With restrictions removed and body kit in place, Hartge's M5 zips to 62 mph in 4.5 seconds, with top speed at 320 kph. The rear apron includes an under-floor diffuser (courtesy Hartge, http://www.hartge.de).

sharper throttle squeeze sees a switch to alternate maps. Hartge doesn't touch fuel rail pressure, preferring longer injector duration instead, which preserves fuel pump life. ECU tuning is done on a custom basis. The original electronic files are emailed to Hartge in Germany, where the files are then modified, encrypted and emailed back. They are then downloaded to the car's ECU, with the standard BMW warranty being unaffected.

Thanks to Hartge the 520d jumps to 212 bhp and 354 lbs./ft., the 535d to 335 bhp and 498 lbs./ft. at the same respective 4,000/2000 rpm engine speeds shared with stock e60s. Hartge does all e60/e61 V-8 owners a favor by jettisoning the 155 mph limiter. In addition to Hartge's ECU tuneup the firm offers stainless steel mufflers with round or oval pipes. For more, go to UK Hartge agent Birds; they offer tuning solutions under their in-house "Make it fly" slogan Spirit brand.

Birds will convert your N62TU V-8-powered e60/e61 into a 5.2-liter hellraiser with their S62-412 stroker kit. For the money one gets a special crank, higher 10.5-to-one CR pistons, conrods, exhaust manifold and racing cats/mufflers. The completed motor has a 92 mm bore and 97 mm stroke, displaces 5,156 cc with 412 bhp at 6,100 rpm and 405 lbs./ft. at 3,900 rpm. Fitted with this engine the 5 series is limited to 300 kph or 186 mph, and Hartge have a 300 kph speedo with silver dial/red needle, plus a 200 mph equivalent to complement S62-412.

Hartge's special dials are no doubt intended for their own H5.0 Complete Conversion directed at the e60 M5. The company opens the taps on the Motorsport Five so it makes 544 bhp at 7,500 rpm and 409 lbs./ft. at 6,000 rpm. One can top the dial with this pack,

AC Schnitzer takes this e61 525d Touring onto 204 bhp. The tuner's sports suspension lowers the 5 series by 30 mm (courtesy AC Schnitzer, http://www.ac-schnitzer.de/en/).

since with speed limiter removed the sedan is good for 320 kph and 0–62 mph in 4.5 seconds. Hartge also offers a 30 mm lowering kit for the M5, plus a front spoiler lip and special rear apron.

Hartge has a sports suspension kit for regular gasoline/diesel I6 and V-8-powered sedans and Tourings, even with all-wheel drive. This also lowers ride height by 30 mm, and goes well with Hartge's body kit with front spoiler and rear apron with under-floor diffuser, which visually blends more favorably with the stock standard or Hartge tailpipes. One can also enjoy the short gearbox throws produced by Hartge's short shift kit, as well as the visual thrills of Hartge emblem hood/trunk badging, 3-spoke leather sports steering wheel with carbon inserts, and Hartge carbon steering wheel cover.

Accessory fetish types can even select a Hartge aluminum emblem for the Hartge sports steering wheel. Hartge's carbon interior trim panels include dashboard, door handles and gear shifter, or one can have the gear shifter in aluminum, leather trim or zebrano wood. The handbrake can have leather or the "Hartge" name engraved in aluminum trim to go with Hartge's aluminum footwell pedals. Then there is the TV facility and other multimedia options.

Hartge doesn't fear the runflat; these tires can be combined with Hartge wheels on request. This is understandable, because all Hartge wheel sets can be equipped with a "Tire Pressure Control" monitor, as well as sets of lockable wheel bolts. Start with 18 × 8.5-inch Classic or 19-inch Classic 2 radial spoke rims, integrated with a diamond-turned outer rim to make the wheel appear larger than it really is. The ultimate is the Classic 2 21-inch rim set fitted to the M5, with 21 × 9.5-inch wheels with 255/30 tires at the front, and 21 × 10.5-inch wheels with 295/25 tires out back. They make any e60 M5 just a bit more special!

Based on the e60 M5, the ACS5 has some unique touches, such as carbon fiber spoiler flippers with aluminum webs (courtesy AC Schnitzer, http://www.ac-schnitzer.de/en/).

Don the AC Schnitzer Racing Helmet

AC Schnitzer does its own ECU diesel tuning mods. The M57D25TU 525d's output rises to 204 bhp at 4,000 rpm, with torque now equaling 333 lbs./ft. at 2,000 rpm. With the M57D30TU-motivated 218 bhp 530d, power increases to 253 bhp at 4,000 rpm, with torque changed to 407 lbs./ft. at 2,500 rpm. The latter power chip application produces a top speed of 252 kph and 0–62 mph in 6.8 seconds. AC Schnitzer recommends power increases be combined with their Nürburgring-tested sports suspension that lowers the 5 series 30 mm. This set can also be combined with a strut tower brace and sway bar kit that has two firmness options.

For the body beautiful, AC Schnitzer has its own front spoiler, side skirts, rear roof spoiler, rear spoiler, and rear apron, plus sports reversing mirrors, body graphics and a "Chromeline Set." The AC Schnitzer modified 5 series is called ACS5, but the one based on the e60 M5 is known as ACS5 Sport. The latter receives a sports rear muffler, special exhaust outlets, 25 mm sports spring lowering set and unusual carbon fiber flippers attached to the front spoiler via chromed aluminum webs. The ACS5 Sport's rear apron has a carbon fiber diffuser.

AC Schnitzer's titanium interior trim set includes an aluminum cover for BMW's iDrive Controller, with the top in the shape of AC Schnitzer's trademark 5-spoke alloy rim design, which leads us to wheel sets. There is the 18 × 8.5-inch Type II called "The Classic,"

Accessories

AC Schnitzer aschtray 8223 00 40
"J. Winkelhock"

Replica of a central wheel lock of the BMW 318i winner of the British touring car championship 1993 with "Jockel" Winkelhock, with J. Winkelhock autograph engraved

Miniature car - scale 1 : 43
Driver: Manfred Wollgarten

AC Schnitzer BMW M3 Gr. N 8223 00 52
DTT 1994

AC Schnitzer BMW M3 Gr. A 8223 00 54
Langstreckenpokal 1995

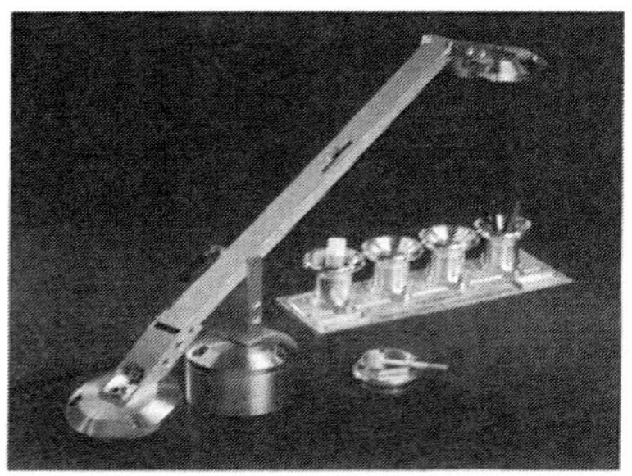

AC Schnitzer desk lamp 8223 00 60
made in aluminium
made in the look of the
AC Schnitzer strut brace

AC Schnitzer desk set 8223 00 65
Replica of the intake trumpet of
the Schnitzer Formula II-engine
(J. Lafitte 1975 European Champion)

AC Schnitzer motorsport literature

Touring car story 8222 00 11

BTCC Year book 1996 8222 00 10
(in english language)

AC Schnitzer M3 book 8222 00 30
„Scenes of a career"
(in german language)

AC Schnitzer Poster
DIN A 1

S3 silhouette 8222 00 08

S8 (BMW 850i) 8222 00 01

„superultraturbostark" (BMW 2002) 8222 00 09

AC Schnitzer 4-colour grafik (print)
DIN A 1
S5 silhouette 8222 00 02

AC Schnitzer Chronograph
Chrono S1 9060 50 10
Automatik Chronograph
in limited Edition

An e60 530i flying the flag for MK-Motorsport. When fitted with the tuner's supercharger kit, outputs rocket to 330 bhp and 311 lbs./ft. (courtesy MK-Motorsport, http://www.mk-motorsport.de).

"The Innovative" Type III available with open or closed spokes, as a one-piece or multi-piece rim and "The Avant Garde" Type IV available in silver only and involving 21 × 9.5-inch front and 21 × 10.5-inch rear rim sizes when fitted to the e60 M5. Finally, there is AC Schnitzer's "Forged Wheel," which comes in bi-color finish, part polished and part lacquered. As a 20 × 9-inch rim the Forged Wheel weighs a mere 22 lbs.!

MK-Motorsport Masters Motorsport's M5

MK-Motorsport continues with the MK-streamline system I for the e60 520i/525i and 530i gasoline I6s. This entails a streamline header, steel cat and sports rear muffler with 76 mm chrome exit pipes, power chip, sports air filter and speed delimit for an extra 30 bhp and 30 lbs./ft. For the 530i streamline, system II adds a sports cam/special power chip

Opposite: **The accessory eccentricities continue with a central wheel locknut novelty ashtray, commemorating "Smokin' Jo" Winkelhock's 1993 BTCC-winning BMW 318iS (courtesy AC Schnitzer, http://www.ac-schnitzer.de/en/).**

for 50 bhp and 37 lbs./ft. more. A supercharger kit for the 530i takes things to 330 bhp and 311 lbs./ft. The kit includes a sports air filter and intercooler.

Don't ignore the diesel. MK provides diesel engine kits for the 525d/530d and 535d. These kits include a sports air filter, rear muffler, power chip and top speed delimit, claimed to bring a 35/40 bhp gain. More comes from this tuner's 5.2-liter conversion for BMW's 4.4-liter V-8, creating 420 bhp and 414 lbs./ft. at 3,700 rpm. Stir the gears using MK's short shift kit, with stainless steel shift knob or in black leather. The "evolution" shifter has black leather and carbon fiber parts.

MK has different 5 series spring sets for gasoline/diesel models, as well as for sedan and Touring. It is also considered if the car has M-Technic shocks. Expect a 30 mm lowering job, though with the Touring only the front springs are changed. In light of the e60's stock single-pot caliper brakes, MK's upgrades are welcome, but one must be using at least 19-inch rims. Front brakes can be uprated with BS355/6, BS370/6 or BS380/6. The first three digits stand for rotor size in mms, and the "6" denotes the 6-piston aluminum calipers. One would be remiss to not also include the tuner's rear 4-piston caliper BS342/4 upgrade set. All sets involve stainless steel brake lines with calipers in blue, or in the same color as the car.

For rolling stock MK has its MK-3 19 × 9-inch 245/35 ZR-shod rims at the front, followed by equally sized rear rims with 275/30 ZR rubber. For a few euros more they can be enjoyed in "chromeline" finish. An MK-4 20-inch design is also in the works. MK's front spoiler lip and racing side mirrors complete the picture. Breyton Design offers a front spoiler for the e60 too, as well as a rear spoiler and sports suspension with 35 mm lower ride height and claimed excellent ride comfort.

Breyton Does Bangle's Five

Breyton Design's rim base has stainless steel covering, with their Magic Sport sized 20 × 9.5 inches front and 20 × 10.5 inches rear, with 255/30 and 295/25 tires front and rear respectively. Breyton also offers the same sized Spirit rim style. The focus of the company's tuning is the popular 530d, available with rear stainless steel muffler and D-Box control box ECU modifier, claimed to provide 40 bhp and 74 lbs./ft. more fun. Breyton Design also has supercharger kits for the e60/e61 gasoline I6 models, and aluminum or carbon fiber interior trim panel sets.

Hamann Helps the e60/e61

Laupheim's Hamann will power chip your 520d to make 196 bhp at 4,000 rpm and 302 lbs./ft. at 2,000 rpm, dropping the 0–62 mph time from 8.6 to 8.1 seconds. Their ECU manipulated 525d reaches 212 bhp and 363 lbs./ft. The 218 bhp 530d chips onto 263 bhp and 422 lbs./ft., with BMW's updated 231 bhp 530d making 276 ponies and a huge 600 Nm or 444 lbs./ft. All-wheel-drive xDrive 5 series variants post faster 0–62 mph times than their rear-drive counterparts, regardless of whether stock or modified cars are at hand. Top of the Hamann diesel pyramid is its chipped 267 kph 535d with 319 bhp and 466 lbs./ft., a sport version raises those figures to 350 bhp and 488 lbs./ft.

If the regular e60 M5 doesn't make a strong enough statement, then fit Hamann's DTM style "EDITION RACE" wide body kit (courtesy Hamann, http://www.hamann-motorsport.de).

The Hamann 535d Sport can do 0–62 mph in 5.8 seconds and 276 kph. Impressive, yes, but there is a nagging doubt. If the rated hp and torque gains through ECU diesel mods are so impressive, why are the performance gains over stock relatively small? As mentioned by engineer Lee Rehorn, turbo outputs, like diesel outputs, fantastic as they are on paper, are all about peaks. The Hamann HM 3.3 with 3,268 cc makes 286 bhp at 6,200 rpm and 263 lbs./ft. at 4,000 rpm; try it on your 525i or 530i. For the 545i the HM 5.2 gives 5,156 cc, 412 bhp at 6,100 rpm and 407 lbs./ft. at 3,900 rpm.

Enjoy the "HM 5.2" insignia on the engine shrouding, but do so safely. That implies selecting Hamann's front 365 × 34 mm slotted and vented disks with red 8-pot calipers (with a surcharge for other colors) and special pads/Stahlflex brake lines. For the racing look, Hamann's front spoiler fits on the standard front bumper, and there is a more radical front spoiler with built-in ellipsoid fog lamps, plus a "Competition" front spoiler for M-Technic-equipped 5 series. There is a single rear trunk spoiler and a twin rear spoiler equivalent for extroverts. Roof spoilers and side skirts are also available for the e60/e61.

The Hamann rear aprons have diffusers to accept their 2-pipe and 4-pipe rear sports mufflers. For wheels the Edition Race is easy on the eye; it's an ultra-light forged 3-piece cross spider-spoke design in black with titanium screws and polished flange. The PG3 is a 5-spoke split-rim style in silver with polished flange in 19- and 20-inch sizes. The 19- and 20-inch Anniversary I one-piece has a split-rim multi-spoke design, available in silver; the outer rim has polished INOX and stainless steel protection lip. Hamann's Threaded Sports Suspension involves coilovers front and rear, adjustable for height, 4 sport shocks and progressive springs that can lower by 25 mm at the front and 55 mm rearwards.

The e60 generation saw the first M5 to get a "Paddle Controller" gearbox. This, plus all the other special buttons abounding, means that tuners trim around, rather than replace, interior items (courtesy Hamann, http://www.hamann-motorsport.de).

The lowering kit for the e60/e61 sees the front and rear lowered by 40 and 20 mm respectively for the sedan, and just 35 mm for the Touring's front, the rear staying unchanged. Hamann raises the performance of the e60 M5 by 60 bhp and 40 lbs./ft. Since April 2006 their "HM/M+60 sport-kit" for the M5 has comprised headers, metal cats, rear muffler, special air filter and superchip with delimit for 320 kph. Combine this with Hamann's DTM look "EDITION RACE" wide body kit, which goes well with the tuner's 90 mm round exit 4-pipe rear muffler. Hamann sports suspension lowers the M5 30 mm at the front and 25 mm at the rear. Hamann's finest 380 mm disk/8-pot caliper upgrade kit is most appropriate. Perfect for the wide body set is the "EDITION RACE" rim set: 21 × 9 inches with 255/30 tires front and 21 × 10.5 inches with 295/25 tires rear. Hamann's checkered flag profile body decals and inscribed "Hamann" aluminum trim handbrake lever are the icing on the cake!

Motorsport's V-10 e60/e61 M5

The e60 M5 came out as a 2005 MY car in Europe, 2006 MY in North America. Like the e39 M5 it was also Dingolfing assembled, but used a 4,999 cc 90-degree V-10 with Double Vanos and what was the most powerful ECU on the planet, Siemen's MS S65. Special computer hardware and software was Motorsport prepared. The motor had a 92 mm bore and 75.2 mm stroke, had a 8,250 rpm redline, and weighed 528 lbs, making 507 bhp at 7,750 rpm and 383 lbs./ft. at 6,100 rpm. The V-10 had 10 computer-controlled throttle bodies and was designed/built at the same plant as the former BMW F1 V-10. By meeting Euro 4 and ULEV II emissions regs it was a truly "green" power plant!

The e60 M5 utilized the world's first 7-speed sequential manual gearbox in a series production car, known as SMG III. The e46 M3 had the 6-speed SMG II. As an alternative, a conventional 6-speed manual has been offered in North America as a no-cost option since the 2007 MY. By November 10, 2006, the U.S. e60 M5 retailed for $83,195 with a $3,000 gas-guzzler tax for SMG III and an equivalent $3,700 surcharge for the 6-speed. The 4,012-lb. M5 was EPA rated at 12 mpg city/18 mpg highway and used a 70-liter tank. The 6-speed was slightly slower in acceleration and one couldn't turn DSC off fully as with SMG III.

SMG III had its hydraulic unit and actuators integrated in the transmission housing, with shift by wire and 11 options, 6 manual (S mode) and 5 for the automated D mode. Rely on the Hill Ascent Assistance (HAA) to stop the M5 from rolling back during hillside starts. SMG III considered gradients and gave engine braking, the main CPU told of gas pedal position, wheel/engine speeds, temps and steering angle to SMG and DSC, where DSC worked with SMG. Lots of gadgets, but you wouldn't find Dynamic Drive, Active Steering or runflats. Motorsport chose normal Continental Sport Contact 2s or Michelin Pilots.

The e60 M5 did use the e60's Servotronic with 2.4 turns lock-to-lock, and the rear e60 floorpan was modified to accept the big stainless steel exhaust system. The usual e60 aluminum suspension basics were there, with stronger rear subframe mounting points. For braking hardware the M5 used drilled 14.7-inch front rotors with twin-pot calipers, and 14.6-inch rotors with single-pot calipers at the back. There was also Brake Pretensioning that cut braking response time in a full-brake scenario, plus Brake Drying, which skimmed water from the disks. The stock M5 brakes did fade with heavy usage. A variable differential lock provided 100 percent locking when required.

Around the M5's shifter were buttons for M Drive power setting (2 stages of engine tune), SMG Drive Logic (11 modes — 6+5), EDC (electronically cycled between standard, comfort and sport) and DSC. One could select M Dynamic Mode for full-on ten-tenths action via a steering wheel button too. Adjustable launch control, shift speed and other performance functions could be dialed in using the M Drive menu, which came up on the iDrive screen. A warning lamp indicated when 10/10ths mode was engaged, and M Dynamic Drive allowed a power slide with electronic driver aids coming on only when the performance envelope had been breached, so one could leave DSC III on and still have fun safely.

The M5 always started from cold in 400 bhp mode; the 500 bhp mode had to be selected. The regular e60 econometer gave way to an oil temperature gauge, with HUD showing "M oriented info," like gear selected, speed, tach revs, with a Formula 1-style warning light telling the driver to change up at the redline. The speedo and tach had chrome trims with white corona ring illumination, and the yellow/red "go easy" tach zone warning lights telling the driver to take things gently with a stone-cold V-10. SMG III shift paddles were located on the left (-) and up on the right (+) of the tiller, so both hands could remain on the wheel at all times.

Special body kit and registration plate trim made the e60 M5 stand apart. So did the

Top: The e60 M5 arrived in North America for the 2006 MY, and this car was in the first shipment. The 2006 M5 shown uses a Dinan 3.91 ratio differential. Focusing on getting a grip, DSC had 3 settings: ON, M Dynamic Mode and OFF (courtesy Mike Hooven). ***Bottom:*** A tire-smoking display performed by a Swedish e60 M5 SMG III 7-speeder. This act was theoretically impossible on U.S. e60 M5s with the no-cost option conventional 6-speed manual, since one couldn't fully deactivate DSC on such cars (courtesy Kleiv).

With a nod to the family guy, BMW Motorsport introduced a Touring (e61) version of the M5 in Germany on May 26, 2007 (courtesy Bob Harper and *BMW Car* magazine, http://www.bmwcarmagazine.com/).

4 Motorsport exclusive racetrack colors Silverstone II Silver, Interlagos Blue, Sepang Bronze, and the later-released Indianapolis Red. Inside, perforated Merino Extended Leather in Black, Silverstone or Light Sepang Bronze covered the center of the instrument panel, center console, handbrake lever and armrests. Merino Complete Leather came in 5 colors, including Indianapolis Red and Portland Natural Brown with the instrument panel completely covered. The e60 M5 sported Alcantara anthracite headlining, with the BMW Individual program extending option customization choices.

For getting a grip DSC has three settings: ON, M Dynamic Mode and OFF. Performance settings (launch control ferocity, transmission shift speed, etc.) can be activated and saved by depressing the tiller's "M" button. To switch to 500 bhp mode one needs to visit the M Drive menu, using the "M" button.

The e60 M5 came with factory figures of 0–62 mph in 4.7 seconds and a top speed of 155 mph with limiter, or a claimed 205 mph without. BMW Motorsport boss Gerhard Richter stated, "This car was always going to have 500 bhp, nothing less." The 507 ECE hp conveniently became an even 500 bhp in U.S. SAE net terms, but who chooses advertised power ratings for appearance's sake? The selection of a V-10 over a V-8 may mostly have been for technical reasons. More cylinders means more piston area and accelerative potential for a given displacement, but consider this: when the e60 M5 was being drawn up, the BMW Williams F1 V-10 was picking up steam.

The halo effect generated by the 1990s Dodge Viper for the V-10 format also can't be ignored. M stands for Motorsport, but marketing also starts with "M." In auto mode SMG III's suburban shift behavior was variable and slow, but this wasn't an automatic, and it wasn't an AMG. None of the e60 M5's foibles stopped it from circling the "Old Ring" in 8 minutes flat. In that arena SMG III was your friend.

The M5 could also be a load-hauling buddy, if one chose the e61 edition. On May 26, 2007, the like-engined e61 M5 Touring was launched in Germany, capable of 0–62 mph in 4.8 seconds and with a power-to-weight ratio of 3.7 kg per bhp versus 3.5 kg for the sedan. At a time when the M5 sedan retailed for 91,600 euros, the e61 M5 Touring was slightly pricier at 94,100 euros. Either way, sedan or wagon, the M5 puts you in the driver's seat!

Appendix. The Fastest and Slowest Fives

A side-by-side comparison of different 5-series cars, showing the variation of performance between the two due to technological improvements.

	e12 518 (1974–81)	*e12 M535i (1980–81)*
Engine	1,766 cc, 90 bhp, 4 cyl, M10 single Solex 38 PDSI downdraft carb	3,453 cc, 218 bhp, 6 cyl, M30 Bosch L-Jetronic fuel injection
Suspension	(front) independent MacPherson strut, coil (rear) independent semi-trailing arm, telescopic damper, coil	M535i: front & rear sway bar, 518 front only
Brakes	(front) 10.7 inch solid disk (rear) 9.84 inch drum	(front) 11 inch vent disk (rear) 10.7 inch solid disk
Gearbox	4 speed manual	5 speed (close ratio)
Trunk capacity	16 cu ft	
Length/width/height	181.9/66.5/56.1 inches	
Weight	2,711 lbs	2,971 lbs
0–60 mph	14.1 scconds	7.1 seconds
Top speed	100 mph	139 mph
Overall mpg	21.6	20.2
	Autocar 10 May 1975	*Autocar* 30 August 1980

	e28 518i (1985–87)	*e28 M5 (1985–87)*
Engine	1,766 cc, 105 bhp, 4 cyl, M10 Bosch LE-Jetronic fuel injection	3,453 cc, 286 bhp, 6 cyl, M88 Bosch ML-Jetronic fuel injection
Suspension	(front) independent MacPherson strut, coil (rear) independent semi-trailing arm, telescopic damper, coil	518i & M5 have double pivot front. M5 has 13 degree rear trail angle, trac link + rear sway bar
Brakes	(front) 11.2 inch vent disk	(front) 11.8 inch vent disk

	e28 518i (1985–87)	*e28 M5 (1985–87)*
	(rear) 9.84 inch drum	(rear) 11.2 inch solid disk + ABS
Gearbox	5 speed overdrive manual	5 speed overdrive manual
Trunk capacity	16.1 cu ft	
Length/width/height	181.9/66.9/55.7 inches	
Weight	2,514 lbs	3,064 lbs
0–60 mph	11.8 seconds	6.2 seconds
Top speed	112 mph	153 mph
Overall mpg	25.4	24.9
	Autocar 3rd September 1986	BMW factory data

To show technical progress over the e12, the e28 518i has been chosen as the tortoise, instead of the e28 518.

	e34 518i (1990–95)	*e34 M5 3.8 (1993–1995)*
Engine	1,796 cc, 115 bhp, 4 cyl, M40, Bosch DME fuel injection	3,795 cc, 347 bhp, 6 cyl, S38B38, Bosch DME M3.3 fuel injection
Suspension	(front) independent MacPherson strut, coil sway bar (rear) independent semi-trailing arm, telescopic damper, coil sway bar	518i & M5 have double pivot front, 13 degree rear trail angle + trac link
Brakes	(front) 11.9 inch vent disk (rear) 9.84 inch drum + ABS (optional)	(front) 13.6 inch vent disk (rear) 12.8 inch vent disk + ABS
Gearbox	5 speed manual overdrive	6 speed manual (5 speed prior to '95MY) both overdrive
Trunk capacity	16.1 cu ft	
Length/width/height	185.8/68.9/55.6 inches	
Weight	2,998 lbs	3,795 lbs
0–60 mph	11.5 seconds	5.8 seconds
Top speed	120 mph	166.1 mph (in delimited 5th gear)
Overall mpg	24.1	17.7
	Autocar 12th September 1990	*CAR* January 1995

	e39 520i (1996–2003)	*e39 M5 (1999–2003)*
Engine	1,991 cc, 150 bhp, 6 cyl, M52, Bosch DME fuel injection	4,941 cc, 400 bhp, V8, S62, Siemens MSS 5.2 fuel injection
Suspension	(front) independent MacPherson strut, coil, sway bar	M5 — reinforced elements

	e39 520i (1996–2003)	*e39 M5 (1999–2003)*
	(rear) independent multi-link, telescopic damper, coil sway bar	
Brakes	(front) 11.65 inch vent disk (rear) 11.7 inch solid disk + ABS	(front) 13.6 inch vent disk (rear) 12.9 inch vent disk + ABS

	e39 520i (1996–2003)	*e39 M5 (1999–2003)*
Gearbox	5 speed manual close ratio	6 speed manual overdrive
Trunk capacity	16.1 cu ft	
Length/width/height	188/70.9/56.5 inches	188.3/78.3/56.4 inches
Weight	3,267 lbs	3,863 lbs
0–60 mph	9.7 seconds	5.3 seconds
Top speed	133 mph	161 mph (6th) (limited in 5th gear)
Overall mpg	20.2*	13.4*
	Autocar 27th August 1997	*Autocar* 20th January 1999

	e60 520i (2004–05)	*e60 M5 (2005–10)*
Engine	2,171 cc, 170 bhp, 6 cyl, M54, Siemens MS 45 fuel injection	4,999 cc, 507 bhp, V10, S85, Siemens MS S65 fuel injection
Suspension	(front) independent MacPherson strut, coil sway bar (rear) independent Integral IV, multi-link telescopic damper, coil sway bar	520i & M5 use double pivot front + aluminum component Integral IV (reinforced on M5)
Brakes	(front) 12.2 inch vent disk (rear) 12.6 inch vent disk + ABS	(front) 14.7 inch vent disk (rear) 14.6 inch vent disk + ABS
Gearbox	6 speed overdrive	7 speed SMG III
Trunk capacity	19.5 cu ft (runflat)	19.5 cu ft (U.S.)
Length/width/height	190.6/72.7/57.8 inches	191.1/80.2/57.8 inches (width with mirrors)
Weight	3,432 lbs	4,026 lbs
0–60 mph	8.9 seconds	4.6 seconds
Top speed	143 mph	161 mph (limited in true top)
Overall mpg	31.4*	14.5*
	BMW factory data	*Autocar* 2nd November 2004

**Economy figures use Imperial gallon, equivalent to 4.546 liters (U.S. gal. = 3.785 liters).*

Chapter Notes

Chapter 1

1. R. Bacon, *The Illustrated History of BMW Motorcycles* (Promotional Reprint, 1995), p. 6.
2. *Thoroughbred & Classic Cars* 13, No. 11 (August 1986): pp. 36–37.

Chapter 2

1. *Management Today* (January 1971): p. 55.
2. *Road & Track on Volvo 1957–74* (Brooklands Books), p. 85.
3. *BMW Magazine* (Australian edition, Issue 2 1992): p. 82.
4. *Thoroughbred & Classic Cars* 19, No. 10 (July 1992): p. 96.
5. *Autocar* 141, No. 4062 (August 31, 1974): p. 15.
6. *Thoroughbred & Classic Cars* 20, No. 6 (March 1993): p. 16 (supplement section).
7. *Management Today* (September 1974): p. 65.
8. *Autocar* 141, No. 4062 (August 31, 1974): p. iv (color section).
9. *Autocar* 141, No. 4062 (August 31, 1974): p. 15.
10. *Consumer Reports* 43, No. 1 (January 1978): p. 40.

Chapter 3

1. *European Car* 24, No. 8 (August 1993): pp. 54–55.

Chapter 4

1. *Motor* 160, No. 4102 (June 17, 1981): p. 38.
2. *Autocar* 162, No. 1 (October 10, 1984): p. 53.
3. *What Car?* (June 1988): p. 72.

Chapter 6

1. *CAR* (August 1984): p. 55.
2. *What Car?* "Crash Test!" (Reprint, December 1990).
3. *Consumer Reports* 55, No. 6 (June 1990): p. 410.
4. *Ibid.*, pp. 420–421.
5. *Daily Express Guide to 1987 World Cars*, p. 18.

Chapter 7

1. *BMW Magazine* (Australian edition, Issue 3 1992): p. 20.
2. *CAR* (January 1995): pp. 91–92.
3. *BMW Magazine* (Australian edition, Issue 3 1992): pp. 19–21.

Chapter 8

1. *Daily Express 1997 World Car Guide*, p. 24.

Chapter 9

1. *BMW Magazine* (Australian edition, Issue 1 1992): pp. 62–63.
2. *BMW Magazine* (Australian edition, Issue 3 1993): p. 36.
3. *CAR* (February 1993): p. 15.
4. *BMW Car*, No. 27 (September 1996): p. 9.
5. *Consumer Reports* 65, No. 6 (June 2000): p. 50.

Bibliography

Autocar 141, No. 4062 (August 31, 1974).
Autocar 162, No. 1 (October 10, 1984).
Bacon, Roy. *The Illustrated History of BMW Motorcycles.* London: Promotional Reprint, 1995.
BMW Car, No. 27 (September 1996).
BMW Magazine (Australian edition, January 1992).
BMW Magazine (Australian edition, February 1992).
BMW Magazine (Australian edition, March 1992).
BMW Magazine (Australian edition, March 1993).
CAR, August 1984.
CAR, February 1993.
CAR, January 1995.
Consumer Reports 43, No. 1 (January 1978).
Consumer Reports 55, No. 6 (June 1990).
Consumer Reports 65, No. 6 (June 2000).
Daily Express Guide to 1987 World Cars. Harpenden: Pedigree Books, 1987.
Daily Express 1997 World Car Guide. Harpenden: Pedigree Books, 1997.
European Car 24, No. 8 (August 1993).
Management Today (January 1971).
Management Today (September 1974).
Motor 160, No. 4102 (June 17, 1981).
Road & Track on Volvo 1957–74. N.p.: Brooklands Books, 1991.
Thoroughbred & Classic Cars 13, No. 11 (August 1986).
Thoroughbred & Classic Cars 19, No. 10 (July 1992).
Thoroughbred & Classic Cars 20, No. 6 (March 1993, supplement section).
What Car? (June 1988).
What Car? "Crash Test!" (Reprint; December 1990).

Index